The Art of Cooking and Serving

Plum Pudding (Page 194)   *Pumpkin Pie* (Page 184)

Mince Pie (Page 183)

Thanksgiving Desserts

THE ART OF
Cooking and Serving

Procter & Gamble

CINCINNATI, OHIO

ACKNOWLEDGMENT

*The accessories shown in our photographs of correctly set tables were supplied by the following famous
shops in New York:* THE GORHAM COMPANY—*Solid silver;* OVINGTON BROTHERS COMPANY—
Plated silver, china and glass; JAMES McCUTCHEON AND COMPANY—*Linen;* JOSIAH WEDGEWOOD
AND SONS—*China;* JOSEPH HEINRICHS—*Brass samovar;* STERN BROTHERS—*Furniture, ship
model and screen.*

FOREWORD

HOMEMAKERS, it would appear, are in need of a brief, authentic reference book on modern cooking and serving. Though our standards of living are higher today than they ever were, they are simpler, for common sense and the new knowledge about health have shaped them. The lavish, formal table customs of twenty or even ten years ago now seem pretentious and out of date.

With these facts in mind this book has been written. Besides information on nutrition and table service, it contains more than five hundred recipes, all of which were carefully tested before they were permitted a place here. The majority of them call for Crisco—but there are recipes for foods, too, in which no shortening is used, because it is desired that this book shall be a rounded-out cooking guide of the greatest possible value to the average homemaker.

Procter & Gamble

CONTENTS

GOOD NEWS OF A GRAND NEW CRISCO

CRISCO is an old friend to most women who have begun housekeeping in the past 25 years. A friend whose familiar blue and white wrapper has been seen in their kitchens for years and is there today—the most popular shortening on the market.

Of course, improvements have been made from time to time in Crisco. But many good cooks don't realize that today a new kind of Crisco is being made and sold which surpasses anything produced before—*a genuinely super-creamed Crisco*. This new Crisco has all the fine qualities of the old Crisco plus many new advantages. You will find it now, at your dealers, in the same familiar blue and white wrapped can.

CUTS CREAMING TIME IN HALF

New, super-creamed Crisco has been creamed and blended over and over again at the spotless Crisco factory to make it the lightest, fluffiest shortening ever made. You know what an arm-tiring task it used to be to blend a shortening with the sugar in making a cake. You could stir and stir, and it wasn't until you were practically worn out that the mixture was ready for the flour and milk.

Suppose it is a whole egg cake you are making. All you have to do is to measure your Crisco and sugar directly into your mixing bowl, break in your eggs—or yolks as the recipe may state—and stir briskly. In less than half a minute you will find the ingredients are thoroughly blended together and ready for the addition of flour and milk. Quite different, isn't it, from the old method of first creaming up a hard, stiff shortening, then adding the sugar little by little and finally beating in the eggs?

MAKES RICH TENDER PASTRY

You'll be surprised to find this new super-creamed Crisco mixes so lightly and smoothly, so easily, with flour it gives your pastries a real rich, creamy lightness . . . makes them meltingly tender.

Good cooks are discovering everywhere that pies made with new Crisco are more digestible too. Their tender, flaky light crust, free from sogginess, is the answer.

CRISP AND GREASELESS FRIED FOODS

Everyone wants crisp and greaseless fried foods . . . light and easy to digest. This new super-creamed Crisco won't smoke at proper frying temperatures. It forms a crisp, tender crust on the surface of the food, sealing it instantly, so that no grease can soak in, and the fine delicate flavor of the food itself is preserved. Crisco fried foods are crisp on the outside, tender and well cooked on the inside—really digestible. More and more good cooks are using Crisco for deep frying and pan frying as well as for their cakes.

FIT FOR DELICATE STOMACHS

Doctors and nurses as well as some 11,000,000 good cooks and Crisco enthusiasts find that Crisco foods agree with delicate digestions. If you haven't tried the improved new super-creamed Crisco, you can't imagine how light and easy to digest fried foods and pastry can be.

KEEP IT ON THE PANTRY SHELF

There is no need to keep Crisco in the refrigerator. It keeps sweet on the pantry shelf, and, kept at room temperature, is always ready for cake or pie making and for frying. Crisco used for frying can be strained and used over and over again.

TRY NEW CRISCO——SEE FOR YOURSELF

Naturally, you'll want to find out for yourself just how Crisco has been improved. You'll want to test out the new Crisco in your own kitchen with these recipes. All we ask is that you will give the new Crisco a real trial not only for cakes or pastry, but for cookies, biscuits, fritters, deep fat frying and pan frying—for everything you cook and bake. The 3-lb. can with its lower price per pound, is the economical size to buy.

HOME ECONOMICS DEPT.

CHAPTER I

Table Service in the Servantless House

THREE things a meal must be when you are your own cook and waitress: it must be nourishing, it must be reasonably easy to prepare and it must give your family pleasure in the way it is served.

Since well-bred people avoid display, especially display that is out of keeping with their means, the mistress of the servantless house does not attempt the formalities of table service observed by the Richest-Family-in-Town. The old proverb that advises us to bite off only as much as we can chew applies very aptly to serving. It is a sign of good taste to do only as much as we can do well, and to leave the extreme expressions of style to those who have money and servants to carry them out.

The intelligent woman fits her service to her pocketbook and strength. Certain fundamental rules she observes to the letter, of course, but beyond that she is given a wide latitude to work out her own taste and convenience. She may choose, for instance, to bring broiled chops to the table in a covered earthenware casserole, instead of on the platter which matches her dinner set, but what sane person would find fault with this method when it is the only way of keeping the food piping hot on the long journey from *her* particular kitchen?

This matter of serving hot foods *hot* and cold foods *cold* happens to be one of those fundamental rules which no woman who aspires to be a good housekeeper can make light of. It just *has* to be done, however it is accomplished.

Quite as hard and fast is the edict about clean linen and shining silver. Better never to use anything but doilies, and keep *them* immaculately fresh, than to cover the table for even one meal with a cloth having a single spot on it. In many

For breakfast in the house without a maid you will put the fruit course on the table before your family assembles. The fruit plate or saucer is placed on the breakfast plate

homes of wealth tablecloths, as a matter of fact, are no longer seen; lace or even linen runners and place mats have supplanted them. This type of linen demands a well-finished table top, of course, either of paint or of natural wood smoothly polished. Probably the latter is the more practical, as hot dishes will not mar it if it is left unvarnished and rubbed down frequently with oil or wax.

Table silver will always be bright if washed in hot suds made with Ivory Soap and dried at once with a soft clean towel. Silver polish should be kept close to the kitchen sink so that stained pieces may be rubbed up after each meal. This plan consumes only a few extra minutes each day, but how it reduces the labor of the weekly silver cleaning!

Just one more adamantine law. Each place, or cover, as one sometimes sees it called, must be carefully set with the knife at the right of the place plate and the fork at the left. The sharp edge of the knife *must* be turned toward the plate and the fork must be placed with its prongs pointing upward. The water glass takes its stand about one inch above the point of the knife, while the bread-and-butter plate goes to the opposite side of each place just above the fork. The small butter knife is placed on the bread-and-butter plate, either across the top or the right-hand edge.

This is the skeleton arrangement of a place. Additional silver and glass is added to it according to the meal and the kinds of food to be served, and a napkin always puts in its appearance, sometimes on the plate, at other times to the left of the fork. But these are details which are easily remembered once you understand the reasons for them. And it is high time to discuss them now.

BREAKFAST

In most households breakfast, on week days at any rate, is a scramble with everyone coming down at the last minute and wanting to be waited on at once. But it is the meal, too, that starts the day right or wrong for each member of the family

A breakfast place

and so you, the homemaker, manage to have the table looking pretty, to wear your most serene manner and to serve food that looks absolutely irresistible.

If the condition of your table top permits, you will use a small breakfast cloth or a runner and place mats, which may be all white or embroidered or woven in gay colors. Their variety is infinite, ranging all the way from an excellent quality of brightly checked gingham to a hand-woven linen embellished with lace and Italian cutwork. The napkins are small, matching the color of the cloth or runner.

For the center of the table a bowl or vase with just a few flowers of the garden variety is better than a tight mass of formal hothouse flowers. Or fruits of several kinds piled together in a bowl make a colorful decoration. When neither fruit nor flowers are available you may devise a charming center-piece of some tiny ferns combined with a bit of partridge vine or other colored woodsy thing in a low bowl or delicate wicker basket.

At each place is a plate—breakfast size—a knife, fork, bread-and-butter plate, butter knife and a water glass. Here again, you see, is our skeleton place arrangement.

But you are going to have grapefruit or baked apple for your first course. You will need a spoon for it—so lay it at the right of the knife. If you have children you will certainly serve cereal. A dessert spoon is the generally accepted implement for this food. Put it between the knife and fruit spoon. Boiled eggs would necessitate the addition of a teaspoon. This tea-spoon would be given the place next to the knife, and the cereal and fruit spoons would be moved to the outside places, since it is considered more convenient for silver to be laid in the order of its use—the fork, spoon or knife for the first course being found on the outside of the row, while the pieces for the last course are on the inside, nearest the plate.

If you pour the coffee at the table, as you probably will want to do, you will lay a teaspoon on each saucer before you pass it.

For breakfast in the house without a maid you will put the fruit course on the table before your family assembles, so as to save yourself as many steps as possible after the meal has begun. The fruit plate or saucer will be placed on the breakfast plate. And just here the reason becomes perfectly evident as to why the breakfast napkin, neatly folded, must repose at the left of the place, just beside the fork. If it were put on the plate it would be covered by the dish of fruit!

The coffee service is beside *your* place. An electric perco-lator is a wonderful possession, permitting, as it does, the coffee to be made on the table. But if one is not so fortunate as to own this convenient device, the coffee is strained in the kitchen into a well-heated china or silver coffee pot and brought to the table.

Toast or hot bread is usually served on a bread tray or in a basket which has been lined with a fresh napkin large enough to fold over the contents and keep them warm.

Alcove breakfasting for the small family is more and more popular as our form of living becomes condensed and simplified, and the breakfast alcove is being added to many new houses and apartments. The alcove is part of, or very close to, the kitchen and it makes the serving of the meal a much easier affair.

The setting of the alcove table is the same as that of the ordinary breakfast table, but one has to beware of crowding. It is well to call into play the tea-wagon or a small table on which the extra things may be placed. The used plates may be put out of sight on the lower shelf of the tea-wagon.

And, by the way, a tea-wagon is one of the best servants the servantless house can have. It may be trained to carry things to and from the kitchen under your guiding hand, or to stand faithfully beside the dining room table holding fresh china and silver for the last course on its upper shelf, and amiably receiv-ing used plates on its concealed under shelf.

With a small family one may vary the breakfast, or the luncheon either, in many ways. The mistress of a perfectly charming little house in the country has a way of surprising her family occasionally by serving breakfast or luncheon on her spotless marble-topped kitchen table, which looks out over an

There are all sorts of alluring breakfast sets

expanse of green lawn. I shall never forget one breakfast there in her kitchen when I was a week-end guest in the Spring. We had golden popovers and home-made marmalade for breakfast and I looked out upon a glory of white and pink apple blossoms on the wide-spreading apple tree that presses close to the house. The kitchen is as immaculate as a drawing-room and its blue-and-white freshness adds to one's appetite. To achieve such an effect with a kitchen breakfast one cannot be a cluttery person.

Another homemaker frequently transfers breakfast on a warm day to the side porch with its lovely view of the winding river and the white church spire sailing out of the trees on the opposite bank. All three of her family lend a hand at the carrying and for the extra steps there is a soul-satisfying half-hour of matchless peace and beauty.

ENTERTAINING AT BREAKFAST

When there are guests for breakfast one may add a few special touches as a tribute to the festive occasion. Dressing up the fruit by serving it in baskets made of the shell of the grapefruit or orange, or scooping melon out in balls and serving it in sherbet glasses, or laying a handful of luscious red strawberries on a bed of fresh grape or nasturtium leaves, enlivens the first course; while eggs baked in individual casseroles or an omelette garnished with parsley or mushrooms give a "company" air to a quite simple meal.

More and more it is becoming a custom when one has guests to serve breakfast on a tray either in the bed-room or down-stairs—in winter, before an open fire, in summer, on the porch. It gives a guest—usually it is a woman who welcomes this pleasant little courtesy—a bit more freedom about her hour of waking and in the end it is much more convenient for the host-ess, permitting her to send her family off about their day's work and to get her own duties well under way.

There are all sorts of alluring breakfast sets, costly and in-expensive, but the important point is that everything should match and that the tray should not be a conglomeration of odd bits of china. One needs, of course, a small cream pitcher and sugar bowl, a covered dish for toast, a tall glass for orange juice, which is preferable to the orange served whole, or an individual fruit dish and a small tea or coffee pot. A very small vase with one flower is a touch that completes the tray breakfast, the keynote of which should be daintiness.

THE FAMILY LUNCHEON

The homemaker who from choice or necessity serves dinner at night has need of all her ingenuity in making the mid-day luncheon an inspiring meal. Nearly always there are left-overs to be used up and only a woman with a glowing imagina-tion and the true housekeeping instinct can make them look and taste enticing.

Everything must be done to make the luncheon table at-tractive. There should always be a pretty centerpiece and, as at breakfast, the low bowl with a few flowers in a holder in the Japanese fashion or a bowl of gaily assorted fruit is better than the more pretentious centerpiece. In one household where the mistress "can make anything grow" a succession of tulips,

The informal type of table covering is the only correct thing for luncheon and no end of variety is possible

daffodils and narcissi is kept blooming indoors throughout the winter and the vivid blossoms in a deep-toned blue or an ivory bowl make a lovely bit of color in the center of the table when all the world outside is gray.

The informal type of table covering is the only correct thing for luncheon and no end of variety is possible. Pretty luncheon cloths or sets of runners are being made now of all sorts of materials besides linen—of checked ginghams, or of a fine quality crepe or even of closely woven straw and grass.

The table is set with the silver necessary to the meal. If soup or bouillon in cups is the first course, the bouillon spoon will be placed at the right of the knife, just as the fruit spoon was for breakfast. The salad fork, if needed, will occupy the place immediately to the left of the plate, with the meat fork beyond it, following the rule that the last piece to be used shall be nearest the plate.

If layer cake or pie happens to be the dessert, an extra fork will be required and this may either be placed before each person just before the dessert is served or it may be put on the table in the beginning, in which case it will take up its position next the plate, causing the salad and meat forks to be shifted to the left. Theoretically, silver for the last course is not supposed to be placed on the table until the time comes to serve that course, but such a ruling is very sensibly modified for the maidless house.

Comfortingly enough, it is no great blunder, either, to serve soup *in plates* at an informal family luncheon, though for a formal one only cups with double handles (bouillon cups) would be possible. Soup in plates demands a soup spoon, of course, so place it to the right of the meat knife and omit the bouillon spoon.

When the family assembles, the soup will be at each place, in plates as hot as they can be made, or in summer icy cold cantaloupe or fruit cocktail will substitute for it. If there is no introductory dish, then the main course will be on the table so that the housewife may sit down with the rest of the family and *stay* seated. If the dessert is one that does not need to be

A luncheon place

The formal dinner napkin may be of heavy damask with embroidered initial or monogram, or, if a fancy cloth is being used, the napkin should match the cloth. For breakfast and luncheon the napkins are smaller as also are those used for the informal, or family, dinner. For afternoon tea a simple Madeira or filet lace-edged napkin not much larger than a handkerchief is in good taste kept hot it should be placed on the serving table or tea-wagon before the meal begins and served from there.

Where there are small children requiring something different from the regular menu, it is a good plan to supply their plates in the kitchen and bring them in ready for immediate consumption, so saving the children's patience and one's own steps.

In some households there are children of an age sufficiently dependable to be trained as waitresses (or butlers). A wise mother will encourage her girls and boys to assume this share of the family responsibilities, and will cultivate their pride in doing their task well and in saving her so many steps.

ENTERTAINING AT LUNCHEON

There is no happier way of entertaining one's women friends than at luncheon. (Men, as a rule, are not devotees of this pleasant indoor sport.)

Naturally if one has no maid one does not attempt a luncheon on a very large scale, although in nearly every community it is possible to draft for the occasional gala meal a helper who will either stay in the kitchen or help out as waitress. But let us suppose the worst; no "accommodator" is available, and you, in your one person, must perform in the triple role of cook-waitress-hostess.

The first consideration is to choose a menu that will be as delightful as possible without presenting undue complications in serving. Dishes with "trailers" or sauces, gravies and condiments must be sternly foregone, but a simplified service does not mean that the food cannot be both delicious and interesting. When you next contemplate a luncheon you will find the menu on page 232 helpful, since it purposely avoids the pitfalls not foreseen by the unwary.

It goes without saying that you will do all your marketing and as much preparation of the food as is possible on the day before the party.

For a formal luncheon the table is spread with the handsomest luncheon cloth, or runners and place mats, or center-

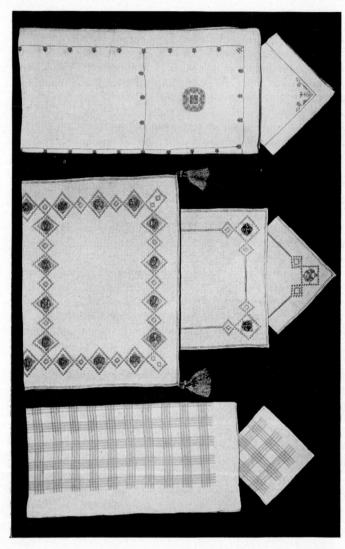

Pretty breakfast and luncheon cloths, or sets of runners and mats are being made now of all sorts of materials—choice gingham, fine crepe, heavy Italian linen or Chinese lawn

piece and doilies that the hostess possesses. (A large white damask cloth is suitable only for dinner.) A handsome bowl or vase in the center holds some of the more delicate varieties of garden or hothouse flowers arranged loosely, their stems cut at uneven lengths, so that the effect is of grace and fragility rather than of the profuse costliness which fairly shrieks at one's guests: "count-me-there-are-two-dozen-of-me."

If the table is very long and narrow it may be necessary to place two smaller bowls of the same flowers between the central bowl and the ends of the table. Or if the table is large and square you may want as many as four small vases ranged around the bigger one. Small dishes, or compotes, of salted nuts and candy complete the table decorations and it is needless to say that these compotes must be placed on the table in positions symmetrically related to the centerpiece and to each other, not plumped down anywhere with irregular intervals between them.

For a small luncheon there is no real need of place cards, but you may choose to have them because of the festive touch they give. Where to put them depends upon the type of card you choose. The most conservative card is a small plain white oblong which is placed on top of the folded napkin at the left side of each place. But there are others which are designed to cling to the edge of the water glass or to the individual container for salted nuts. The most important point to remember in the choice of your place cards is that if decorated they must harmonize with your general color scheme.

In entertaining either at luncheon or dinner it is the better part of wisdom not to string out the silver in a bewildering row at each place but to have the dessert spoons brought on when the last course is served. Put all extra silver on the serving table or tea-wagon in advance of the luncheon.

When your guests come into the dining-room they find the first course on the service plates, half a grapefruit, melon, a cocktail or bouillon. When they are ready for the next course you will rise quietly, remove the used plates but *not* the service plates and carry them two at a time into the kitchen or pantry.

From the last trip you will return with hot plates for the main course. Long before the luncheon you will have arranged with one of your guests, probably an intimate friend, to be a sort of assistant hostess, and so you have given her the place opposite your own at the other end of the table. Now you take away her service plate and put the hot plates in front of her. Then you bring on the main dish and place it before her to serve.

While she is performing this duty you are free to refill the glasses and gather up each service plate as it is replaced by the hot plate. If there are vegetables to be passed, try to have one of the two-compartment dishes which may be bought either in china or Sheffield Plate. They make serving wonderfully expeditious.

When your guests have been supplied with meat and vegetables you will be free to sit down. A plate or small basket of bread may be passed from hand to hand around the table as it is needed, and jelly, nuts and relish may fare likewise.

At the end of this course you will remove the used plates, taking one in each hand, but never piling them. Strict etiquette demands that you replace the used plate with a fresh service plate which would give way in a moment to the salad plate. But in a servantless house such a plan is not practical and, therefore, the place in front of each guest will be bereft of a plate for a few moments until you can fill it again with the salad plate.

If tea or chocolate is to be served it is probably more successful for the hostess to pour it at the table from the prettiest service she can beg, borrow or buy, rather than to bring it in from the kitchen in cups.

Finger bowls with a doily beneath are brought in on dessert plates. Each guest lifts the finger bowl, together with the doily, and places it on the table at her left, leaving the plate ready for the dessert. This may be ice cream in sherbet glasses brought in from the kitchen on a small tray, or it may be a delicate custard of some sort served by the hostess in glass saucers at the table, or an especially delicious tart or cake may

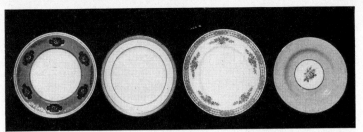

A few of the many good designs to be found in the higher grades of china. From left to right: a handsome service plate for the formal dinner; a plain gold band design in Lenox china; a pleasing pattern in English china; a tea plate in solid color with center decoration

In less expensive china or ware it is always safe for the housewife to choose of fine old patterns which have stood the test of time

In excellent taste are these attractive flower and fruit holders of Spanish ware, white Wedgewood, silver, opalescent glass and Italian pottery

*Nothing so contributes to a pleasant dinner hour as a pretty table.
The centerpiece may be a little more elaborate than for luncheon. The
cloth is smooth and spotless*

be the ending to the luncheon—this last would be served on
the dessert plates, of course.

THE FAMILY DINNER

The family dinner should be the clearing house for the best
of the day's experiences of each member of the family. Dinner
should be a relaxing meal, an end of the day affair to which
each person contributes his most cheerful and amusing "yarns."
On no account must it be the place where the day's troubles
and disappointments are unloaded.

A pretty table is the first requirement for a pleasant dinner
hour. The centerpiece may be a little more elaborate than for
luncheon. The cloth is smooth and spotless—of white damask
that reaches almost to the floor—and a thick white "silence"
cloth is stretched smoothly under it. (Runners and place mats

of linen or lace are also suitable.)   Candles, which should never
be used for luncheon, are perfect for dinner, casting a golden,
flattering glow on objects and people.   Such little touches
as these make dinner a ceremony which warms the soul to
think about all day.

For the rest, everything is much as it is at luncheon.   While
at a formal dinner you would not use the small bread-and-
butter plate you would, no doubt, have difficulty in making
your family subscribe to this principle when they are alone.
So by all means let them have this very wholesome food and
the equipment necessary to its use.   A detail photograph of a
correctly set dinner place is shown below.

The carving will, of course, be done on the table and in
many households the homemaker will do well to see that the
carver does not give all the choicest pieces to the rest of the
family while keeping the toughest, least attractive scraps for
himself.   Not infrequently fathers are quite as unselfish as
mothers!

Vegetables may be kept hot in covered dishes during the
meal.   Just before dessert is placed on the table all salt and
pepper holders, bread-and-butter plates and condiment dishes

A detail photograph of a correctly set family dinner table

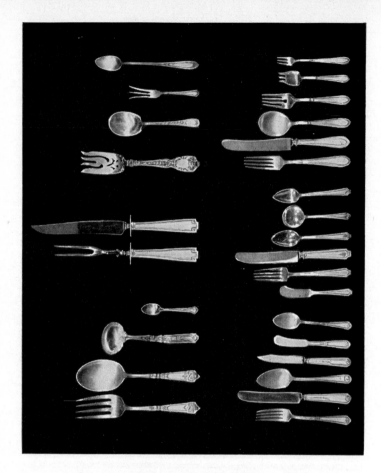

Good designs in both solid and plated silver. Upper row: serving fork and spoon, gravy spoon, after-dinner coffee spoon, carving knife and fork, cold meat fork, jelly spoon, lemon fork, iced tea spoon. Lower row: from left to right, three different patterns showing pieces selected for breakfast, luncheon and dinner are removed, the cloth is crumbed with a folded napkin and plate, and the water glasses are refilled.

ENTERTAINING AT DINNER

To the woman with no maid entertaining at dinner is the very ultimate test of skill. Where more than two guests are added to the usual family it is wise to have some help if it can be obtained, but without help it *is* possible to achieve a successful dinner by careful planning. There is much that may be done in the morning to clear the tracks and keep the last hours from being rushed.

The dessert may nearly always be prepared in advance; if it is to be ice cream from a caterer it is even more easily disposed of. The vegetables may be cleaned and partly prepared in the morning, the salad washed and put on ice, salad dressing made, often the soup may be made and reheated just before the meal. The dishes may all be wiped and laid out and a working plan fully organized so that the hostess may face the dinner hour calmly.

For her table she uses her best linen cloth and her best embroidered napkins. The centerpiece is a handsome silver or porcelain vase or a fragile affair of engraved or colored glass. Flowers may be arranged in it by mid-afternoon, and they must harmonize in color with the decorations of the dinner china and dining-room. Four single candlesticks or two candelabra will supply all the light that is needed on the table.

Salted nuts and candies are in small dishes placed at orderly intervals on the cloth. Each place is laid at an exactly equal distance from the adjoining places, for here, too, order is the first law.

On the serving table extra plates, finger-bowls and water pitcher are all set out, the last two to be filled just before dinner is announced.

When the guests enter the dining-room they find the first course on the table. For the hostess without a maid the best choice for a first course is probably a cold food like fruit,

Sherbet or cocktail glasses, long or short stemmed, in crystal or colored glass are in good taste. Salad and dessert plates, finger bowls, candlesticks and other pieces of glassware should match in color and design

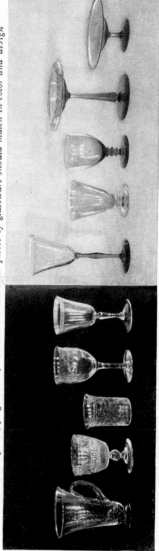

There is an infinite variety of stemmed goblets, tumblers and iced tea glasses in both crystal and colored glass. There are also long and short stemmed compotes for candies and salted nuts

oysters or an hors d'oeuvre, since none of these will lose any of
its palatability during the slight delay which occurs while the
guests find their places. The plate on which the first course
is served rests on the service plate and the napkin (folded as in
the illustration on page 17) lies at the left of the place.

The wise hostess plans a menu that requires the minimum
of passing. Vegetables are a part of some meat dishes, as
chicken casserole, but when they must be passed separately
the two or three compartment dish will be found of the greatest
help. It should be presented to each guest from his left side
and he should be allowed to help himself.

For the dinner of small proportions it is both pleasant and
convenient to serve the coffee in the living-room. The host
may take the coffee things in on a tray on which the cups and
saucers and sugar bowl have been arranged in advance. It is a
pleasant final ceremony, especially if there is a big wood fire
around which everyone can gather.

AFTERNOON TEA

For the woman without a maid no form of entertaining is
more practical than the gathering together of two or three
choice friends over a cup of tea. It involves no wear and tear
of preparation, she can express her very innermost yearnings
of daintiness and it comes at the most leisurely hour of the day.

Everywhere afternoon tea is wedging into popularity—with
hot tea served in the winter and iced beverages in the summer.
It calls for the simplest accompanying dainties if you invite
only two or three friends, and if you have no maid you won't
attempt more than eight or ten guests even in your most ex-
pansive mood. For such an occasion you will press a close
friend into service to help with the passing and replenishing
of the tea cups.

The more intimate and individual an afternoon tea, the more
delightful it is. Mrs. Armington, who is one-fourth American
and three-fourths English, always brings her pot of tea from
the kitchen with the tea all brewed—a special blend of her own,
by the way—and serves with it nothing but the crispest, thin-

For the woman without a maid no form of entertaining is more prac-
tical than the gathering together of two or three choice friends over a
cup of tea

nest pieces of buttered toast and delicious home-made jam.
Everything is so perfect that one would never think of wanting
anything else—which is as well, since it is all she ever serves.
Needless to say she rarely invites more than four guests at
once for the very first mandate of tea is that a guest shall have
a real chance to chat with her hostess.

Everything that one has for tea, unless it is toast, usually
may be prepared ahead so that there is no need for flutter.
Ordinarily it seems simpler to bring the hot water in from the
kitchen and coax it to a final boil in an alcohol or electric kettle.
If you have inherited or been presented with a silver service
you are fortunate, but a samovar or a copper kettle serves
splendidly. You have out, of course, your most delicate cups
and saucers, a pretty white tea-cloth covers the tea table,

and the cream pitcher, sugar bowl, plates, small napkins, a strainer, a tea caddy and teaspoons complete the list of *inedible* necessities.

A tea wagon is invaluable in saving steps but a prettily arranged tray on a small firm table looks really more interesting. If you own a nest of small tables, distribute them among your guests, keeping the largest one for the tea tray.

In summer, tea on the porch is very much the same, except that iced tea or punch is served. The preparation of the beverage necessarily takes place behind the scenes where the ice may be cracked and the tea or ginger ale or grape juice poured in. Then everything is brought in on a tray, the beady pitcher sprigged with mint, the cakes and sandwiches. It is a little more of a ready-made affair, but it gives the hostess that much more freedom once she settles herself with the tray. The iced drink is a peculiarly American development, and consequently being without old-world traditions almost any variation and accompaniment that one likes is correct.

SUNDAY NIGHT SUPPER

The very term, "Sunday night supper" has a special flavor of its own. Immediately it conjures up freedom from the usual routine. Often the man of the family who has secret yearnings to cook has his chance on Sunday night, and turns out something staggering to the imagination of the family. One nationally known literary man has made almost as much of a reputation among his intimate friends for his Welsh rarebit as for his novels of contemporary life. Almost anything is likely to go into the making of it, while his wife stands by in apprehension. But the result without fail is delightful.

In no way can a family more truly express hospitality than by giving a standing invitation to their friends to "drop in" for Sunday night supper. Especially can the family without a maid entertain easily in this way, making the Sunday evening at home an occasion of real delight to their friends.

For the dinner of small proportions it is both pleasant and convenient to serve coffee in the living room. The host can carry the coffee things in on a tray on which everything but the coffee has been arranged in advance

The dining table should be prettily set and lighted with candles. If there are a number of guests it is best to serve the meal "buffet" style—that is, the food is placed on the table, the guests help themselves and carry off their plates to small tables (card tables with luncheon cloths will do) scattered through the dining room and possibly the living room.

The fare usually consists of cold meat, salad, a hot food prepared in the chafing dish, or scalloped potatoes, or Boston baked beans or spaghetti with a wonderful Italian sauce, brought very hot from the kitchen. Tea and coffee are available and there are lots of hot rolls or biscuits. The dessert may be layer cake or cream puffs or delicate home-made tarts. Someone, usually the host or hostess, replenishes the hot dish and biscuits from time to time, but with this exception very little service is necessary. It is an easy and a delightful way to gather together a number of friends who "mix" well.

If the guests are few on Sunday night the dining table will be set just as it is for luncheon and everyone will sit down at a regular place.

CHAPTER II

Table Service
in the House with a Servant

THE house with a maid! What delectable pictures of faultless service it conjures up to the young housekeeper not yet saddened by experience. But the older homemaker is deceived by no such illusions. Rare indeed is the perfect maid; if she exists our friends are the lucky possessors, and such as fall to our lot need training and endless encouragement.

But one can transform an untidy, inexperienced girl into a well-groomed, professional servant if one is patient and kind and fair. She will never be able to accomplish the work of three people—nor even as much as one, if that one happens to be her mistress, all of whose love and interest are naturally enough centered upon the household.

Any maid worth having wants to look her best in the diningroom and to wait on table properly. She should be supplied with well-fitting uniforms of washable cotton for the morning, of black or gray material for the evening, with plenty of white aprons and collars and cuffs.

There are two distinct forms of serving a meal. That which has gradually gained favor in this country is the Russian style by which everything is brought in from the kitchen and presented to each person at the table, who serves himself. The dish is then carried to the serving table or pantry until wanted again. Except in homes where there is more than one servant or where the family is very small a compromise is usually effected between this and the second form of serving where the roast, bread, celery and any other small dishes are placed upon the table. Vegetable dishes are presented at the left and all plates are set down and removed from the right. The maid

Uniforms from Lord & Taylor, New York

The correctly dressed maid wears this finely striped percale uniform in the morning (green, pink or blue) with collar, cuffs and large apron of white cambric. In the afternoon and evening she appears in this attractive uniform of suede-rayon (black, gray, deep blue or maroon) with dainty collar, cuffs and apron of patterned organdie holds a dish on the palm of her left hand, with a folded napkin beneath it.

Where there is but one maid several small dishes, such as olives, celery and sauces, may be passed at one time on a tray. A meal must be served without long pauses and it is better to compromise with the formal code of serving than to go through the agony of seeing the last relative or guest supplied just as the first one finishes.

THE FORMAL LUNCHEON

The setting of a luncheon table is very much the same whether one has a maid or not, charm being the object rather than ceremoniousness. The table can be colorful in its appointments and permits of far more individuality than for dinner.

In the last chapter we went into the matter of centerpieces and decorations. If the luncheon is a small affair, one may place upon the table besides the nuts and bonbons, the dishes of relishes and the rolls or bread to be passed by the guests to one another.

Each place is laid with a service plate, the prettiest the hostess has, and with the necessary knives and forks with the single exception of the dessert fork and spoon. A small napkin matching the cloth or runner is folded and laid on the service plate. A bread-and-butter plate with small butter knife is placed at the left side of the place just beyond the forks. Butter may be placed on the plate but, preferably, it is served by the waitress while the guests are eating the first course. The water glass is at the tip of the knife.

The moment the guests are seated the first course is served—soup, oysters or hors d'oeuvre, being placed on the service plate. This plate remains until the main course, when it is removed and a hot plate from the kitchen is substituted. Except when the salad plate is removed and the table is cleared and crumbed in preparation for the dessert course, there is always a plate of some kind before the guest.

With the bringing in of the dessert service, everything is removed from the table except the candies and nuts. The

The dinner party, whether it be a small affair of half a dozen people, or stretches the table to the last limit of extra leaves, will always be the entertainment par excellence in our social calendar

dessert plates usually have been gotten ready beforehand with the spoon or fork, or both, on them. The finger bowl with doily beneath is always on the dessert plate. One or two small blossoms or flower petals are often seen in the finger bowl.

Luncheon usually consists of not more than four courses and unless there is bridge afterwards it is a short affair, the guests, unless they are intimate friends, making their adieus by three o'clock.

THE FORMAL DINNER

The dinner party, whether it be a small affair of half a dozen people, or stretches the table to the last limit of extra leaves and brings out the reserves of the family china and silver, will always be the entertainment par excellence in our social calendar. Served in the glow of candlelight, with men and women

[28]

of congenial tastes together, there is a sparkle about it that no
other form of entertainment can ever quite rival.

As befitting the more formal meal a dinner expresses a certain
stateliness and dignity in its appointments. What guest is
not subtly flattered to know that the yellow gleam of candles
in the silver candelabra shines upon one's best silver and prized
Wedgewood and that the tea roses in the bowl in the center of
the table have been especially selected to give him pleasure?

Seat your guests with thought as to which ones "match up"
well, plan the best dinner of which your house is capable, and
then settle back with a calm mind to contribute the very best
of yourself to the great event.

A place at the dinner table is set very much as it is for
luncheon except that there is no bread-and-butter plate, that
some extra knives or forks are seen and that the napkin is a
large one to match the cloth. If there are any other beverages
to be served than water, the extra glasses are arranged in a
semi-circle to the right of the water glass.

*A place at the dinner table is set very much
as it is for luncheon except that there is no
bread-and-butter plate, that some extra
knives or forks are added and that the napkin is a large one, matching the cloth*

The roast is carved in the kitchen, then skillfully put together again so that its appearance is not harmed. It is then brought in and offered to each guest who serves himself

All serving dishes are presented at the left side of the person seated. A fork and spoon are needed for convenience

Vegetables are a part of some meat dishes, as they are in the case of this planked steak, garnished and ready to be carried to the table

The salad course may be arranged in a pretty salad bowl and passed for each person to help himself

For a dinner of more than eight it is almost necessary to have two maids and a double service, each dish of food being exactly duplicated. For a small dinner use the divided dish in which two vegetables can be offered at one time. Each dish when it is brought in is passed first to the hostess.

If there are two maids one serves one side of the table and the other the opposite side and usually they vary the ends at which they begin so that one guest is not every time left until the last. At a formal dinner things are passed but once; at a smaller affair they may be passed twice.

How to serve the meat course is entirely a matter for individual choice. If a hostess abides by the letter of the law of fashion the roast is carved in the kitchen, then skillfully put together again so that its appearance is not harmed. It is then brought in and offered to each guest who serves himself. But even with a retinue of servants some households prefer to have the carving done at table, and there is no good reason why this should not be done.

Coffee is usually served in the living-room. In very formal houses the women would leave the men in the dining-room to drink their coffee and to smoke, while they went to the drawing-room for their coffee. (It would *have* to be called a drawing-room in such a house!) There the men would join them later. But in these informal days comparatively few houses follow this plan.

THE LARGE TEA

The formal reception as a form of entertaining has been relegated to the past along with bustles and hips and ping-pong and has been replaced by the jollier, less formal afternoon tea. This may be of any proportions from the two or three intimates gathered together over a small tea table to the large affair introducing a society bud.

For the larger functions the dining-room table is laid with a pretty cloth, the tea service is at one end, and if men are invited, a service of coffee is surely at the other. (If just women are coming, chocolate might be provided instead.) If the time is

For the larger tea the dining room table is laid with a pretty cloth, the tea service is at one end, and if men are invited, a coffee service is surely at the other

summer, the table is usually out on the veranda or on the lawn, and the tea becomes an even less formal affair.

But for an indoor tea, the shades are drawn and the table is lighted with candles. There is a handsome centerpiece of flowers, and both on the table and the sideboard or buffet are small dishes of various kinds of candies and salted nuts so that a guest may help herself. Dishes of small and delicious sandwiches and cakes are either on the table within easy reach or they are passed by maids or by friends who are assisting.

The tea or coffee service is presided over by an intimate friend of the hostess who usually knows most of the guests and says something agreeable to them as they pause beside her. While there are irreverent men who call this kind of party a "tea-fight" it will always be dear to the hearts of women, who find it an easy as well as a satisfactory way of dispensing hospitality.

CHAPTER III

Helpful Cooking Equipment

AFTER you have the indispensable "pots and pans" for your kitchen and it's a question of what to add *next*, do you sometimes wonder what to buy?

Or perhaps you realize that the preparation of food is a lot more trouble than it should be. When you begin to look around for ways and means to make it easier, do you know which of the up-to-date devices save labor?

Or possibly you're a thrifty housewife who doesn't like to see food wasted, and yet that old casserole has been so overworked the family sighs on seeing it. What you need is a new baking dish or a few individual ones to give those unavoidable left-overs an appearance of exciting novelty.

On the other hand, you may have solved these particular difficulties and want to know just what equipment you will need to add attractive, original touches and tempting garnishes to your dishes. A little "dressing-up" will often make the simplest food a delight to the eyes of your family and friends. For instance, potatoes—most prosaic of foods!—take on a new interest when you cut them with a fancy cutter before frying them; a plain pudding or molded dessert prepared in a fancy mold gains a prestige it never had before; and the most easily made vegetable, meat or fish salad becomes a party dish if a few fancy-cut garnishes of beet, pimento or green pepper are added.

Whatever your problem this chapter will help you. It has many suggestions from the most efficient equipment for deep fat frying to the latest implements for making fancy cake icings and the vegetable garnishes.

This does not mean that you will need them all, but certain of them you will surely want, and a few minutes of "eye" shopping here will save you many hours of wearisome looking in the stores.

FOR ACCURATE RESULTS: Standard measuring cups and spoons; a spatula for making measurements level; an oven thermometer to insure perfect baking if you have no oven regulator; a glass thermometer to give correct temperatures of boiled mixtures, candy, yeast bread dough, etc., and kitchen scales for weighing meats and poultry to determine length of cooking time

FOR MIXING CAKES, BREADS AND PASTRIES: Nests of bowls in glass, crockery or enamel; large and small sifters; spatula and knife for cutting Crisco into flour for pastry; large and small rotary beaters and wire whisks for beating eggs; plain and slotted mixing spoons; wooden spoons and a rolling pin

FOR DEEP FAT FRYING: An iron kettle (round or square bottomed); a wire basket for draining and lifting out cooked food; a deep-fat thermometer to gauge correct temperature of fat; a long handled spoon and wire dipper for lifting food from fat if no basket is used; a fork for removing food from basket; a shallow pan lined with unglazed paper on which to drain food, and a bowl, strainer and cheesecloth to use in clarifying Crisco after each frying

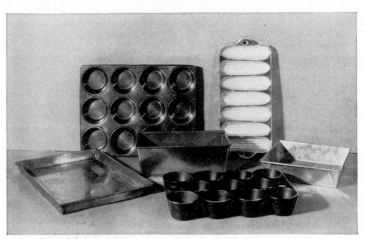

FOR BAKING BREADS, MUFFINS AND POPOVERS: A flat pan for biscuits, rolls and scones; loaf and square pans for yeast, quick loaf and cornbread; muffin or gem pan and fancy cornbread pan and iron pans for popovers

FOR THE FANCY TOUCH: Back row—a batter forcer with perforated change-able ends for making ornamental cookies; a pastry tube with fancy tips to make decorative frosting, whipped cream or Duchess potato garnishes, and for shaping French doughnuts, eclairs and cream puffs; an icing gun and tips for making ornamental frostings; fancy cutters for cookies and sandwiches. Front row—a pastry jagger; a pie-crust cutter-and-marker and patty pans

FOR MOLDED SALADS, DESSERTS AND ICES, STEAMED BREADS AND PUDDINGS: Covered molds with center tubes for steaming breads and puddings; covered melon and ring molds for frozen desserts and salads; and open molds—large, individual, border, fluted or in designs for molding desserts and jellied salads

OTHER INDISPENSABLE TOOLS: A small grater; pan lifter; set of small fancy cutters for vegetable garnishes; a broad spatula for lifting cookies, turning fried foods, etc.; an apple corer; strawberry huller; snip for removing pine-apple eyes; knife sharpener; brush for greasing pans; pair of scissors for shred-ding lettuce, etc., and a board for kneading bread, rolling out pastry, etc.

CASEROLES AND BAKING DISHES: Large-size casseroles of glass, porcelain and earthenware; individual scallop shell, casseroles, baking dishes and custard cups in which foods can be cooked and served

FOR BAKING CAKES, PIES, TARTS AND COOKIES: Layer cake pans with and without removable bottoms; plain and fluted tube pans; glass loaf and shallow cake pans; small muffin tins; enamel pie pan; open-end cookie sheet; fluted tart shell tins; a Mary Ann shortcake pan and a wire rack for cooling cakes

FOR PREPARING VEGETABLES AND GARNISHES: Front row, left to right—a Julienne knife for making Julienne potatoes; an egg slicer; two types of slicers for making shoestring or lattice potatoes and potato chips; small scoops for making melon and potato balls; vegetable fork and paring knives. Back row—a Handy slicer for vegetables; a Roller mincer for parsley, onions, etc.; large and small chopping bowls and knives; a rice boiler and potato ricer

CHAPTER IV

How to Plan Your Meals

DON'T you sometimes wonder what you have to show for the time and thought you spend on the family meals? Three meals a day, seven days a week—on and on, year after year! No business man cares to "plod away" unless his work gains significance, and why should you, you may have thought resentfully. Yet yours more than any other occupation has compensations to offer.

Look at your children's rosy cheeks and happy dispositions; your husband's good health, the general feeling of content and happiness that pervades your home. All these are a result of your thought and planning, and surely they are worth all the energy they cost.

And you have accomplished all this in spite of the bewildering technical information hurled at your devoted head when all you needed to know were a few large embracing facts.

Here they are, then!

The body needs food for these purposes: (1) To build new bone and tissue, (2) to supply energy, (3) to regulate the processes of digestion, elimination, respiration and so forth.

Just which foods are best equipped to do this work are shown in the following table:

WHAT FOODS DO FOR YOU

These build Bone and Tissue

PROTEINS		MINERALS	
Eggs	Poultry	Fruits	Eggs
Milk	Legumes	Vegetables	Cereals
Cheese	(peas, beans	Meats	
Meat	and lentils)	Milk	
Fish	Nuts		

These supply Energy

FATS	CARBOHYDRATES—(*Starch and Sugar*)
Crisco	Cereal foods—breakfast cereal,
Salad oil	rice, hominy, macaroni,
Cream and butter	potatoes
Nuts	Sweets—sugar, candy, sweet
Fatty meats, bacon,	desserts, molasses, syrups,
sausage, etc.	honey

These regulate Your Body's Processes

ROUGHAGE	MINERAL MATTER
Coarse breads and cereals	Fruits
Vegetables	Vegetables
Fruit	Meats
Nuts	Milk
	Eggs

VITAMINS

Milk and eggs	Raw vegetables (celery,
Cooked green leafy vegetables	tomatoes, cabbage, etc.)
(chard, spinach, beet tops, etc.)	Fruits

WATER

Do you see how simple this chart makes menu planning? Be sure to give your family a food from *each* of these classifications at least once a day if you want them to have a well balanced diet.

An even easier guide to complete nutrition is what is known as the "protective diet." Leading physiological chemists have proven beyond a doubt that a quart of milk, a cooked leafy vegetable and some raw vegetable food *in each person's diet each day* are a complete protection against under-nourishment.

To make this statement a more practical guide to the planning of meals let's say that everyone should eat twice each day a salad of some uncooked fruits or vegetables, once each day a liberal serving of a cooked green vegetable, and in addition not less than a pint (if possible, a quart) of milk or its equivalent.

The reasons for this choice of foods are several. In the first place, *salads* contain vitamins in considerable amounts. Most of them also encourage chewing, which helps to keep the teeth in good condition.

The cooked leafy vegetables contain important vitamins, as well as necessary mineral elements.

The milk supplies lime and calcium and other mineral constituents of the body and is rich in the health-producing vitamin A. There are also proteins of high quality. *Milk is the only food which can adequately supply certain building material for the growing child.*

And, so, if this protective scheme is followed, you can serve whatever other foods you choose. It does not deprive your family of their favorite dishes.

The "protective diet" is not expensive because the most nutritious vegetables are often quite low priced. Green cabbage, for instance, contains all three vitamins and the important mineral salts. It is also valuable for its "roughage" qualities, which keep the intestines scoured out and in a healthy condition. Other cheap but nutritious vegetables are spinach, kale, tomatoes, yellow turnips, yellow squash and carrots. These are all within the scope of every family's budget and one or another of them should not fail to appear on the menu every day.

If you have raw fruit for breakfast or serve it as dessert for luncheon or dinner you need not have two salads that day; *one* will be sufficient. The point is to get some raw food into your diet, and salads seem a safe and popular way of getting it.

In some localities salad greens, such as lettuce and romaine, may not be obtainable at all seasons, but fortunately cabbage, one of the most nutritious and economical salad plants, can always be had. It is delicious shredded and served very crisp and cold with cooked or mayonnaise dressing. Or it can be used as the foundation for other more hearty salads.

It may sound more difficult to carry out the "quart of milk" schedule, but when you consider the many ways other than drinking that milk can be included in the diet, it is not so formidable as it sounds. Cereals use lots of milk, as do cream

soups. Vegetables, meat and fish served in white sauce are
a means of getting a little into the diet and there are many
desserts such as baked custards, blanc mange, ice creams,
tapioca, rice and bread puddings, which are made almost
entirely of milk.

Evaporated milk, diluted with water, or milk powder may
be substituted for fresh milk in cooking if desired, but will not
take the place of whole milk as a beverage for children.

Besides providing proper nourishment the ideal meal should
furnish variety in flavor, texture, form and color. Eye appeal
is almost synonymous with appetite appeal, and a meal con-
sisting of cream of celery soup, creamed chicken, mashed
potatoes, cauliflower and baked custard might fulfill all nutrition requirements but would be so monotonous in appearance
that it would completely fail in its mission. Some sharp
contrast in flavor, like currant jelly, and in texture, like crisp,
green lettuce, would add much to the interest of this meal.

When there are left-overs to be used up, plan to disguise
them. Soufflés and croquettes are not recognizable as Sunday's
roast, and crisp fritters with cheese sauce will be spurned by no
one even if they *are* the survivors of last night's vegetables.
And whenever your ingenuity fails look into this little book for
friendly help.

(*Seasonable menus will be found on pages 220 to 231. They
are based on the foregoing principles and will prove suggestive
both for hot and cold weather.*)

To measure flour or any dry ingredient accurately heap up the material in a cup and then level it off with a knife or spatula

To measure quarter or half spoonfuls of Crisco or dry ingredients when one doesn't possess a set of measuring spoons shown in Chapter III, level off an ordinary spoonful with a knife, cut lengthwise through the center to make a half spoonful, and again crosswise (as shown in illustration) for a quarter spoonful

CHAPTER V

Deep Fat Frying

FRYING is the one phase of cooking of which the average housewife has still a lot to learn. Either she fries food haphazardly, ignorant of the scientific principles back of the process, and with sad results to her family's digestions; or, believing that all fried foods are indigestible, she veers to the other extreme and entirely avoids frying.

Of deep fat frying she oftens knows nothing. And yet foods, properly fried, have a savor and delicacy which almost no other form of cooking can develop, and they hold no terrors for the digestion. In that one word, "properly," lies the whole secret.

One cannot speak of frying without differentiating between the two forms of frying, sautéing and frying in deep fat. They are two distinct methods, each with its fine points. Sautéing is cooking in a small amount of hot fat; deep fat frying means cooking in a kettle of hot fat, in which the food is immersed. In both of these forms of frying the French are past masters and this is one of the reasons why their food has such delicacy, flavor and variety.

The sautéing method is frequently used to sear over the outside of meat and poultry which are to be cooked in water, as for stews, fricassees and meat pies, the hot Crisco causing a coating to be formed over the surface which prevents loss of flavor in the process of stewing or simmering. Fish cakes, hash and fried eggs are just a few of the familiar foods cooked by this method. Fritters and croquettes may also be sautéed if preferred, but the appearance is not quite so perfect as when cooked in deep fat and the food is more likely to absorb Crisco, so the latter method is recommended in this book.

*Roll the food to be fried in crumbs, then dip it into beaten egg, and
once again in the crumbs*

Certain fish cut in small pieces, such as fillets, and thin fish,
like butter fish, are usually sautéed instead of cooked in deep
Crisco. Just as for deep frying the Crisco should be hot—but
not smoking—when the food is put into it.

To wipe out that bugaboo of the indigestibility of anything
that is fried, one must keep in mind two cautions, first—as to
the *kind* of fat used for frying and the *way* it is used; second—
as to the preparation of the food to be fried. A fact to be
learned by heart is that *when fat begins to smoke it begins to
decompose*. It then tends to become less digestible and to lose
some of its nutritive value. Crisco does not smoke at proper
frying temperatures. There is no reason, therefore, why it
should be heated to the decomposition point.

In frying, the hot Crisco seals the surface of the food immediately, thereby preventing sogginess and grease soaking.
Crisco fried foods are crisp and crusty on the surface, well
cooked inside. They are readily digestible not only because
they are properly cooked but because the new super-creamed
Crisco in itself is readily digestible.

Various fine points are worth remembering in preparing food
to be fried in deep fat. "Egging and crumbing," for instance,

[45]

When rolling out doughnuts take care to have dough stiff enough so that you will need very little flour on the board, as this extra flour is likely to cook off in frying fat and discolor it

prevent fat from being absorbed by the food, because heat coagulates egg proteins and quickly forms a protective coating through which grease cannot penetrate. Such foods as oysters, scallops, croquettes and cutlets are always dipped in egg and crumbs before frying.

The egg for this purpose should be beaten slightly and mixed with two tablespoons of water. For the crumbs use dried bread, rolled out and sifted, or you can buy crumbs in a package if you have no stale bread on hand. Roll the food to be fried in the crumbs, then dip it into the egg mixture and roll again in crumbs. This makes a heavy coating and a crisp, tender outside crust is formed when the food comes in contact with hot Crisco. A second important point is that foods for frying should be *as dry as possible* before they are put into the kettle. If you soak French fried potatoes in cold water before frying—as you should to remove some of the starch—dry them thoroughly in a clean towel before dropping them into the Crisco. This makes them wonderfully crisp and tender.

The vessel for deep fat frying should contain enough Crisco to float the food without being so full that it will bubble over. Also it is essential to drain all fried foods as they are taken

Be sure Crisco is the proper temperature before putting in the dough-nuts. It may be necessary to reheat the fat before starting each batch

from the hot Crisco. This is easily done by dropping them into a pan lined with unglazed paper.

With these few definite facts in mind a housewife can successfully add to her culinary program a number of dishes which lend a welcome variety to the family menus. Not only does deep fat frying open up new and interesting avenues in cooking, but it offers ways for subtly disguising and utilizing leftovers which the family might otherwise reject. It is a very economical process as well, because it means short cooking with a consequent saving of time and fuel. And one more point in its favor—food immersed in hot fat has all of its juices closed in and so retains its full flavor.

Crisco which has been used for frying is not discarded but may be used again and again without losing its sweetness. It should be cooled rather rapidly, not left to simmer indefinitely on the back of the stove. On the other hand it should not be plunged into the ice box, but merely set in some cool place. When partly cooled, it should be strained through a fine sieve or cheesecloth to free it from any particles of food.

Pour a little of the timbale batter in a cup (fill about half full). Dip the heated timbale iron into it until the iron is nearly covered with the batter, then dip immediately into the hot fat. (See recipe for Swedish Timbales, page 61)

If later any taste or odor should be discerned in Crisco which has been used for frying, it is safe to prophesy that particles of food, which should have been carefully strained out, have been left in it to become stale and rancid.

Clarify Crisco more thoroughly by occasionally melting it over a gentle heat. When melted drop in slices of raw potato, allowing them to cook slowly until brown. The potato, being porous, will absorb small particles of food material. The Crisco should then be strained through a double thickness of cheesecloth and allowed to cool quickly. The fact that Crisco can be used so many times makes it very economical.

One should not keep Crisco in the ice box. It does not become rancid in average temperature.

SUCCESS SECRETS

1. Never allow Crisco to get hot enough to smoke.

2. Do not fill frying kettle more than two-thirds full of Crisco.

3. Allow Crisco to heat gradually, starting it in a cold utensil.

4. Use a wire basket, fitting loosely into the kettle, to lift food in and out of the hot fat. A long handled slit spoon or skimmer will serve the purpose if you haven't a basket.

5. Do not attempt to cook too much food in the fat at one time. Always test the temperature of the fat *just* before adding each batch of food.

6. When food is cooked remove it immediately and drain on unglazed paper to absorb any excess fat.

7. Always strain Crisco after using; then cool it quickly.

8. Be sure that all food to be fried, which has been previously washed or soaked in cold water, is thoroughly dried.

9. When testing the temperature of hot fat with a thermometer hold it in the center of the kettle so that the mercury bulb is covered but does not touch the bottom.

10. If a thermometer for testing temperature of fat is not available, use the following tests with a cube of soft bread:

TEMPERATURE	BREAD TEST	KIND OF FOOD
340° F.–375° F.	Cube of bread turns light brown in 50 to 60 seconds	Uncooked mixtures as doughnuts and fritters, also small pieces of raw foods, as oysters, clams, etc.
375° F.–400° F.	Cube of bread turns light brown in 40 to 50 seconds	Previously cooked mixtures as croquettes, fish cakes, also French fried potatoes, potato chips

11. Cook frequently in deep, hot Crisco. It is an economical method of cooking, as well as a means of bringing delicious, digestible foods to your table.

APPLE FRITTERS

1 cup flour	½ teaspoon salt
1½ teaspoons baking powder	½ cup milk
2 tablespoons sugar	1 egg

5 or 6 tart apples

Mix and sift flour, baking powder, sugar and salt. Add milk and well-beaten egg. Mix well. Pare and core apples. Cut in sections. Dip each piece of apple in the batter and fry in deep hot Crisco until brown. Drain on unglazed paper and sprinkle with powdered sugar.

BANANA FRITTERS

Peel bananas. Cut through lengthwise and again in pieces 1½ to 2 inches long. Follow recipe for Apple Fritters.

PINEAPPLE FRITTERS

Cut pineapple in suitable sized pieces. Follow recipe for Apple Fritters.

PEACH OR APRICOT FRITTERS

Cut halves of peach or apricot in quarters. Follow recipe for Apple Fritters.

ORANGE FRITTERS

Separate sections of orange. Follow recipe for Apple Fritters.

FRIED BANANAS

Remove skins from 3 bananas, cut in halves lengthwise and crosswise. Sprinkle with salt and lemon juice. Dip in flour, then in slightly beaten egg, diluted with 2 tablespoons water. Roll in fine crumbs and fry in deep hot Crisco 3 or 4 minutes or until brown. Drain on unglazed paper. Serve with roast meats.

CHEESE BALLS

½ pound grated American cheese	⅛ teaspoon salt
2 cups soft bread crumbs	Few grains cayenne
3 eggs	1 egg
1 teaspoon Worcestershire sauce	2 tablespoons water

½ cup dry bread crumbs

Mix cheese, crumbs, 3 beaten eggs, Worcestershire sauce, salt and cayenne. Form into balls. Dip in slightly beaten egg diluted with water, roll in crumbs and fry in deep hot Crisco until a delicate brown. Drain on unglazed paper. Serve hot with Tomato Sauce (page 116).

FRIED CREAMS

2 eggs	1 teaspoon Crisco
½ cup sugar	1 teaspoon vanilla
6 tablespoons flour	¾ cup fine dried bread crumbs
¼ teaspoon salt	1 egg
2 cups scalded milk	2 tablespoons water

Beat 2 eggs and add sugar, flour, salt and milk. Mix well and cook over hot water until thick, stirring constantly. Remove from fire, add Crisco and cool slightly. Add vanilla. Pour into a small greased pan to ¾ inch thickness. Put in ice box over night. Cut into pieces 2 inches long and 1 inch wide. Roll each piece in crumbs, dip in beaten egg diluted with water and roll again in crumbs. Fry in deep hot Crisco until a delicate brown. Drain on unglazed paper. Serve with powdered sugar or maple syrup.

CROÛTONS

Cut stale bread in thick slices. Remove the crust and cut bread in small cubes. Drop in deep hot Crisco and fry until a delicate brown. Remove with a skimmer and drain on unglazed paper. Serve a few croûtons in each portion of soup.

CROUSTADES

Cut stale bread in 2½ inch slices, and the slices in squares, oblongs or circles. Scoop out the centers with a fork leaving cases ¼ inch thick. Fry in deep hot Crisco until a delicate brown. Drain on unglazed paper. Fill with creamed vegetables, meat or fish.

FRENCH CRULLERS

4 tablespoons sugar	1 teaspoon grated orange rind
1 teaspoon salt	1 cup hot water
4 tablespoons Crisco	1 cup flour

3 eggs

Put sugar, salt, Crisco, orange rind and water in a saucepan. Bring to the boiling point, add flour and mix well. Cook until thick, stirring constantly. Cool slightly. Add one egg at a time, beating hard after each egg is added. Press through a pastry bag, using a rose tube, onto a well-greased square of heavy paper, one at a time. Turn paper upside down to let cruller drop into deep hot Crisco and fry 6 to 7 minutes or until well puffed up and a delicate brown in color. Ice with Confectioners' Frosting (page 169).

This recipe makes 18 crullers.

DOUGHNUTS

⅓ cup sugar
1½ tablespoons Crisco
1 egg
⅓ cup milk
2 cups flour

2 teaspoons baking powder
⅛ teaspoon cinnamon
⅛ teaspoon clove
1/16 teaspoon mace
½ teaspoon salt

Cream sugar and Crisco together. Add well-beaten egg and milk and mix well. Mix and sift flour, baking powder, cinnamon, clove, mace and salt. Add to the first mixture and mix thoroughly. Turn out on slightly floured board and roll to ½ inch thickness. Cut with a doughnut cutter and fry in deep hot Crisco until a delicate brown. Drain on unglazed paper. Sprinkle with confectioners' sugar before serving.

This recipe makes 24 doughnuts.

RAISED DOUGHNUTS

⅔ cup sugar
3 tablespoons Crisco
1 teaspoon salt
1 cup scalded milk

1 yeast cake
2 tablespoons lukewarm water
5 cups flour
2 eggs

1 teaspoon nutmeg

Add sugar, Crisco and salt to the scalded milk. When lukewarm add the yeast cake mixed with warm water. Add enough flour to make a sponge (about 2 cups). Set in a warm place to rise. When light add well-beaten eggs, nutmeg and enough flour to make a soft dough. Cover and let rise until double in bulk. Knead until free from large air bubbles. Roll out on a slightly floured board to ½ inch thickness. Cut with a doughnut cutter, cover and set in a warm place to rise again until double in bulk. Put them top side down in deep hot Crisco. Fry on one side, turn and fry on the other side. When a delicate brown remove from fat and drain on unglazed paper. Just before serving sprinkle with confectioners' sugar.

This recipe makes 30 doughnuts.

PRUNE DOUGHNUTS

Follow recipe for Raised Doughnuts. After the second rising, roll out on a slightly floured board to ⅛ inch thickness. Cut with a cooky cutter. Put a teaspoon of prune mixture in the center of one round. Moisten edge, cover with another round and press edges together. Cover and set in a warm place to rise until double in bulk. Fry in the same way as Raised Doughnuts.

PRUNE MIXTURE

Soak ½ pound prunes over night. Cook until soft. Drain off liquid. Remove stones and cut in small pieces. Add the grated rind of 1 lemon and 2 teaspoons of lemon juice.

JELLY DOUGHNUTS

Follow recipe for Raised Doughnuts. After the second rising, roll out on a slightly floured board to 1/8 inch thickness. Cut with a cooky cutter. Put 1 teaspoon currant jelly in the center of one round, moisten edges with water and place another round on top. Press edges lightly together. Cover and set in a warm place to rise until double in bulk. Fry in the same way as Raised Doughnuts.

This recipe makes 24 doughnuts.

FRIED PIES

Follow recipe for Plain Pastry (page 178) made with 1/2 cup Crisco. Roll out pastry to 1/8 inch thickness. Cut in large circles. Put a tablespoon of seasoned apple sauce in center of pastry. Moisten edges with cold water. Fold over so as to make a semi-circle. Press edges together with tines of a fork. Fry in deep hot Crisco until a delicate brown.

BEEF CUTLETS

2 cups chopped cold beef	1 cup very thick white sauce
1/2 teaspoon onion juice	1 egg
1 tablespoon chopped parsley	2 tablespoons water
3/4 cup fine bread crumbs	

Put beef through meat grinder. Add onion juice, parsley, and hot White Sauce (page 113), and mix well. Season more if necessary. Chill. Form into cutlets. Roll in crumbs, dip in slightly beaten egg diluted with water, and roll again in crumbs. Fry in deep hot Crisco about 5 minutes. Drain on unglazed paper.

CHICKEN CROQUETTES

2 cups chopped cold chicken	1 cup very thick white sauce
2 tablespoons finely chopped celery	1 egg
Few grains nutmeg	2 tablespoons water
3/4 cup fine bread crumbs	

Put chicken through meat grinder. Add celery, nutmeg and hot White Sauce (page 113), and mix well. Season more if necessary. Chill. Form into croquettes or cutlets. Roll in crumbs, dip in slightly beaten egg diluted with water, and roll again in crumbs. Fry in deep hot Crisco about 5 minutes. Drain on unglazed paper.

(1/2 cup chopped cooked mushrooms may be added to this recipe if desired.)

EGG CROQUETTES

Follow recipe for very thick White Sauce (page 113). Add to it 4 hard cooked eggs, chopped fine, 1/2 teaspoon salt, 1 tablespoon chopped parsley. Chill. Shape into croquettes, of any size or form. Roll each in fine dried bread crumbs, dip in well-beaten egg diluted with 2 tablespoons cold water, and roll again in crumbs. Fry in deep hot Crisco until a delicate brown. Drain on unglazed paper. Serve hot with Cheese Sauce (page 114) or Tomato Sauce (page 116).

LAMB CROQUETTES

2 cups chopped cold lamb   1 egg
2 tablespoons chopped parsley   2 tablespoons water
1 cup very thick white sauce   ¾ cup fine bread crumbs

Put lamb through meat grinder. Add parsley, and hot White Sauce (page 113), and mix well. Season more if necessary. Chill. Form into croquettes. Roll in crumbs, dip in slightly beaten egg diluted with water, and roll again in crumbs. Fry in deep hot Crisco about 5 minutes. Drain on unglazed paper.

LOBSTER CROQUETTES

2 cups cold lobster   1 cup very thick white sauce
1 tablespoon chopped parsley   1 egg
2 tablespoons finely chopped celery   2 tablespoons water
                ¾ cup fine bread crumbs

Chop lobster, add parsley, celery and hot White Sauce (page 113), and mix well. Season more if necessary. Chill. Form into croquettes or cutlets. Roll in crumbs, dip in slightly beaten egg diluted with water, and roll again in crumbs. Fry in deep hot Crisco about 5 minutes. Drain on unglazed paper.

SALMON CROQUETTES

2 cups cold salmon   1 cup very thick white sauce
2 tablespoons chopped parsley   1 egg
½ teaspoon lemon juice   2 tablespoons water
                ¾ cup fine bread crumbs

Flake salmon, add parsley, lemon juice, hot White Sauce (page 113), and mix well. Season more if necessary. Chill. Form into croquettes or cutlets. Roll in crumbs, dip in slightly beaten egg diluted with water, and roll again in crumbs. Fry in deep hot Crisco about 5 minutes. Drain on unglazed paper.

VEAL CROQUETTES

2 cups chopped cold veal   1 egg
2 tablespoons chopped parsley   2 tablespoons water
1 cup very thick white sauce   ¾ cup fine bread crumbs

Put veal through meat grinder. Add parsley and White Sauce (page 113), and mix well. Season more if necessary. Chill. Form into croquettes. Roll in crumbs, dip in slightly beaten egg diluted with water, and roll again in crumbs. Fry in deep hot Crisco about 5 minutes. Drain on unglazed paper.

SOFT SHELL CRABS

Remove the eyes and the stomach (the soft portion under the eyes) if this has not already been done. Wash and dry the crabs. Dip in flour seasoned with salt and pepper. To one egg add 2 tablespoons water and beat slightly. Dip crabs in egg, then in fine, sifted bread crumbs and fry in deep hot Crisco 5 to 8 minutes. Drain on unglazed paper. Serve with parsley and slices of lemon.

FRIED CLAMS

1 pint clams	Flour
Salt	1 egg
Pepper	2 tablespoons water

½ cup cracker or stale bread crumbs

Pick over clams and remove pieces of shell. Dry between towels. Sprinkle with salt, pepper and flour. Dip in slightly beaten egg diluted with water, and roll in crumbs. Fry in deep hot Crisco about 5 minutes. Drain on unglazed paper.

FRIED CLAMS IN BATTER

1 pint clams	¼ cup milk
2 eggs	¼ cup clam liquor
1 teaspoon salt	1 cup flour
⅛ teaspoon pepper	½ teaspoon baking powder

Pick over clams and remove pieces of shell. Dry between towels. Beat eggs, and add salt, pepper, milk and clam liquor. Mix and sift the flour and baking powder, add the liquid mixture and beat until well mixed. Dip clams in the batter, and fry in deep hot Crisco about 5 minutes. Drain on unglazed paper.

CLAM FRITTERS

1 cup flour	¼ cup milk
¼ teaspoon salt	¼ cup clam juice
⅛ teaspoon pepper	1 dozen clams, cleaned and
2 eggs	chopped

1 teaspoon melted Crisco

Mix and sift flour, salt and pepper. Add beaten eggs, milk and clam juice and mix until smooth. Add Crisco and clams and mix well. Drop by tablespoons in deep hot Crisco and fry about 5 minutes or until brown. Drain on unglazed paper and serve with Tartar Mayonnaise (page 140).

CODFISH BALLS

6 medium sized potatoes	2 eggs
2 cups shredded salt cod	⅛ teaspoon pepper

½ cup milk

Pare potatoes and boil in unsalted water. Drain and mash. Add codfish and unbeaten eggs, one at a time, and mix well. Add pepper and milk and beat until mixture is light and fluffy. Drop by tablespoons in deep hot Crisco and cook 10 to 12 minutes or until brown. Drain on unglazed paper. Serve very hot.

This recipe makes about 24 fish balls.

FRIED EELS

Skin eels.   Split down middle and clean.   Cut in 3 inch lengths and wipe dry.
Roll in crumbs, dip in slightly beaten egg diluted with 2 tablespoons water, and
roll again in crumbs.   Fry in deep hot Crisco 6 to 8 minutes.   Garnish with
parsley and slices of lemon.

FRIED OYSTERS

1 pint oysters	Flour
Salt	1 egg
Pepper	2 tablespoons water

½ cup cracker or stale bread crumbs

Pick over oysters and remove pieces of shell.   Dry between towels.   Sprinkle
with salt, pepper and flour.   Dip in slightly beaten egg diluted with water and
roll in crumbs.   Fry in deep hot Crisco about 5 minutes.   Drain on unglazed
paper and serve hot with Tartar Mayonnaise (page 140).

FRIED OYSTERS IN BATTER

1 pint oysters	¼ cup milk
2 eggs	¼ cup oyster liquor
1 teaspoon salt	1 cup flour
⅛ teaspoon pepper	½ teaspoon baking powder

Pick over oysters and remove pieces of shell.   Dry between towels.   Beat
eggs and add salt, pepper, milk and oyster liquor.   Mix and sift flour and
baking powder and stir the liquid into it.   Beat until well mixed.   Dip oysters
in batter.   Drop in deep hot Crisco and cook about 5 minutes.   Drain on
unglazed paper and serve hot, garnished with parsley and slices of lemon.

OYSTER FRITTERS

1 cup flour	¼ cup milk
¼ teaspoon salt	¼ cup oyster liquor
⅛ teaspoon pepper	1 dozen oysters, cleaned and
2 eggs	chopped

1 teaspoon melted Crisco

Mix and sift flour, salt and pepper.   Add beaten eggs, milk and oyster liquor.
Mix until smooth.   Add Crisco and oysters and mix well.   Drop by tablespoons
in deep hot Crisco and fry about 5 minutes or until brown.   Drain on unglazed paper.

FRIED SCALLOPS

1 quart scallops	Flour
Salt	1 egg
Pepper	2 tablespoons water

¾ cup fine bread or cracker crumbs

Wash scallops and dry between towels.   Sprinkle with salt, pepper and flour.
Dip in slightly beaten egg diluted with water and roll in crumbs.   Fry in deep
hot Crisco about 5 minutes.   Drain on unglazed paper and garnish with slices
of crisp bacon and watercress.

FRIED SMELTS

1½ pounds smelts   1 egg
     Salt   2 tablespoons water
     Pepper   ¾ cup fine bread crumbs

Wash the smelts and make a slight opening at the gills with a sharp knife or
scissors. Draw them between the thumb and finger from tail to head to press
the intestines out at the gill opening, keeping the fish whole. Wash and dry
and sprinkle with salt and pepper. Dip in crumbs, then in slightly beaten egg
diluted with water, and again in crumbs. Fry in deep hot Crisco 3 to 5 minutes. Drain on unglazed paper and serve with Tartar Mayonnaise (page 140).

FRENCH FRIED CALVES' LIVER

Soak 1 pound calves' liver in salt water ½ hour. Scald with boiling water.
Drain and cut in 3 inch strips. Moisten with French Dressing (page 139), and
let stand 1 hour. Drain. Dry, and fry in deep hot Crisco 3 to 5 minutes.
Drain on unglazed paper. Garnish with crisp bacon and serve hot.

VEGETABLE FRITTERS

1¾ cups flour   ½ cup milk
  1 teaspoon salt   ½ cup cooked carrots, chopped
     Few grains pepper   ¼ cup cooked peas
3½ teaspoons baking powder   ¼ cup cooked lima beans
  2 eggs   1 tablespoon chopped parsley
                    2 tablespoons melted Crisco

Mix and sift flour, salt, pepper and baking powder. Beat eggs and add milk.
Add to the flour mixture and beat thoroughly. Add carrots, peas, lima beans,
parsley and Crisco and mix well. Drop by tablespoons into deep hot Crisco
and fry until a delicate brown. Drain on brown paper. Serve hot with
Cheese Sauce (page 114).

FRIED CARROTS

Cut off small tips of cooked carrots. Cut in halves or quarters, according to
the size of the carrot. Dip pieces in milk, and roll in flour until thoroughly
covered. Fry in deep hot Crisco until a delicate brown. Drain on unglazed
paper. Sprinkle with salt and serve hot.

FRENCH FRIED ONIONS

Cut 4 or 5 Bermuda onions in thin slices. Fry in deep hot Crisco until brown.
Drain on unglazed paper. Sprinkle with salt.

Parsnip Puffs (Recipe on page 60)

Egg Croquettes (Recipe on page 53)

POTATO PUFFS

3 medium sized potatoes	2 eggs
½ cup boiling water	1 teaspoon salt
½ cup Crisco	⅛ teaspoon pepper
½ cup flour	Few grains nutmeg

Pare potatoes and cook in boiling salted water. When done put through a ricer or coarse sieve. Put water and Crisco over the fire and bring to boiling point. Add flour and cook, stirring constantly until the mixture leaves the sides of the pan. Cool. Add eggs one at a time, beating well after each egg is added. Add potatoes to this mixture with salt, pepper and nutmeg. Season more if necessary. Drop by tablespoons in hot Crisco and fry 8 to 10 minutes or until brown. Drain on unglazed paper.

This recipe makes 9 puffs.

FRENCH FRIED POTATOES

Pare 5 or 6 potatoes. Cut in strips ½ inch thick and soak in cold or ice water 1 hour. Drain. Dry between towels and fry in deep hot Crisco until a delicate brown. Drain on unglazed paper. Sprinkle with salt.

SARATOGA CHIPS

Pare 5 or 6 potatoes. With a sharp knife or potato cutter cut in very thin slices, crosswise. Soak in cold or ice water ½ to 1 hour. Drain. Dry between towels and fry in deep hot Crisco until a delicate brown. Drain on unglazed paper. Sprinkle with salt. These may be served hot or cold.

SHOESTRING OR JULIENNE POTATOES

Pare 5 or 6 potatoes. Cut in ¼ inch strips making them as uniform as possible in size and length. Soak in cold or ice water ½ to 1 hour. Drain. Dry between towels and fry in deep hot Crisco until a delicate brown. Drain on unglazed paper and sprinkle with salt.

POTATO SURPRISE

2 cups seasoned mashed potato	1 egg
1 cup cooked peas	2 tablespoons water
½ cup thick white sauce	1 cup fine dry bread crumbs

Form potato into cups, molding them in the palm of the hand and patting the potato to an even thickness. Add the peas to the White Sauce (page 113), and place a spoonful of the mixture in the center of each one and close the hand around it, putting a little mashed potato on top to entirely cover the peas. Roll balls in crumbs, then in beaten egg diluted with water, and again in crumbs. Fry in deep hot Crisco until brown.

POTATO FRITTERS

3 cups hot mashed potato	Few grains pepper
2 tablespoons Crisco	2 tablespoons flour
1 teaspoon salt	1 tablespoon chopped parsley
1 teaspoon sugar	2 eggs

To the potatoes add Crisco, salt, sugar, pepper, flour and parsley. Add beaten egg yolks and mix well. Fold in stiffly beaten egg whites. Drop by tablespoons in deep hot Crisco and fry 5 to 8 minutes or until a delicate brown. Drain on unglazed paper. Serve hot.

FRENCH FRIED SWEET POTATOES

Parboil 4 or 5 large sweet potatoes for 10 minutes. Peel and cut in strips, 3 inches long. Fry in deep hot Crisco until a delicate brown. Drain on unglazed paper. Sprinkle with salt.

SWEET POTATO CROQUETTES

2 cups hot mashed sweet potato	1 teaspoon sugar
2 tablespoons Crisco	2 eggs
1 teaspoon salt	½ cup fine bread crumbs
⅛ teaspoon pepper	2 tablespoons water

Mix sweet potato with Crisco, salt, pepper, sugar and one well-beaten egg. Beat well. If mixture is too stiff, add a little hot milk. Shape into croquettes. Roll in crumbs, dip in beaten egg diluted with water, and roll again in crumbs. Fry in deep hot Crisco until brown and drain on unglazed paper.

A nice accompaniment to baked ham.

PARSNIP PUFFS

5 parsnips	Few grains pepper
3 tablespoons milk	2 eggs
2 tablespoons Crisco, melted	2 tablespoons water
1 teaspoon salt	½ cup dried bread crumbs

Cook parsnips in boiling salted water until tender. Drain and mash and add milk, Crisco, salt and pepper. Add one beaten egg. Set aside to cool. Shape into small balls. Roll in crumbs, then in beaten egg diluted with water and again in crumbs. Fry in deep hot Crisco until brown. Drain on unglazed paper.

FRIED RICE CAKES

2 cups boiled rice	½ teaspoon salt
1 egg	Few grains nutmeg
2 tablespoons flour	½ cup fine bread crumbs
1 teaspoon baking powder	1 egg yolk
1 tablespoon sugar	2 tablespoons water

Mix rice, beaten egg, flour, baking powder, sugar, salt and nutmeg. Mix well. Form into balls. Roll in fine bread crumbs, then in beaten egg yolk diluted with water, and again in crumbs. Fry in deep hot Crisco until a delicate brown. Drain on unglazed paper and serve with jelly, Cheese Sauce (page 114), or Tomato Sauce (page 116).

SWEDISH TIMBALES

1 cup flour	⅔ cup milk
½ teaspoon salt	1 egg
½ teaspoon sugar	1 tablespoon melted Crisco

Mix and sift the flour, salt and sugar. Add milk gradually and slightly beaten egg. Add melted Crisco and beat until mixture is smooth. Put a little batter in a cup. Put timbale iron in melted Crisco and heat Crisco until hot enough for frying. Remove iron from the Crisco and dip in batter nearly to top. (See page 48.) Return again to the hot Crisco and fry 1 to 2 minutes or until batter is a delicate brown. If iron is too hot or too cool the batter will drop off the iron.

This recipe makes 18 to 20 small timbales.

CHAPTER VI

Soups

THERE are two good reasons for serving soup. First, soup can be an appetizer to stimulate the appetite and aid digestion; and second, it can be an actual part of the meal, in which case it must be high in nutritive qualities. The real value of soup lies in this second use.

To the first or appetizer group belong the clear soups, consommés and bouillons. The latter would be served as the first course of a heavy dinner or luncheon. In the second or nutritive group are included all the milk and cream soups, bisques and chowders which are intended to accompany lighter meals or to be served as a main course for luncheon or supper.

Many American housewives throw away the water in which vegetables are cooked. In this water mineral elements and valuable vitamins are held in solution, and when you throw it away you are actually disposing of a certain amount of health. So, save it, and use it later for cream soups.

The best method of making cream soup is to combine the desired vegetable stock with a white sauce of the proper consistency. A most delicious white sauce, rich and absolutely smooth, is made with the new super-creamed Crisco. Crisco, melted, blends easily with flour so that as the milk is added an even-textured sauce results. And is there anything worse than lumps of "thickening" in soup?

The following recipes for cream soups have been worked out in chart form to make them easy for you to use. If you learn to make *one* of these soups well, you will be able to make *all* of them well and to add others of your own choosing if you like. Almost any combination of left over vegetables and the water in which they are cooked may be prepared in the same way.

Cheese Balls (Recipe on page 5c)

Fried Carrots (Recipe on page 57)

SUCCESS SECRETS

1. Never throw away the water in which meat or vegetables are cooked—save it for soup.
2. Save small amounts of left over vegetables. They may be combined and cooked together to make delicious cream soups.
3. Prepare your cream soups ahead of time and reheat them just before serving in a double boiler. This will relieve you of so much "last minute" cooking.
4. In blending ingredients for white sauce be sure that Crisco and flour are well mixed before adding the liquid.
5. Mutton is too strongly flavored to be used as a basis for soup stock. Disguise it by combining it with other meats and vegetables whenever it is to be used.
6. Use the tougher cuts of meat for soup making, such as shoulder, neck, flank, tail and shin. These parts are better flavored as well as more economical to buy.
7. Keep your stock pot perfectly sweet and clean. Empty it often, wash thoroughly and let stand in the sun to dry.
8. Serve soup very hot in heated soup plates or bouillon cups.

THIN WHITE SAUCE

2 tablespoons Crisco	1 teaspoon salt
2 tablespoons flour	1/8 teaspoon pepper

2 cups milk

Melt Crisco, add flour, salt and pepper and mix well. Add milk slowly and bring to the boiling point, stirring constantly to avoid lumping. Keep hot over boiling water until ready to combine with vegetable mixture.

MEDIUM WHITE SAUCE

2 tablespoons Crisco	1 teaspoon salt
4 tablespoons flour	1/8 teaspoon pepper

2 cups milk

Melt Crisco, add flour, salt and pepper and mix well. Add milk slowly and bring to the boiling point, stirring constantly to avoid lumping. Keep hot over boiling water until ready to combine with vegetable mixture.

CREAM SOUPS
Made with Thin White Sauce

Cream of Corn Soup. Cook 2 cups fresh cooked or canned corn with 1 cup water, 1 slice onion, 1 teaspoon sugar and ¼ teaspoon salt in a saucepan 20 minutes. Press through a sieve, mix with the white sauce and add 1½ tablespoons chopped parsley. Serve hot.

Cream of Pea Soup. Cook 2 cups fresh cooked or canned peas with 1½ cups water, ½ teaspoon sugar, ¼ teaspoon salt and 1 slice onion in a saucepan 15 minutes. Press through a sieve and add to the white sauce. Serve hot.

Cream of Cauliflower Soup. Cook 1 small head of cauliflower, broken into pieces, 1 stalk celery, cut in pieces, 1 slice onion, ½ teaspoon salt in enough water to cover until cauliflower is tender. Strain and save 1½ cups stock. Press cauliflower through a sieve and add with the stock to the white sauce. Serve hot.

Cream of Asparagus Soup. Cook 1 bunch of asparagus with 2 tablespoons chopped onion and ½ teaspoon salt in boiling water until tips are tender. Strain and save 1½ cups stock. Cut off tips, press through a sieve and add pulp and stock to the white sauce. Serve hot.

Cream of Potato Soup. Cut 3 medium-sized potatoes in halves and cook with 1 slice onion, 1 stalk celery, cut in pieces, and ½ teaspoon salt in 3 cups boiling water. When tender, strain and save 2 cups stock. Press potatoes through a sieve and add stock and pulp to the white sauce. Sprinkle with 3 tablespoons chopped parsley. Serve hot.

CREAM SOUPS
Made with Medium White Sauce

Cream of Tomato Soup. Cook 2 cups stewed or canned tomatoes, ½ cup water, 2 teaspoons sugar, 2 whole cloves, ½ teaspoon salt and 1 tablespoon chopped onion in a saucepan 20 minutes. Strain and add ⅛ teaspoon soda. Stir well and pour into the hot white sauce. Serve immediately.

Cream of Celery Soup. Cut into small pieces the tops and stalks of 1 small bunch of celery. Put in a saucepan with 5 cups cold water, ½ teaspoon salt and 1 slice onion and cook until celery is tender. Press through a sieve and use 2½ cups strained liquid. Add to the hot white sauce. Serve hot.

Cream of Onion Soup. Slice 4 medium-sized onions, add 2 cups water, ½ teaspoon salt and $\frac{1}{16}$ teaspoon pepper. Cook until onions are tender. Press through sieve and use 2 cups liquid. Add to hot white sauce. Serve hot.

Cream of Spinach Soup. Wash and pick over 1 quart spinach. Cook with ½ teaspoon salt and 3 cups boiling water for 20 minutes. Press through a sieve and use 2½ cups liquid and pulp. Add to the hot white sauce. Serve hot.

Cream of Mushroom Soup. Peel ¾ pound mushrooms, using caps and stems. Slice thin and cook with ½ teaspoon salt and 3 cups boiling water for 20 minutes. Press through a sieve and use 2½ cups liquid and pulp. Add with ½ cup cream to the hot white sauce. Serve hot.

Cream of Watercress Soup. Wash and cut fine leaves of 1 bunch watercress, reserving 2 tablespoons to sprinkle on the soup. Cook with ½ teaspoon salt and 2 cups water for 10 minutes. Add liquid to the hot white sauce. Serve hot.

LOBSTER BISQUE

Remove meat from a 2-pound cooked lobster (see Boiled Lobster, page 84). Add 2½ cups cold water to the shell and claws and cook 25 minutes. Drain and reserve 2 cups stock. Cut lobster meat in small pieces. Add lobster and stock to 2 cups medium white sauce (page 64). Heat and serve immediately.

CLAM BISQUE

2 dozen clams	5 tablespoons flour
Liquor from clams	1 teaspoon salt
½ cup celery, cut in pieces	⅛ teaspoon pepper
2 tablespoons parsley, chopped	1 cup thin cream
2 tablespoons Crisco	1 cup milk

Strain liquor from clams through cheesecloth and add enough water to make 2 cups liquid. Remove all particles of shell and chop clams fine. Cook clams, celery, parsley and liquid together 10 minutes. Press through a sieve and keep hot. Melt Crisco, add flour, salt and pepper and mix to a smooth paste. Add cream and milk and bring to boiling point, stirring constantly. Add the strained clam liquid. Serve immediately.

CONSOMMÉ

4 pounds fowl	1 teaspoon peppercorns
2 pounds knuckle veal	2 whole cloves
2 pounds beef	1 allspice berry
4 quarts water	1 small bay leaf
1 tablespoon salt	2 sprigs parsley
½ cup carrots, cut in pieces	1 sprig thyme
½ cup onions, cut in pieces	1 sprig savory
½ cup celery, cut in pieces	1 sprig marjoram

Clean, disjoint and cut up fowl. Saw knuckle bone in pieces and cut up veal and beef in small pieces. Put in a covered soup kettle and add water. Let stand 1 hour to draw out juices. Put over the fire and bring quickly to the boiling point. Reduce heat at once to simmering and cook 6 or 7 hours. Add salt, vegetables and seasonings the last hour of cooking. Strain. Remove any fat when cold. Season more if necessary and clear by the following method:

Put cold stock in a saucepan and add 2 slightly beaten egg whites. Put over fire and stir constantly until it boils. Boil 5 minutes. Let stand until it settles. Strain through 2 thicknesses of cheesecloth. Heat thoroughly and serve with toasted crackers.

BOUILLON

3½ pounds beef, chopped	2 stalks celery
3½ quarts water	½ bay leaf
1 onion	2 cloves
1 carrot	6 peppercorns
1 sprig parsley	1 teaspoon salt

Use beef from lower round. Put it in saucepan with water and let stand 1 hour. Place over the fire in covered pot and bring to boiling point. Skim. Reduce heat and simmer 3 hours. Chop onion, carrot, parsley, celery and add to soup with the bay leaf, cloves, peppercorns and salt. Let simmer an hour longer. Strain into a bowl and cool quickly. This stock will not jelly as no bones are cooked with it. When ready to serve, remove fat and clarify by method used in Consommé.

CHICKEN SOUP

1 fowl	1 sprig parsley
4 quarts water	1 teaspoon salt
½ onion	6 peppercorns
3 stalks celery	½ cup rice

Dress and cut the fowl in pieces and put into a saucepan. Add water, cover and bring to the boiling point. Reduce heat and simmer slowly 3 hours. Add onion, celery, parsley, salt and peppercorns. Cook for another hour. Take out fowl, strain stock and cool. Remove fat when cold. Cut 1½ cups meat from the breast in small cubes and add to the soup. Steam the rice in 2 cups water in a double boiler about 30 minutes. Add to the soup. Season more if necessary and serve with crisp crackers.

This soup may also be made from a chicken carcass but will not be as rich a stock.

TOMATO PURÈE

1 quart fresh tomatoes	1 slice onion
2 cups water or meat stock	½ teaspoon salt
½ bay leaf	⅛ teaspoon pepper
2 stalks celery	1 tablespoon sugar
1 sprig parsley	1 tablespoon Crisco

2 tablespoons flour

Wash and cut tomatoes in quarters, add water (or stock), bay leaf, celery, parsley, onion, salt, pepper and sugar and cook slowly until tomatoes are soft. In another saucepan melt Crisco, add flour and mix well. Add tomato mixture and stir until thick. Press soup through a fine sieve. Reheat over boiling water. Season more if necessary and serve with crisp croûtons.

Canned tomatoes may be used in this recipe.

BLACK BEAN SOUP

2 cups black beans	1 teaspoon salt
2 quarts water	⅛ teaspoon pepper
3 tablespoons Crisco	Few grains cayenne
1 small onion	2 tablespoons flour
1 carrot	3 tablespoons water
2 stalks celery	1 hard-cooked egg
2 sprigs parsley	1 lemon

Soak beans over night. Drain. Put Crisco in saucepan, slice onion into it and cook slowly 5 minutes. Add the beans, water, sliced carrot, celery, parsley, salt, pepper and cayenne. Simmer slowly 3 or 4 hours. Add more water if necessary. Press through a sieve. Reheat over boiling water. Mix flour and water to a smooth paste and add, stirring constantly until soup is thick and smooth. More seasoning may be added if needed. Strain again if necessary. Chop egg fine or mash with a fork and add to soup. Cut lemon in thin slices and serve a slice in each soup plate.

SPLIT PEA SOUP

1½ cups dried split peas
3 quarts water
Ham bone
⅛ teaspoon pepper

1 onion, sliced
2 cups scalded milk
2 tablespoons Crisco

Wash and pick over peas and soak over night. Drain. Add water, ham bone and onion. Cover and cook slowly 3 hours or until peas are soft. Press through a sieve. Add milk, Crisco and pepper and heat thoroughly.

GERMAN VEGETABLE SOUP

½ cup dried lima beans
½ cup dried peas
2 tablespoons barley
2 tablespoons rice
2 tablespoons kidney beans
2 quarts cold water
½ cup celery, cut in pieces
1 ham bone or 1 frankfurter

2 potatoes, sliced
2 onions, sliced
1 white turnip, diced
1 cup stewed or canned
    tomatoes
1 teaspoon salt
¼ teaspoon pepper

Wash beans, peas, barley, rice and kidney beans and soak over night in cold water. Bring to boiling point. Add celery, potatoes, onions, turnip, tomatoes, salt and pepper. Simmer slowly 2 hours. Add water as it cooks away. About half hour before serving add ham bone and more seasoning if necessary. Remove bone before serving. This soup should be quite thick and is a meal in itself.

CLAM CHOWDER

1 dozen clams
4 tablespoons chopped onion
2 tablespoons Crisco
3 cups cooked potatoes, cut in cubes

1½ teaspoons salt
⅛ teaspoon pepper
4 cups scalded milk
2 tablespoons flour

Strain liquor from clams and set it aside. Clean and pick over clams, removing all particles of shell. Chop fine and put into a saucepan with the liquor. Cook 10 minutes. Fry onion in Crisco until a delicate brown and strain Crisco into the clams. Add potatoes, salt, pepper and milk and bring to the boiling point. Mix flour with a little cold water to make a smooth paste and add to the chowder. Stir gently until it thickens. Serve at once.

OYSTER CHOWDER

1 dozen oysters
4 tablespoons chopped onion
2 tablespoons Crisco
3 cups cooked potatoes, cut in cubes

1½ teaspoons salt
⅛ teaspoon pepper
4 cups scalded milk
2 tablespoons flour

Strain liquor from oysters and set it aside. Clean and pick over oysters, removing all particles of shell. Chop fine and put into a saucepan. Fry onion in Crisco until a delicate brown and strain Crisco into the oysters. Add potatoes, salt, pepper and milk and bring to the boiling point. Mix flour with a little cold water to make a smooth paste and add to the chowder with the oyster liquor. Stir gently until it thickens. Serve at once.

CORN CHOWDER

4 tablespoons chopped onion	4 cups milk
3 tablespoons Crisco	1½ teaspoons salt
3 cups cooked potatoes, cut in	⅛ teaspoon pepper
¼ inch slices	Few grains cayenne
2 cups cooked or canned corn	6 small pilot crackers

Fry onion in Crisco until a delicate brown. Strain Crisco into a saucepan. Add potatoes, corn, milk, salt, pepper and cayenne. Bring to the boiling point. Serve a cracker in each portion of soup.

CHAPTER VII

Cereals and Cheese

MANY homemakers do not realize that certain other foods furnish the same amount of nourishment as meat.

Cheese and milk are the two most valuable foods which may be substituted for meat in the meatless menu as they are rich in protein, the element usually supplied by meat. But to give them variety it is necessary to combine them skillfully with other things.

The cereal foods lack just the elements which milk and cheese contain and are therefore well suited to combine with them, especially if fat is added to make up for the lack of meat fat. Crisco, which is a pure vegetable fat, supplies this deficiency and helps to make a perfectly balanced dish of real nutritive value.

Some of the recipes in this chapter are for "one-dish meals" and if followed by a light salad of greens or fruit they will supply the full amount of nourishment for one meal. Among those which will be found most appetizing are baked samp and cheese with tomato sauce, Italian spaghetti and Mexican cheese.

For your convenience a chart giving directions for cooking the most familiar breakfast cereals has been included in this chapter.

_____

SUCCESS SECRETS

1. Buy cereals in small quantities and keep in tightly covered jars or cans.

2. After five minutes of cooking over direct fire place cereal in a double boiler and cook until done.

3. Save your cereal left over from breakfast! Mold or slice it and fry in hot Crisco. Serve with syrup as a dessert for luncheon or supper.

4. Use cheese more often in your menu. It is a concentrated source of protein (building food) and in combination with other foods makes a good substitute for meat.

5. Serve "one-dish" meals occasionally to your family. They save fuel and labor and are an economical way of using left over food material.

6. Cheese cooked at too high a temperature becomes tough and leathery. Bake dishes containing cheese in a moderate oven or over hot water.

GENERAL RULES FOR COOKING CEREALS

Kind of Cereal	Amount	Water	Salt	Method of Cooking	Time
COARSE— Oatmeal Samp Cracked Wheat	1 cup	4 cups	1 teaspoon	Steam— (double-boiler or fireless cooker)	3 hours or over night in fireless cooker
ROLLED— Hominy Rolled Oats	1 cup	3 cups	1 teaspoon	Steam— (double-boiler)	1 hour
FINE— Wheatena Cream of Wheat Farina, etc. Cornmeal	1 cup	4 cups	1 teaspoon	Steam— (double-boiler)	½ hour

1. Sprinkle dry cereal slowly into actively boiling salted water, stirring constantly.

2. Cook directly over fire for 5 to 10 minutes or until cereal thickens slightly, stirring occasionally to prevent lumping. Finish cooking as directed above.

3. Consult chart for quantity and length of time required for cooking.

FRIED HOMINY

Sprinkle 1 cup hominy into 3 cups actively boiling salted water, stirring constantly.   Cook directly over fire until thick, stirring occasionally to prevent lumping.   Put in double boiler or over hot water and cook 30 minutes. Pour into a greased mold.   When cold, cut in thin slices.   Dip in slightly beaten egg mixed with 1 tablespoon cold water, then in flour.   Fry slices in a small amount of Crisco until a delicate brown.

BOILED MACARONI

Cook macaroni in boiling salted water until tender.   Drain in sieve or colander. Pour boiling water over the macaroni to prevent sticking.   Keep hot over hot water.

Spaghetti and noodles are cooked the same way.

MACARONI AND CHIPPED BEEF
EN CASSEROLE

4 cups cooked macaroni	2 cups thin white sauce
1 cup chipped beef	¼ cup bread crumbs

Put a layer of macaroni in a greased baking dish or casserole, then a layer of chipped beef and a layer of White Sauce (page 113).   Repeat until all the ingredients are used.   Sprinkle top with seasoned bread crumbs and bake in hot oven (400 degrees F.) 20 to 25 minutes.

BAKED NOODLES, CHEESE AND HAM

4 cups cooked noodles	⅔ cup grated cheese
1 cup ham, cut fine	2 cups thin white sauce

Put a layer of noodles in a greased baking dish.   Sprinkle with ham and cheese, then cover with a layer of White Sauce (page 113).   Repeat until all the ingredients are used.   Sprinkle top with cheese.   Bake in hot oven (400 degrees F.) 20 to 25 minutes.

BOILED RICE

Wash 1 cup rice and soak in a quart of water over night.   Drain.   Add slowly to 1½ quarts boiling salted water and boil until soft, about 30 minutes.   Stir occasionally while cooking, using a fork to avoid breaking the kernels.   Drain in a sieve.   Pour boiling water over it to prevent sticking.   Put into the pan in which it was cooked, cover and let stand over hot water 5 minutes.

STEAMED RICE

Wash 1 cup rice and soak in a quart of water over night.   Drain.   Add slowly to 2½ cups boiling salted water.   Boil 5 minutes.   Steam over boiling water until tender, stirring occasionally with a fork.

RICE AU GRATIN

3 cups cooked rice   1 cup grated cheese
1½ cups thin white sauce

Put a layer of rice in a greased baking dish. Sprinkle with cheese and cover with a layer of hot White Sauce (page 113). Repeat until all the ingredients are used, having a layer of cheese on top. Bake in a hot oven (400 degrees F.) 20 to 25 minutes.

BAKED SAMP AND CHEESE
WITH TOMATO SAUCE

2 cups cooked or canned tomatoes	Few grains cayenne
2 tablespoons chopped onion	3 tablespoons Crisco
2 cloves	2 tablespoons flour
½ teaspoon salt	2½ cups cooked samp
1 tablespoon sugar	½ cup grated cheese

½ cup bread crumbs

Cook tomatoes, onion, cloves, salt, sugar and cayenne together slowly 20 minutes. Strain. Melt 2 tablespoons Crisco, add flour and mix well. Add the strained tomato juice and bring slowly to the boiling point, stirring constantly. Put a layer of samp in a greased baking dish. Add a layer of cheese and a layer of tomato sauce. Repeat until all the ingredients are used. Sprinkle top with crumbs and dot with small bits of Crisco. Bake in a hot oven (400 degrees F.) 25 minutes, or until crumbs are brown.

BAKED SPAGHETTI

½ pound spaghetti	1 teaspoon salt
2 tablespoons Crisco	⅛ teaspoon pepper
1 tablespoon chopped onion	⅛ teaspoon paprika
2 tablespoons chopped green pepper	2 teaspoons sugar
2 cups tomatoes	1 cup grated cheese

Cook spaghetti in boiling salted water until tender. Drain. Melt Crisco, add onion and green pepper and cook until soft. Add tomatoes, salt, pepper, paprika and sugar and cook 10 minutes. Mix spaghetti with sauce. Add ½ cup cheese. Put in a greased baking dish, sprinkle the top with remaining cheese and bake in a hot oven (400 degrees F.) 20 to 25 minutes or until cheese is brown.

ITALIAN SPAGHETTI

1 onion, sliced thin	1½ tablespoons Crisco
4 tablespoons chopped green pepper	1 can tomato paste
¼ pound mushrooms, chopped	1½ cups water
½ pound chopped beef	½ teaspoon salt

½ pound spaghetti

Fry onion, green pepper, mushrooms and meat in Crisco until a delicate brown, stirring constantly. Add tomato paste, water and salt and cook 20 minutes. Cook spaghetti in boiling salted water until tender. Drain. Serve on a hot platter and pour the hot sauce over it.

CHEESE DREAMS

Cut thin slices of bread and trim off crusts. Sprinkle thin slices of American cheese with salt, paprika and cayenne and put between two slices of bread. Cut in halves and dip in a mixture of 1 beaten egg, ½ cup milk and ¼ teaspoon salt. Fry in hot shallow Crisco until brown on both sides. Drain on unglazed paper and serve hot.

CHEESE FONDUE

1½ cups milk
2 cups soft bread crumbs
3 eggs
1½ cups grated cheese

1 teaspoon salt
⅛ teaspoon pepper
⅛ teaspoon paprika
1 tablespoon melted Crisco

Pour milk over the bread crumbs. Add beaten eggs, cheese, salt, pepper, paprika and Crisco. Mix well. Pour into greased individual baking dishes and bake in moderate oven (350 degrees F.) 20 to 25 minutes.

MEXICAN CHEESE

2 tablespoons Crisco
2 tablespoons chopped green pepper
2 tablespoons flour
1 teaspoon salt
¼ teaspoon mustard

Few grains cayenne
1 cup strained tomato juice
1 cup cooked or canned corn
1½ cups grated cheese
1 egg

Melt Crisco, add green pepper, and cook until soft. Add flour, salt, mustard and cayenne and mix well. Add tomato juice slowly and cook until thick, stirring constantly. Add corn and cheese and cook until cheese is melted. Remove from fire. Beat the egg well and pour the hot sauce on it. Mix well. Serve hot on toast.

CHEESE SOUFFLÉ

1 cup grated cheese
1 cup very thick white sauce

3 egg yolks
3 egg whites

Add the cheese to the hot White Sauce (page 113), and stir until melted. Cool. Add the beaten egg yolks. Fold in the stiffly beaten egg whites. Pour into a greased baking dish. Stand in a pan of warm water and bake in a moderate oven (325 degrees F.) 50 to 60 minutes.

RING-TUM-DIDDY

½ pound grated American cheese
½ teaspoon salt

Few grains cayenne
1 can tomato soup

Toasted crackers

Melt cheese in a saucepan over a slow fire. Add salt, cayenne and tomato soup. Stir until well mixed and heat thoroughly. Serve on toasted crackers.

WELSH RAREBIT

2 tablespoons Crisco
2 tablespoons flour
1/4 teaspoon mustard
1/2 teaspoon salt

Few grains cayenne
1 cup thin cream
1 cup grated cheese
1 egg

Toast

Melt Crisco. Add flour, mustard, salt and cayenne and mix well. Add cream slowly and bring to the boiling point, stirring constantly. Add cheese and stir until melted. Remove from fire. Beat the egg well and pour hot sauce on it. Mix well. Serve hot on toast.

CHAPTER VIII

Eggs

EGGS are an important source of iron, phosphorus and vitamins, but they are not a complete food in themselves and should be used in combination with other foods which supplement them.

When eggs are used as a breakfast dish—scrambled, fried, baked, poached or in an omelet—their possibilities are merely begun. With a cream sauce and a few hard cooked eggs one has the makings of an endless range of luncheon and supper dishes. An ingenious cook will add anything to eggs from minced green pepper or pimento to cheese and mushrooms and, presto, with a pretty garnish she has something to be proud of.

A hostess famous for her salads always introduces hard cooked eggs as a finishing touch and as an emergency measure usually keeps one or two on hand ready cooked. Eggs offer any number of possibilities for salads.

In soups, eggs are a bit of culinary wisdom everyone should cultivate. A raw egg added at the last minute, or a chopped hard cooked egg lends both flavor and nourishment to soup.

New super-creamed Crisco is the ideal fat to use in egg dishes of all kinds because of its delicate flavor. For frying, scrambling or making omelets eggs properly cooked in Crisco are apt to be more easily digested than when cooked in a fat which burns easily.

SUCCESS SECRETS

1. For "hard cooked" eggs allow them to stand for twenty to thirty minutes in water kept just below the boiling point. For "soft cooked" eggs allow them to stand from five to eight minutes. Never allow the water in which eggs are cooked to reach the boiling point, as it makes the white tough and leathery.

2. The whites of eggs beaten until stiff and "folded in," as for omelets and soufflés, make the mixture puff up and become light.

3. Include eggs frequently in your menu. They are especially valuable as a body building food because of the protein and mineral matter they contain.

4. Use only strictly fresh eggs for boiling and poaching.

5. Test eggs for freshness: (a) if they rattle when shaken they are stale. (b) When placed in a glass of water a perfectly fresh egg will sink to the bottom, a half stale one will rise slightly at one end and if very stale it will float.

6. Buy eggs when they are plentiful and cheap, and put them away in water glass solution, or pack them in sawdust against the season when the price is high.

7. Use Crisco, instead of butter, for all egg cookery. Eggs require slow cooking and butter is apt to burn before they are done, making them unsightly and indigestible.

8. Wash dishes in which eggs are cooked first in cold water to loosen the egg, then in hot water.

9. Keep eggs in a cool place, but not in the refrigerator unless in a covered dish, because their porous shells readily absorb odors.

FRIED EGGS

Heat an iron frying pan and put enough Crisco in it to cover the bottom of the pan generously. When melted drop eggs into it. Fry slowly until the white is set. Serve hot. If a harder yolk is desired the eggs may be turned and cooked on the other side.

SCRAMBLED EGGS

6 eggs	¾ teaspoon salt
½ cup milk	⅛ teaspoon pepper

1 tablespoon Crisco

Beat eggs slightly and add milk, salt and pepper. Heat iron frying pan. Melt Crisco and pour in the egg mixture. Cook slowly, stirring constantly with a fork until creamy. Serve hot on toast.

SHIRRED EGGS

Grease individual custard cups. Cover bottom and sides with dried bread crumbs. Break eggs into a saucer, one at a time, and carefully slip into the custard cups. Sprinkle with a little salt and pepper. Cover top with well seasoned crumbs. Bake in a slow oven (275 degrees F.) 15 to 20 minutes or until the egg white is firm and the crumbs are a delicate brown.

FRENCH OMELET

6 eggs	¾ teaspoon salt
⅛ cup milk	⅛ teaspoon pepper

1½ tablespoons Crisco

Beat eggs slightly, just enough to blend yolks with whites. Add milk, salt and pepper. Melt Crisco and pour in the egg mixture. Cook slowly and prick up with a fork until it thickens. Fold and turn out on a hot platter.

CHEESE OMELET

Follow recipe for French Omelet. Sprinkle ½ cup grated cheese on the omelet and put in a very hot oven (475 degrees F.) until cheese melts.

PUFFY OMELET

5 egg yolks	Few grains cayenne
1 teaspoon salt	5 tablespoons hot water
Few grains pepper	5 egg whites

1 tablespoon Crisco

Beat egg yolks until thick and add salt, pepper, cayenne and hot water. Mix well. Fold in lightly the stiffly beaten whites until thoroughly blended. Melt Crisco in an iron frying pan or omelet pan. Pour in the egg mixture and spread evenly. Cook over a slow fire, moving the pan occasionally so as to distribute the heat evenly. When a delicate brown underneath put in a moderate oven (350 degrees F.), and bake 10 to 15 minutes or until top is firm. Fold and serve on a hot platter. Garnish with parsley.

JELLY OMELET

Follow recipe for Puffy Omelet. Beat ½ cup jelly with a fork to the right consistency for spreading. As soon as the omelet is baked spread quickly with the jelly and fold. Serve immediately.

SPANISH OMELET

2 tablespoons Crisco	3 tablespoons chopped celery
3 tablespoons chopped green pepper	¼ cup chopped mushrooms
3 tablespoons chopped onion	¾ teaspoon salt
1 large tomato	Few grains pepper

Few grains cayenne

Melt Crisco, add green pepper and onion and fry slowly until soft. Peel tomato, and cut in small pieces. Add tomato, celery, mushrooms, salt, pepper and cayenne to the first mixture. Cook over a low fire until the tomato is tender. Follow recipe for Puffy Omelet. Put the hot tomato mixture on one-half of the omelet and fold over. Garnish with parsley. Serve immediately.

EGG FLUFF

1 slice of bread	½ tablespoon Crisco, melted
Milk	½ teaspoon salt
4 eggs	Few grains cayenne

Break bread in pieces and put in a cup. Fill the cup with milk. Pour into a bowl and add beaten eggs, cayenne, salt and Crisco. Fill greased custard cups ¾ full and bake in a moderate oven (325 degrees F.) about 30 minutes. Serve at once.

EGG SOUFFLÉ

3 egg yolks	1 tablespoon chopped parsley
1 cup medium white sauce	3 egg whites

Add beaten egg yolks to the hot White Sauce (page 113), and add the parsley. Cool. Fold in the stiffly beaten egg whites. Put into a greased baking dish. Set in pan of hot water and bake in a moderate oven (325 degrees F.) 45 to 50 minutes. Serve immediately.

CURRIED EGGS

Follow recipe for medium White Sauce (page 113), adding ½ teaspoon curry powder and 1 teaspoon chopped onion to the melted Crisco. Add 3 sliced hard cooked eggs. Heat thoroughly and serve on toast.

DEVILLED EGGS

6 hard cooked eggs	½ teaspoon salt
3 tablespoons Crisco Spread	⅛ teaspoon mustard
1 tablespoon vinegar	Few grains cayenne

Cut eggs in halves lengthwise. Put yolks in a bowl, add Crisco Spread (page 145), vinegar, salt, mustard and cayenne and mash to a smooth paste. Fill egg whites with the mixture. Serve with cold cuts of meat.

GOLDEN EGGS

6 hard cooked eggs	Toast points
1½ cups thin white sauce	2 teaspoons chopped parsley

Separate yolks from whites. Chop whites fine and add to the hot White Sauce (page 113). Pour sauce into a platter and arrange toast points around edge. Press egg yolks through a sieve over the sauce and sprinkle with parsley. Serve immediately.

SCALLOPED EGGS

6 hard cooked eggs	1½ cups soft bread crumbs
¼ teaspoon salt	2 cups thin white sauce

Chop eggs fine and add salt. Put a layer of crumbs in the bottom of a greased baking dish. Add a layer of egg and one of White Sauce (page 113). Repeat until all the ingredients are used, having a layer of crumbs on top. Bake in a moderate oven (350 degrees F.) 20 minutes or until crumbs are brown.

BAKED EGGS IN TOMATO SAUCE

2 cups cooked or canned tomatoes	Few grains pepper
1 slice onion	2 tablespoons Crisco
½ teaspoon salt	3 tablespoons flour
2 teaspoons sugar	6 eggs

½ cup grated American cheese

Cook tomatoes, onion, salt, sugar and pepper together 20 minutes. Press the pulp through a sieve, discarding seeds. Melt Crisco, add flour and mix well. Add the tomato juice slowly and bring to the boiling point, stirring constantly. Pour the sauce into six individual baking dishes. Break eggs, one at a time, into a cup and slip carefully into each dish. Sprinkle with cheese. Bake in a moderate oven (325 degrees F.) 15 minutes or until eggs are firm.

BAKED EGGS WITH CHEESE SAUCE

Put a thin layer of Cheese Sauce (page 114), in the bottom of a greased baking dish or individual baking dishes. Break eggs, one at a time, into a cup and drop carefully on the sauce. Cover them with another layer of cheese sauce. Sprinkle top with well-seasoned soft bread crumbs. Bake in a moderate oven (325 degrees F.) 15 to 20 minutes or until the egg whites are firm and the crumbs are brown.

EGGS AND SPINACH EN CASSEROLE

1½ cups cold chopped spinach	6 eggs

1 cup cheese sauce

Put 4 tablespoons well-seasoned spinach in bottom of individual baking dishes. Drop a raw egg on top of each. Sprinkle with salt and pepper. Cover with Cheese Sauce (page 114). Cook in a moderate oven (325 degrees F.) 15 to 20 minutes or until eggs are set.

EGGS AND MUSHROOMS EN CASSEROLE

½ pound mushrooms	Few grains pepper
1½ cups water	Few grains cayenne
1 tablespoon Crisco	1 cup milk
4 tablespoons flour	6 hard cooked eggs, sliced
1 teaspoon salt	2 tablespoons dried bread crumbs

Wash mushrooms, drain and peel, and remove stems. Cook stems and peelings together in the water 15 minutes. Strain liquid into a cup. Slice mushrooms and fry slowly in the Crisco until tender. Mix flour, salt, pepper and cayenne together and add milk slowly to make a smooth paste. Add the cup of mushroom stock and cook over a slow fire, stirring constantly until thick. Add mushrooms. Put a layer of eggs in a casserole then a layer of the mushroom mixture. Repeat this process until all the ingredients are used. Sprinkle top with crumbs. Bake in a moderate oven (350 degrees F.) 20 minutes or until crumbs are brown.

CHAPTER IX

Fish

HAVE you ever wondered why fish has been called "brain food?" There is no actual foundation in fact for such a statement. But because most kinds of fish are low in energy-producing materials (fats, carbohydrates) and rich in general health materials (proteins, vitamins) they are considered good food for people who live sedentary lives. Fish is also easily digested, and so persons who do not get sufficient exercise to digest more hearty food can readily take care of well-cooked and temptingly served fish.

Wherever it can be had at low cost, fish should be used frequently to help furnish the protein requirements of the family. It may be a little more trouble to prepare and require a little more care than a lamb chop, still the difference in price and the pleasing variety added to the menu make it quite worth the extra effort.

Fish appears on the market fresh and preserved by freezing, canning, salting and smoking. One must be careful in selecting fish that it is perfectly fresh, as it decomposes readily.

If one is not fortunate enough to live in a locality where she can purchase fresh fish, storage fish is almost always available and, if it has been properly preserved, is even more reliable than "uncertain" fresh fish. Cold storage fish should never be purchased unless frozen solid and fully enclosed in a jacket of ice. When it comes home from the market put it in a covered pan in the ice box and allow it to thaw gradually, but *do not* soak it in water. Use it as soon as possible after it has thawed out. Salted and smoked fish are always available, as are also good brands of canned fish.

The preparation and cooking of fish is simple and quickly accomplished and if properly prepared at the market it requires very little attention by the cook. Whole fish should be carefully washed in plenty of cold water, while sections, such as fillets and slices, should be wiped with a clean damp piece of cheesecloth.

As most fish is deficient in fat it should be cooked so that fat enters into its preparation in some way. In every case Crisco "just fills the bill." In baking, bits of Crisco dotted over the top make it rich and tender; in broiling, the pan rubbed with Crisco keeps the fish from sticking; and for deep fat frying and sautéing, cooking in the new super-creamed Crisco is the best possible means of securing delicious, easily digested sea food.

SUCCESS SECRETS

1. Fish, as a source of tissue-and-bone-building material, is cheaper than meat. Substitute it once or twice a week for the ever-present roast and stews.

2. When boiling white fish add a little vinegar or lemon juice to the water to keep the flesh white and firm.

3. Narrow strips of muslin, greased with Crisco and put across the bottom of the pan in which fish is to be baked, make it easy to remove the fish from the pan without breaking. The ends of the strips must extend beyond the fish.

4. In selecting fish remember that (a) fresh fish should not give off an offensive odor, (b) the eyes of fresh fish should be bulgy, bright and shiny, (c) the flesh of fresh fish should be firm and the gills reddish in color.

5. When fish comes from the market remove it from the paper and, if it has not been cleaned, clean it at once. Wash and salt it slightly and put in a covered dish.

6. Keep fish in a part of the refrigerator from which odors cannot be carried to other foods.

7. Cook fish as soon as possible after it comes from the market.

8. See Chapter V for additional fish recipes.

SAUTÉED BUTTERFISH

Wipe the fish with a damp cloth. Sprinkle with salt, pepper and flour. Cook in a small amount of Crisco in a frying pan 8 to 10 minutes or until brown on both sides. Sprinkle with chopped parsley and juice of half a lemon. Garnish with watercress and serve with slices of lemon.

BOILED CODFISH

1 tablespoon Crisco	2 quarts water
1 stalk celery, chopped	½ bay leaf
1 small onion, chopped	1 tablespoon vinegar
1 small carrot, chopped	1 teaspoon salt
1 sprig parsley, chopped	⅛ teaspoon pepper

2½ pounds codfish

Melt Crisco, add celery, onion, carrot and parsley. Cook 2 minutes, stirring frequently. Add water, bay leaf, vinegar, salt and pepper and bring to boiling point. Wrap fish in cheesecloth, and drop into the boiling water. Reduce heat and simmer 30 minutes. Remove cheesecloth from the fish and serve on hot platter garnished with parsley. Serve with Egg Sauce (page 115).

CREAMED CODFISH

3 cups cooked cod, flaked	2 tablespoons chopped parsley
2 cups medium white sauce	1 tablespoon chopped pimento

Heat the flaked fish in the White Sauce (page 113). Add parsley and pimento and more seasoning if necessary. Serve on hot toast with baked potatoes.

SAUTÉED CODFISH

Remove the skin and backbone and cut fish in square pieces. Season with salt and pepper and roll in fine cornmeal or cracker crumbs. Cook in a small amount of Crisco in a frying pan 8 to 10 minutes or until brown on both sides. Drain on unglazed paper and serve with Tartar Mayonnaise (page 140).

STUFFED HADDOCK

1 haddock (about 4 lbs.)	1 teaspoon chopped onion
2 tablespoons Crisco	1 teaspoon chopped parsley
1½ cups bread crumbs	½ teaspoon salt
2 tablespoons chopped sour pickle	⅛ teaspoon pepper
1 teaspoon chopped capers	⅛ teaspoon paprika

Wipe fish with a damp cloth and remove head and tail. Split down the middle, clean, remove backbone and as many other bones as possible. Season with salt and pepper. Melt Crisco and add bread crumbs, pickle, capers, onion, parsley, salt, pepper and paprika. Mix well. Put this stuffing between the two halves of fish, sandwich style. Put in a baking pan with ½ cup water, brush top with melted Crisco, sprinkle with salt and pepper and bake in moderate oven (350 degrees F.) 50 to 60 minutes. Baste occasionally while baking with melted Crisco.

HALIBUT STEAK

Wipe slices of halibut with a damp cloth, sprinkle with salt and pepper and dust with fine cracker crumbs. Cook in a small amount of Crisco in a frying pan 8 to 10 minutes or until brown on both sides. Drain on unglazed paper. Garnish with parsley and slices of lemon and serve with Hollandaise Sauce (page 115).

STUFFED HALIBUT STEAK

1 dozen oysters	1 cup bread or cracker crumbs
2 tablespoons Crisco, melted	½ teaspoon salt
1 tablespoon chopped parsley	⅛ teaspoon pepper
2 slices halibut, cut from the middle of fish	

Drain oysters. Add Crisco, parsley, crumbs, salt and pepper and mix well. Wipe the fish with damp cloth. Place one slice on a greased piece of muslin. Sprinkle with salt, pepper and lemon juice and spread with the oyster stuffing. Place second slice on top and brush with melted Crisco. Put in a baking pan with a little water. Bake in moderate oven (350 degrees F.) 40 to 50 minutes. Baste frequently with melted Crisco. Remove to hot platter, garnish with potato balls, parsley and slices of lemon. Serve with Hollandaise Sauce (page 115) or Béarnaise Sauce (page 114).

BOILED LOBSTER

Take the live lobster by the back and plunge it in boiling salted water, head first. Have water deep enough to cover. Reduce heat and simmer 35 to 40 minutes. Remove from the water and cool. Turn lobster on back and make a cut with a sharp knife from point under head to tail, through the shell. Take out the large intestine which runs the length of the tail. (This is often colorless.) Crack the claws so that the meat may be easily removed.

Serve ice cold in the shell with cold Hollandaise Sauce (page 115), or Mayonnaise Dressing (page 140).

BAKED MACKEREL

2 tablespoons Crisco	¼ teaspoon salt
1 cup bread crumbs	⅛ teaspoon pepper
1 teaspoon chopped onion	1 teaspoon chopped parsley
1 teaspoon chopped capers	3½ to 4 pounds mackerel

Melt Crisco. Add crumbs, onion, capers, salt, pepper and parsley. Wash the fish and wipe with a damp cloth. Stuff and tie together. Sprinkle with salt and pepper and spread with melted Crisco. Bake in moderate oven (350 degrees F.) 50 to 60 minutes. Baste often with Crisco and water.

BROILED OYSTERS

Dry 24 oysters with a clean soft cloth. Heat broiler and grease well, using melted Crisco. Dip oysters in melted Crisco, then in dried bread crumbs, and arrange on broiler. Broil about 3 minutes. Have ready 6 slices of toast, cut in uniform pieces. Moisten toast with hot oyster juice. Place 4 broiled oysters on each slice of toast and season with salt, pepper and a few drops of lemon juice.

SCALLOPED OYSTERS

2 tablespoons Crisco   1 teaspoon salt
1½ cups soft bread crumbs   ⅛ teaspoon pepper
30 oysters   ½ cup milk
½ cup oyster liquor

Grease baking dish with Crisco and cover bottom with a layer of crumbs. On this put 10 oysters. Sprinkle each layer with salt and pepper and dot with small bits of Crisco. Repeat this process until all the ingredients are used, having a layer of crumbs on top. Pour the milk and oyster liquor over it and bake in moderate oven (350 degrees F.) 30 minutes. Serve with slices of crisp bacon.

FRIED PICKEREL

Wipe the fish with a damp cloth. Leave whole or cut in pieces of uniform size. Sprinkle with salt, pepper and flour. Cook in a small amount of Crisco in a frying pan 20 to 30 minutes, according to size of fish. Serve with lemon and parsley.

BOILED SALMON

1 tablespoon Crisco   2 quarts water
1 onion, chopped   ½ bay leaf
1 stalk celery, chopped   1 teaspoon salt
1 sprig parsley, chopped   ⅛ teaspoon pepper
1 carrot, chopped   1 tablespoon vinegar
2½ pounds salmon

Melt Crisco, add onion, celery, parsley and carrot. Cook for 2 minutes, stirring frequently. Add water, bay leaf, salt, pepper and vinegar and bring to boiling point. Wrap salmon in cheesecloth and drop into the boiling water. Reduce heat and simmer 30 minutes. Remove cheesecloth and serve fish on hot platter. Garnish with lemon, cut in fancy shapes, and parsley. Serve with Parsley Sauce (page 115).

SCALLOPED SALMON

1 cup thick white sauce   1 tablespoon chopped green pepper
1½ cups cold flaked salmon   ¼ teaspoon paprika
1 cup soft bread crumbs

To the hot White Sauce (page 113), add salmon, green pepper and paprika. Mix well. Put in greased ramekins or a large baking dish. Sprinkle with fine bread crumbs. Bake in a hot oven (400 degrees F.) 20 minutes, or until crumbs are brown.

BROILED SALMON STEAK

Moisten slices of salmon with French Dressing (page 139), and let stand for 1 hour. Put in a broiler and broil on both sides. Brush while cooking with 1 tablespoon melted Crisco, using a little at a time. Cook 12 to 15 minutes. Remove to hot platter. Season with salt, pepper and juice of ½ lemon and sprinkle with 1 tablespoon chopped parsley. Serve with Béarnaise Sauce (page 114).

BROILED SHAD

Wash, remove head and tail from shad, clean and split down the back. Remove backbone with as many other bones as possible. Place skin side down on a greased broiler, spread with melted Crisco and sprinkle with salt and pepper. Broil 20 to 25 minutes, depending on size of fish. Remove to hot platter and garnish with watercress and slices of lemon. Serve at once.

SHAD ROE

Wash and dry the roe, using care not to break the skin. Sprinkle with salt, pepper and flour. Melt 2 tablespoons Crisco in a frying pan. When hot, put in the roe and cook slowly until brown on one side. Turn and brown on the other side. A cover may be put over the frying pan to keep the Crisco from spattering. Cook from 20 to 30 minutes. Garnish with lemon and parsley and serve very hot with crisp bacon.

SHRIMP AND RICE, BAKED

2 cups cooked shrimp, cut in pieces	$\frac{1}{8}$ teaspoon pepper
2 cups cooked rice	Few grains cayenne
2 tablespoons chopped parsley	2 cups medium white sauce
$\frac{1}{2}$ cup dried bread crumbs	

Mix shrimps, rice, parsley, pepper, cayenne and White Sauce (page 113). Pour in a greased baking dish and sprinkle with crumbs. Bake in a hot oven (400 degrees F.) 20 to 25 minutes or until crumbs are brown.

FILLET OF SOLE (FLOUNDER)

1½ pounds fillets of flounder	¾ cup fine bread crumbs
Salt	1 egg
Pepper	2 tablespoons water

Wipe fillets with a damp cloth. Sprinkle with salt and pepper. Dip in crumbs, then in slightly beaten egg diluted with water and again in crumbs. Cook in a small amount of Crisco in a frying pan 8 to 10 minutes, or until brown on both sides. Garnish with lemon and parsley and serve with Tartar Mayonnaise (page 140).

BAKED WEAKFISH

Wash fish, wipe with damp cloth, and sprinkle inside with salt and pepper. Cut gashes across the skin. Spread fish with Crisco and sprinkle with salt, pepper and ½ teaspoon Worcestershire sauce. Place fish in a baking pan on a strip of muslin greased with Crisco. Bake in a moderate oven (350 degrees F.) allowing about 15 minutes to the pound. Remove from the muslin to a hot platter. Garnish with lemon and parsley. The fish may be filled with a bread stuffing if desired.

CHAPTER X

Meat and Poultry

DO YOU know that about one-third of the money spent
on food in the United States is spent for meat? This
seems a high percentage but it is probably due to the
fact that so many of us demand the expensive roasts, steaks
and chops. Fortunately there is just as much nourishment in
the cheaper cuts of meat as in the expensive cuts, and if they
are properly cooked they will be deliciously tender and palat-
able.

The recipes in this chapter call frequently for the cheaper
cuts, and if you follow them you cannot help but notice the
difference in your butcher's bill at the end of a month.

In cooking meats you aim for two things. First, you want
to keep all the juices *in* the meat, and secondly, you want the
tissues to grow tender. Juices will not run out of a piece of
meat if the outside is first seared over by exposure to a very
hot fire; then the heat should be reduced and the meat cooked
rather slowly for the remainder of the required time if you want
to avoid toughness.

During the process of roasting, the meat should be basted
frequently to keep it moist and to concentrate the flavors in
the meat itself. The tougher meats, and in fact any meat or
fowl which is to be cooked in water, should not actually boil.
It should simmer or cook very slowly just below the boiling
point. Slow cooking loosens the connective tissues while the
more rapid cooking hardens and toughens them.

When cooking roasts it is best not to put any water in the
pan at first. If the meat has not enough fat to make liquid for
basting, Crisco will be found a great help. Basting lean meats
with Crisco makes them juicy, tender and deliciously flavored.
Meats basted with Crisco are brown and have a delicately crisp
outside covering.

As poultry is frequently lacking in fat it is sometimes necessary to add extra fat when roasting it. The skin of chicken and turkey should be rubbed over with Crisco before being put in the oven and then the bird should be basted frequently, more Crisco and a little water being added as the pan becomes dry.

SUCCESS SECRETS

1. When meat comes from the market remove it from the paper and place it in the ice box on a china or enamel plate.
2. Do not put meat into water to wash it. Wipe with a clean, damp cloth before cooking.
3. Do not pierce the meat with a fork while it is cooking; this lets out the juices.
4. To draw out the flavor of meats, as for broths, start the cooking in *cold* water, bringing slowly to the boiling point.
5. To keep flavor and juices *in* meat expose it to extreme heat *first*, then reduce the temperature and cook more slowly.
6. Cook the tough and cheaper cuts of meat very slowly and for a long time.
7. Baste meat and poultry often while roasting.
8. Learn to make appetizing, nourishing dishes of the cheaper cuts of meat.
9. Use the internal organs of beef and lamb—liver, kidneys, heart and sweetbreads—to increase the vitamins in your diet.
10. Serve Yorkshire pudding with roast beef, dumplings with stew and fried apples with pork to give your meat course "the perfect touch."

ROAST BEEF

Wipe the meat with a clean damp cloth. Do not wash it. Dredge with flour. Place in roasting pan and put ½ teaspoon salt, ¼ teaspoon pepper and 2 tablespoons Crisco in the pan. Put in a very hot oven (500 degrees F.) for 15 to 20 minutes. Reduce heat to hot oven (400 degrees F.) and cook, allowing 8 to 10 minutes to a pound for standing roast and 10 to 12 minutes for a rolled roast, if it is wanted rare. Baste frequently. Do not add water to the roast. Serve with Yorkshire Pudding (page 101).

BRAISED BEEF

2½ pounds lower part of rump
1 teaspoon salt
⅛ teaspoon pepper
3 tablespoons flour

3 tablespoons Crisco
½ cup carrots, cut in slices
½ cup onions, cut in slices
½ cup celery, cut in pieces

2 cups boiling water

Wipe meat with a clean damp cloth and cut in 3 inch cubes. Sprinkle with salt, pepper and flour. Put Crisco in frying pan and when hot add the meat and brown slightly. Put meat in a baking dish, add carrots, onions, celery and water. Cover tightly and bake in a moderate oven (325 degrees F.) 3 hours or until meat is tender. Thicken the stock with a little flour mixed to a smooth paste with water.

POT ROAST À LA MODE

4 pounds beef (round)
1 teaspoon salt
⅛ teaspoon pepper
2 tablespoons flour
2 tablespoons Crisco

½ cup carrots, cut in cubes
½ cup celery, cut in pieces
½ cup turnip, cut in cubes
½ bay leaf
Sprig of parsley

Wipe meat with a clean damp cloth. Sprinkle with salt, pepper and flour. Melt Crisco in a frying pan and brown the surface of the meat. Put meat in a saucepan, add carrots, celery, turnips, bay leaf and parsley. Add boiling water to half cover the meat. Cover and simmer slowly about 4 hours, until meat is tender. Put meat on a hot platter. Strain liquid from the vegetables and put them around the meat. Thicken the stock with a little flour mixed to a smooth paste with cold water. Add more seasonings, if necessary.

BEEF STEW

1 small onion
2 tablespoons Crisco
2 pounds beef, top round
5 tablespoons flour
3 medium-sized tomatoes
2 tablespoons chopped parsley

3 cups water
6 small onions
1½ cups sliced carrots
⅛ teaspoon pepper
1½ teaspoons salt
Few grains cayenne

⅓ cup water

Slice onion and cook slowly in Crisco 5 minutes. Cut beef in uniform pieces. Sprinkle with 2 tablespoons of the flour and a little salt and pepper. Brown meat in the Crisco, turning often. Add tomatoes, parsley and water and cook slowly about 1 hour. Add onions and carrots, salt, pepper and cayenne and cook 1 hour longer. Thicken gravy with 3 tablespoons flour and ⅓ cup water mixed to a smooth paste and bring to the boiling point. Serve hot.

ROLLED FLANK STEAK

Select a flank steak weighing about 1½ pounds. Wipe meat with a clean damp cloth. Sprinkle with salt. Spread Poultry Stuffing (page 101) on meat. Roll like a jelly roll and fasten ends together with skewers. Put in a baking dish and add 1 cup boiling water. Brown in a very hot oven (500 degrees F.) 15 minutes. Cover and cook slowly in a moderate oven (325 degrees F.) 1 hour or until meat is tender. Remove to a hot platter. Thicken the stock with a little flour mixed to a smooth paste with cold water. Slice meat and serve with the gravy.

SWISS STEAK

2 pounds beef, round	1 small onion, chopped
½ cup flour	2 tablespoons Crisco
½ teaspoon salt	¼ cup chopped green pepper
⅛ teaspoon pepper	1 cup stewed or canned tomatoes

1 cup boiling water

Wipe meat with a clean damp cloth. Cut in 2 inch square pieces. Mix flour, salt and pepper together. Pound flour into the meat with a wooden potato masher. Brown onion and meat in the Crisco. Add green pepper, tomatoes and water. Cover and cook slowly 2 hours or until meat is tender. The stock may be thickened more with a little flour mixed to a smooth paste with cold water.

BEEFSTEAK PIE

2 pounds chuck steak	1 cup cooked carrots, cut in cubes
1 teaspoon salt	2 cups cooked potatoes, cut in cubes
⅛ teaspoon pepper	1 cup cooked celery, cut in pieces
2 tablespoons flour	6 cooked medium-sized onions
3 tablespoons cold water	2 tablespoons Crisco

Wipe meat with a clean damp cloth, cut in 1 inch cubes and sprinkle with salt and pepper. Cover meat with boiling water and simmer for 1 hour or until meat is tender. Put the meat in a baking dish. Thicken the stock with the flour mixed to a paste with the water. Add carrots, potatoes, celery and onions. Pour the gravy over it and dot with Crisco. Add more seasoning if necessary. Cover top with Plain Pastry (page 178). Bake in a quick oven (450 degrees F.) 10 minutes. Reduce the heat to a moderate oven (325 degrees F.) and bake 20 to 25 minutes.

HAMBURG BALLS

1 pound round steak, ground	⅛ cup milk
2 eggs	2 tablespoons chopped onion
⅔ cup soft bread crumbs	1 tablespoon Crisco
1 teaspoon salt	1½ tablespoons flour
⅛ teaspoon pepper	1½ cups boiling water

Mix meat, beaten eggs, bread crumbs, salt, pepper and milk together. Fry onion in Crisco until a delicate brown and add to the meat mixture. Form in small flat circular cakes and sprinkle with flour. Fry on both sides in a small amount of Crisco until brown. Remove the cakes to a hot platter. Add flour to the Crisco in the pan and cook until a delicate brown, stirring constantly. Add water and bring to the boiling point, mixing well. Pour around the meat balls.

SCALLOPED BEEF

3 cups chopped cold cooked beef   1½ cups medium white sauce
1 tablespoon chopped parsley   1½ cups soft bread crumbs
1 teaspoon onion juice

Mix beef, parsley and onion juice with the White Sauce (page 113). Put a layer of crumbs in the bottom of a greased baking dish and cover with layer of meat and sauce. Repeat the process until all the ingredients are used, having a layer of bread crumbs on top. Bake in a hot oven (400 degrees F.) 15 to 20 minutes or until crumbs are brown.

HASH

Chop cold roast beef, or steak, and add an equal amount of chopped cold cooked potatoes. Season with salt, pepper, onion juice and a few drops Worcestershire sauce. Moisten with a small amount of water. Melt a little Crisco in a frying pan, add meat mixture and spread evenly. Cover and fry slowly until a delicate brown on the bottom. Fold over like an omelet and turn out on a hot platter and garnish with parsley. Serve with Tomato Sauce (page 116) if desired.

CREAMED BEEF ON TOAST

½ pound dried beef   2 cups medium white sauce

Pour boiling water over the dried beef to remove some of the salt. Drain. Follow the recipe for White Sauce (page 113), using ¼ teaspoon salt in place of ¾ teaspoon called for in the recipe. Add the beef and heat thoroughly. Serve on hot platter garnished with toast points.

ROAST LEG OF LAMB

Wipe leg of lamb with a clean, damp cloth. Rub with Crisco and sprinkle with salt and pepper. Put in a roasting pan with a little water and 1 teaspoon Worcestershire sauce. Bake in a very hot oven (460 degrees F.) for 15 minutes. Reduce the temperature to a moderate oven (350 degrees F.) for remaining time, allowing 15 to 20 minutes per pound. Baste every half hour, adding more hot water if necessary. Remove lamb to a hot platter. Pour off the fat leaving 2 tablespoons in the pan. Add 4 tablespoons flour and cook until brown. Add 2 cups hot water and bring to the boiling point, stirring constantly. Cook 5 minutes longer. Season with salt and pepper. Serve with the lamb.

STUFFED SHOULDER OF LAMB

1 shoulder of lamb   2 cups soft bread crumbs
Salt   1 teaspoon chopped mint
Pepper   1 tablespoon chopped celery leaves
2 tablespoons chopped onion   ½ teaspoon salt
5 tablespoons Crisco   ⅛ teaspoon pepper

Have the shoulder blade removed. This leaves a pocket for the stuffing. Wipe meat with a clean, damp cloth, spread with 2 tablespoons Crisco and sprinkle the pocket and surface of the lamb with salt and pepper. Fry onion in 3 tablespoons Crisco until a delicate brown. Add bread crumbs, mint, celery leaves, salt and pepper. Mix well. Fill pocket with stuffing. Put in a roasting pan and add a little hot water to cover bottom of pan. Bake in a very hot oven (460 degrees F.) 15 minutes. Reduce the heat to a moderate oven (350 degrees F.) for remaining time, allowing 15 to 20 minutes per pound. Baste every half hour, adding more hot water if necessary.

CURRIED LAMB AND RICE

2½ pounds lamb, shoulder
2 tablespoons Crisco
1 teaspoon salt
⅛ teaspoon pepper

1½ tablespoons curry powder
2 tablespoons flour
2 tablespoons water
3 cups boiled rice

Wipe lamb with a clean, damp cloth. Cut into medium-size pieces and remove the fat. Melt Crisco in a frying pan, add lamb and cook until a delicate brown. Cover with boiling water. Add salt, pepper and curry powder mixed with a little cold water. Cover and simmer for about 2½ hours or until lamb is tender. Make a smooth paste of the flour and water and add enough to thicken the liquid. Mound hot rice in center of a hot platter and pour the curried lamb around it.

IRISH STEW

3 pounds lamb (forequarter)
1 cup carrots, cut in cubes
1 cup turnips, cut in cubes

3 cups potatoes, cut in cubes
1 teaspoon salt
⅛ teaspoon pepper

1 onion, sliced

Wipe meat with a clean, damp cloth, and cut in 2 inch square pieces. Put in a kettle, cover with boiling water and cook slowly for 1½ hours or until tender. Add carrots, turnips, onion, salt, pepper and cook for 30 minutes. Add potatoes and cook 15 minutes longer. Thicken with a little flour mixed to a paste with cold water.

LAMB EN CASSEROLE

3 cups cold cooked lamb, cut in pieces
1 tablespoon Crisco
1 cup cooked carrots, cut in cubes

1 cup cooked potato balls
8 small onions, cooked
Left over gravy

Brown lamb in Crisco. Put in a baking dish. Add carrots, potato balls and onions. Add left over gravy and enough hot water to moisten. Season with salt and pepper. Cover and bake in a hot oven (400 degrees F.) 20 to 25 minutes.

SCALLOPED LAMB

2 cups cooked lamb, cut in small pieces
2 cups medium white sauce

1 cup soft bread crumbs
1 tablespoon chopped parsley

Mix lamb and White Sauce (page 113), together. Put a layer of lamb in a greased casserole or baking dish, add a layer of bread crumbs and sprinkle with parsley. Repeat this process until all the ingredients are used, having a layer of crumbs on top. Bake in a hot oven (400 degrees F.) 20 to 25 minutes or until crumbs are brown.

SHEPHERD'S PIE

Chop cold cooked lamb and moisten with left over gravy. Put in a casserole or baking dish and dot with small pieces of Crisco. Cover with hot Mashed Potatoes (page 109). Spread top with beaten egg yolk mixed with 2 teaspoons cold water. Bake in a hot oven (400 degrees F.) 20 minutes or until brown.
For individual pies bake in small ramekins or custard cups 15 minutes.

MINCED LAMB ON TOAST

Chop cold cooked lamb in small pieces. Follow recipe for medium White Sauce (page 113). To 1½ cups meat add 1 cup sauce, and 1 teaspoon chopped parsley. Serve on hot toast.

BOILED LEG OF MUTTON

Wipe meat with a clean, damp cloth. Put in a kettle and cover with boiling water. Cover the kettle and bring quickly to the boiling point. Boil 10 minutes and skim. Simmer slowly until tender. When half done add salt. Serve with Caper Sauce (page 114).

ROAST STUFFED VEAL

Select a shoulder of veal and have it boned. Wipe with a damp cloth and stuff with Poultry Stuffing (page 101). Put in a baking pan, spread with Crisco and sprinkle with salt and pepper. Brown in a very hot oven (500 degrees F.) 15 minutes. Add 1 cup water. Reduce heat to a hot oven (400 degrees F.) and cook until done, allowing 25 to 30 minutes per pound. Baste occasionally, adding more water when necessary.

INDIVIDUAL VEAL CUTLETS

2 pounds veal cutlet	1 egg
1 teaspoon salt	2 tablespoons water
⅛ teaspoon pepper	2 tablespoons Crisco
¾ cup dried bread crumbs	1 cup hot water

Cut veal into 6 pieces. Wipe with a clean, damp cloth, and sprinkle with salt and pepper. Roll in bread crumbs, dip in well-beaten egg diluted with water and roll again in crumbs. Melt Crisco in an iron frying pan. Put in the cutlets and brown on both sides. Add the hot water and simmer until tender, about 45 to 50 minutes. Remove them and thicken the stock with a little flour mixed to a smooth paste with cold water. Pour the sauce over the cutlets.

VEAL LOAF

3 pounds raw, lean veal, chopped	1½ teaspoons salt
¾ cup cracker crumbs	⅛ teaspoon pepper
1 egg	1 tablespoon chopped onion
1 tablespoon chopped parsley	⅛ teaspoon nutmeg
2 tablespoons melted Crisco	½ cup milk

Mix veal, cracker crumbs, beaten egg, parsley, Crisco, salt, pepper, onion and nutmeg together. Moisten with milk. Pack in a greased small loaf pan.

Spread top with Crisco. Bake in a moderate oven (325 degrees F.) 1 hour. Prick top with fork to allow meat to absorb the Crisco. Baste occasionally with melted Crisco and a little hot water. Serve hot with Tomato Sauce (page 116), or cold with catsup or pickles.

VEAL PIE

2½ pounds knuckle of veal	2 cups water
1 teaspoon salt	½ cup sliced carrots
⅛ teaspoon pepper	2 tablespoons chopped parsley
2 tablespoons Crisco	2 tablespoons flour
2 slices onion	¼ cup water
2 cups celery, cut in pieces	Plain pastry

Cut meat from the knuckle in small pieces (keep bone to use in making soup stock). Sprinkle with salt and pepper. Melt Crisco, add onion and cook slowly 5 minutes. Remove onion from pan and put in the veal. Cook until meat is brown, stirring frequently. Add celery and water, cover and simmer until meat is tender. Add a little water to the meat as liquid boils away. Add raw carrots and parsley and more salt and pepper if necessary. Cook 20 minutes longer. Thicken with the flour and water mixed to a smooth paste. Put in a baking dish and cover with Plain Pastry (page 178). Bake in a quick oven (450 degrees F.) 15 to 20 minutes or until brown.

CURRIED VEAL AND RICE

Follow recipe for Curried Lamb and Rice (page 92), using three pounds of veal (knuckle) instead of the lamb.

VEAL SOUFFLÉ

4 egg yolks	2 cups cooked ground veal
1½ cups very thick white sauce	½ teaspoon salt
	4 egg whites

Add beaten egg yolks to the hot White Sauce (page 113), and mix well. Add the veal and salt. Cool, and fold in the stiffly beaten egg whites. Put in a greased casserole or baking dish set in a pan of hot water and bake in a moderate oven (325 degrees F.) 50 to 60 minutes.

CROWN ROAST PORK

Select the choicest ribs from two loins of pork. Scrape fatty portions from the bone between the ribs as far as the lean meat and trim off. Shape both pieces in a semi-circle having ribs outside and sew pieces together to form a circle or crown. Trim ends of bone evenly and put small cubes of salt pork on them to prevent the bones from burning. Put roast in a roasting pan and add ½ cup hot water. Spread with softened Crisco and sprinkle with salt and pepper. Bake in a very hot oven (460 degrees F.) 15 minutes, reduce the heat to a moderate oven (350 degrees F.) and bake until well done, allowing 20 to 25 minutes per pound. Baste every 15 minutes while cooking, adding more hot water if necessary.

PORK CHOPS EN CASSEROLE WITH POTATOES

7 medium-sized potatoes   ⅛ teaspoon pepper
2 tablespoons flour   3 tablespoons Crisco
1 teaspoon salt   3 cups milk
                    6 pork chops

Wash and pare potatoes and cut in thin slices. Put a layer in a greased baking dish and sprinkle with flour, salt and pepper. Dot with small bits of Crisco. Add another layer of potatoes and seasoning and repeat until all the ingredients are used. Pour the milk over it. Lay pork chops on top. Bake in a moderate oven (325 degrees F.) 1 to 1½ hours or until potatoes are tender.

STUFFED PORK TENDERLOIN

2 pork tenderloins   Salt
2 cups poultry stuffing   Pepper
                    Crisco

Have each loin split but not cut through. Open out flat. Sprinkle one loin with salt and pepper. Cover the other with Poultry Stuffing (page 101). Put the two together and tie securely. Spread with Crisco and sprinkle with salt and pepper. Bake in a moderate oven (350 degrees F.) 50 to 60 minutes. Baste often with Crisco melted in hot water. Garnish with Fried Apple Rings (page 101).

SAUSAGES AND SWEET POTATOES

2 pounds sweet potatoes   ¼ cup water
½ cup sugar   2 tablespoons Crisco
½ cup brown sugar   1 teaspoon salt
                    1 pound sausages

Parboil sweet potatoes 15 minutes. Peel and slice in strips like French fried potatoes. Put in a greased baking dish. Put sugar, brown sugar, water, Crisco and salt in a saucepan and boil 3 minutes. Pour syrup over the sweet potatoes. Bake in a moderate oven (350 degrees F.) 30 to 40 minutes. Put sausages on top of potatoes. Cook one-half hour longer or until potatoes and sausages are tender.

SAUSAGE TURNOVERS

1 cup sausage meat   1 teaspoon Worcestershire sauce
1 cup chopped ham   1 egg
1 cup cooked rice   Plain pastry

Cook sausage meat in a frying pan, slowly, stirring constantly until done, but not browned—about 10 minutes. Drain off the fat. Add ham, rice and Worcestershire sauce and mix well. Add well-beaten egg. Roll Plain Pastry (page 178) very thin and cut in 4 inch squares. Put 2 tablespoons of the meat mixture in the center of each square. Moisten edges with water and fold over to form triangles. Press edges together with tines of a fork, and prick the tops. Bake in a hot oven (400 degrees F.) 15 to 20 minutes.

BAKED VIRGINIA HAM

Put ham in a deep pot, cover with cold water and bring to the boiling point quickly.   Reduce heat and simmer 2 or 3 hours or until tender.   Take from pot and remove the skin.   Cover with brown sugar and stick whole cloves into the ham about 2 inches apart.   Sprinkle with fine bread crumbs.   Put in a roasting pan with ½ cup water.   Brown in a moderate oven (350 degrees F.) 25 to 30 minutes.

BROILED HAM

Spread thin slices of smoked ham with Crisco and sprinkle generously with brown sugar.   Broil in a very hot oven (550 degrees F.) 10 minutes or until heated thoroughly.   Serve with Fried Bananas (page 50).

HAM SOUFFLÉ

Follow recipe for Veal Soufflé (page 94), using 2 cups ground cooked ham instead of the veal and omitting the salt.

BEEF KIDNEY STEW

2 beef kidneys	3 medium-sized potatoes
2 tablespoons Crisco	1 cup stewed or canned tomatoes
2 cups water	1 teaspoon salt
1 small onion, sliced	½ teaspoon paprika
2 cups sliced carrots	1 teaspoon Worcestershire sauce

Soak kidneys in cold water 1 hour.   Drain.   Pour boiling water over them to blanch.   Remove tubes and skin and cut in pieces.   Sprinkle with salt, pepper and flour.   Melt Crisco in frying pan and sauté kidneys until brown.   Add water, onion and carrots. Cover and cook slowly for 30 minutes.   Add potatoes, cut in slices, tomatoes, salt, paprika and Worcestershire sauce.   Cook 20 to 30 minutes longer or until potatoes are tender.

STUFFED HEART EN CASSEROLE

1 beef heart	INGREDIENTS FOR SAUCE
1 cup dried bread crumbs	
1 tablespoon melted Crisco	1 cup stewed or canned tomatoes
1 slice onion, chopped	1 slice onion
1 teaspoon sugar	½ teaspoon salt
2 tablespoons stewed or canned tomatoes	½ teaspoon paprika
	½ cup celery, cut in pieces
½ teaspoon salt	1 tablespoon Crisco
⅛ teaspoon pepper	

Soak the heart in cold water 1 hour.   Remove the muscles and arteries and every particle of blood.   Parboil for 20 minutes.   Make a stuffing of the bread crumbs, Crisco, onion, sugar, tomatoes, salt and pepper.   Fill the heart with this mixture and tie securely.   Place in a covered casserole.   Mix the ingredients for the sauce and pour over the stuffed heart.   Dot with Crisco and bake in moderate oven (325 degrees F.) for 3 hours.   Add more hot water as liquid cooks away.   Thicken the gravy, if desired, with a little flour and water mixed to a smooth paste.

BOILED BEEF TONGUE

1 fresh beef tongue	2 sprigs parsley
1 carrot, sliced	½ bay leaf
1 onion, sliced	½ teaspoon peppercorns
2 stalks celery, cut in pieces	2 cloves

2 teaspoons salt

Wash tongue thoroughly. Put in a deep kettle. Cover with water and add carrot, onion, celery, parsley, bay leaf, peppercorns, cloves and salt. Bring quickly to the boiling point. Reduce heat and simmer slowly 3 hours or until tongue is tender. Remove from the pot. Cut off the throat part and remove skin from tongue. Serve hot with Almond and Raisin Sauce (page 114). The tongue is delicious cut in slices and served cold. The meat from the throat end makes good hash and the water in which it is cooked is rich soup stock.

SAUTÉED LAMB KIDNEYS

6 small lamb kidneys	⅛ teaspoon pepper
1 teaspoon salt	2 tablespoons flour

1 tablespoon Crisco

Soak kidneys in cold water 1 hour. Pour boiling water over them to blanch. Drain and remove tubes and skin. Cut kidneys in halves and then in quarters. Sprinkle with salt, pepper and flour. Melt Crisco in frying pan and sauté kidneys until tender. Serve on toast with crisp bacon.

BRAISED LIVER

2 cups celery, cut in small pieces	¼ cup water
1½ pounds liver (unsliced)	8 small carrots
1 teaspoon salt	8 small onions
⅛ teaspoon pepper	2 tablespoons flour
2 tablespoons Crisco	Bacon

Put celery in bottom of a greased covered casserole or baking dish. Sprinkle liver with salt and pepper. Put it on top of celery and dot with bits of Crisco. Add the water and cover. Bake in a moderate oven (350 degrees F.) 45 minutes or until liver and celery are tender. Cook carrots and onions in a small amount of boiling salted water until tender and put them in the casserole. Save vegetable stock, thicken with the flour mixed to a smooth paste with a little cold water, and pour over the liver. Cook 15 minutes longer. Serve hot with crisp bacon.

BREADED SWEETBREADS

2 pairs sweetbreads	½ teaspoon salt
1 sprig parsley	1 cup fine dry bread crumbs
1 stalk celery	1 egg

2 tablespoons water

Soak sweetbreads in salt water 1 hour. Drain. Put in saucepan with parsley, celery and salt and enough water to cover. Bring to boiling point. Reduce heat and cook slowly 30 minutes.   Cool in the stock in which they are cooked. Remove fat and connective tissue from the sweetbreads and cut in uniform pieces.   Dip in crumbs then in slightly beaten egg diluted with water and again in crumbs.   Fry in deep hot Crisco until brown.   Drain on unglazed paper.

ROAST CHICKEN

Singe, dress, wash and wipe with a clean, damp cloth a young roasting chicken.   Stuff with Poultry Stuffing (page 101).   Tie securely in shape, with wings and legs close to the body.   Spread with melted Crisco and sprinkle with salt and pepper.   Put in a quick oven (450 degrees F.) 15 minutes.   Add 1 cup water.   Reduce heat to moderate oven (350 degrees F.), and cook until done, allowing 15 minutes to a pound.   Baste often, adding more hot water if necessary.   Serve with Giblet Gravy (page 100).

ROAST CAPON

Prepare and cook the same as roast chicken.   Oyster Stuffing (page 100) is nice with capon.

FRIED CHICKEN

Select 2 young frying chickens weighing about 2½ to 3 pounds each.   Clean, singe and disjoint.   Sprinkle with salt and pepper and roll in flour.   Melt enough Crisco in a large iron frying pan to have it about 1 inch deep.   When hot place the pieces of chicken in it.   Cover and fry slowly until a delicate brown, turning the pieces occasionally.   This will require about 30 minutes. Remove chicken to a hot platter.   Garnish with parsley.

FRICASSEE CHICKEN

Dress, clean, singe and disjoint a year-old fowl.   Sprinkle with salt and pepper and roll in flour.   Melt enough Crisco to cover bottom of a large iron frying pan.   Put in the chicken and fry on both sides until a delicate brown.   Remove to a saucepan and cover with boiling water.   Cover and cook slowly until the chicken is tender, allowing about 20 minutes per pound.   When half done add salt and pepper.   Remove the chicken to a hot platter and sprinkle with a little chopped parsley.   Make a gravy of the stock, thickened with a little flour mixed to a smooth paste with cold water.

CHICKEN PIE

Dress, clean and singe a fowl.   Put in a saucepan with boiling water to cover. Add a sliced carrot, 1 stalk celery, 1 sprig parsley and 1 slice onion.   Bring to the boiling point; cover and simmer until fowl is tender, allowing about 30 minutes to the pound.   When half done season with salt and pepper.   Remove skin of the fowl and cut meat from the bones, keeping it in large pieces.   Put in a baking dish.   Boil chicken stock down to 3 cups, strain and skim off most of the fat.   Mix 4 tablespoons flour to a smooth paste with cold water and add to the stock.   Bring to the boiling point, stirring constantly, and add to the chicken, with ½ pound mushrooms sliced and sautéed in 2 tablespoons Crisco. Cover with Plain Pastry (page 178).   Bake in a quick oven (450 degrees F.) 15 minutes or until crust is brown.

CHICKEN POT PIE

4 pounds roasting chicken	Dumplings
6 medium-sized potatoes	2 tablespoons Crisco
1 teaspoon salt	2 tablespoons flour

⅛ teaspoon pepper

Clean, singe, wash and disjoint chicken. Put in a saucepan, add enough hot water to cover and bring to the boiling point. Cover and cook slowly until chicken is about tender. Add potatoes, salt and pepper and cook until potatoes are soft, about 20 minutes. Place Dumplings (page 101) on top of the chicken and potatoes. Cover tightly and cook 10 minutes longer until dumplings are light. Remove chicken, potato and dumplings to a hot platter. Melt Crisco, mix with the flour to a smooth paste, add to the stock and bring to the boiling point. Serve with the chicken.

AMERICAN CHICKEN CHOP SUEY

2 cups cold chicken	⅛ teaspoon pepper
1 cup cooked celery	1 tablespoon Crisco
1½ cups cooked rice	2 tablespoons flour
1 teaspoon salt	1½ cups chicken stock

Cut chicken and celery in thin strips before measuring. Mix them with the rice, salt and pepper. Melt Crisco, add flour and mix well. Add stock slowly and bring to the boiling point, stirring constantly. Add the chicken mixture and heat thoroughly. One cup of cooked mushrooms may be added.

AMERICAN PORK CHOP SUEY

Follow recipe for American Chicken Chop Suey, using cooked pork instead of the chicken.

ROAST DUCK

Dress, singe, wash and wipe a roasting duck. Stuff with Celery and Olive Stuffing (page 100). Tie securely in shape with wings and legs close to the body. Spread with melted Crisco and sprinkle with salt and pepper. Put in a quick oven (450 degrees F.) for 15 minutes. Add 1 cup water. Reduce heat to moderate oven (350 degrees F.) and cook until done, allowing 20 minutes to a pound. Baste often, adding more hot water if necessary. Serve with apple sauce.

ROAST GOOSE

Select a young goose not over 6 or 7 months old. Singe, dress, wash and wipe dry. Tie securely in shape, with wings and legs close to the body. Rub the cut surface of an onion over the skin. Spread with Crisco and sprinkle inside and out with salt, pepper and powdered sage. Reserve the neck, gizzard and liver and simmer in just enough water to cover, to make the gravy. The goose need not be stuffed unless a stuffing of mashed potatoes is used. Put in a quick oven (450 degrees F.) for 15 minutes. Add 1 cup water. Reduce heat to 350 degrees F., and cook until done, allowing 20 minutes to the pound. Baste often, adding more hot water if necessary. Serve garnished with roasted apples or Fried Apple Rings (page 101). To make the gravy follow recipe for Giblet Gravy below.

ROAST TURKEY

Singe, dress, wash and wipe the turkey with a damp cloth. Slip back the skin from the neck and cut off neck close to body. The skin will turn back and keep in the stuffing. Cut off the tips of wings and cook neck, wings, gizzard and liver in water to cover, to use for the gravy. Fill the turkey with Chestnut Stuffing below. Tie in shape with wings and legs close to the body. Spread with melted Crisco and sprinkle with salt and pepper. Put in a roasting pan in a quick oven (450 degrees F.) for 15 minutes. Add 1 cup water. Reduce heat to moderate oven (350 degrees F.) and cook until tender allowing 15 to 20 minutes to the pound. Baste often, adding more hot water if necessary. A 10 pound turkey will cook in about 3 hours.

GIBLET GRAVY

Pour off the fat from the pan in which the poultry has been roasted, saving 4 tablespoons. Add 3 tablespoons flour and stir until it browns. Measure water in which the giblets were cooked and add enough water to make 3 cups. Add to the browned flour and stir until smooth and thickened. Add liver, gizzard and heart, chopped fine. Season with salt and pepper. Reheat and serve in hot gravy boat with the poultry.

CELERY AND OLIVE STUFFING

3 cups soft bread crumbs	¼ teaspoon pepper
1 cup chopped celery	⅛ teaspoon paprika
½ cup chopped olives	Few drops onion juice
1 teaspoon salt	3 tablespoons Crisco

½ cup hot water

Mix bread crumbs, celery, olives, salt, pepper, paprika and onion juice. Moisten with Crisco, melted in hot water. Mix thoroughly.

CHESTNUT STUFFING

3 cups soft bread crumbs	3 tablespoons Crisco
1 teaspoon salt	¼ cup hot milk
¼ teaspoon pepper	2 cups boiled French chestnuts

Mix bread crumbs, salt and pepper. Moisten with Crisco, melted in the hot milk. Chop the chestnuts rather fine and add to the bread crumb mixture. Mix thoroughly.

OYSTER STUFFING

3 cups soft bread crumbs	1 tablespoon chopped parsley
1 teaspoon salt	25 oysters (1 pint)
⅛ teaspoon pepper	2 tablespoons Crisco
Few drops onion juice	¼ cup oyster juice

Mix crumbs, salt, pepper, onion juice and parsley. Clean oysters, removing particles of shell, and add to the crumbs. Moisten with Crisco melted in hot oyster juice. Mix thoroughly.

PEANUT STUFFING

3 cups soft bread crumbs
¾ cup chopped peanuts
½ teaspoon onion juice
1 teaspoon salt

⅛ teaspoon pepper
1 tablespoon chopped parsley
2 tablespoons Crisco
½ cup stock or water

Mix bread crumbs and peanuts. Add onion juice, salt, pepper and parsley. Moisten with Crisco melted in hot stock or water. Mix thoroughly.

POULTRY STUFFING

1 small onion
3 tablespoons Crisco
3 cups soft bread crumbs

1 teaspoon salt
⅛ teaspoon pepper
1 teaspoon poultry seasoning

Slice onion and fry in Crisco until a delicate brown. Add bread crumbs, salt, pepper and poultry seasoning and mix well.

FRIED APPLE RINGS

Wash, core apples and cut in ⅜ inch slices. Dip slices in sugar. Fry in a small amount of Crisco until apples are tender. Sprinkle with salt. Serve with roast pork.

DUMPLINGS

2 cups flour
1 teaspoon salt

4 teaspoons baking powder
3 tablespoons Crisco

¾ cup milk

Mix and sift flour, salt and baking powder. Cut in Crisco with a knife or rub in with the finger tips. Add milk to make a soft dough. Drop on top of chicken or meat stew, cover closely and steam 15 to 20 minutes without removing the cover.

YORKSHIRE PUDDING

1 cup flour
½ teaspoon baking powder
½ teaspoon salt

1 cup milk
2 egg yolks
1 tablespoon melted Crisco

2 egg whites

Mix and sift flour, baking powder and salt. Add milk, beaten egg yolks and Crisco. Mix well. Fold in the stiffly beaten egg whites. Cover the bottom of an earthenware baking dish with drippings from roast beef. Pour the batter into the baking dish. Bake in a hot oven (400 degrees F.) about 20 minutes. Baste with drippings from the roast after it is well risen. Cut in squares and serve on platter with the roast.

CHAPTER XI

Vegetables

IN THE chapter on nutrition it was explained how important a part vegetables play in the diet. But remember when you buy vegetables that price is no indication of food value. Cabbage, for instance, a vegetable which can be obtained at almost any season of the year and in almost any locality at a low price, is one of the most valuable foods we have, whereas mushrooms, almost the highest priced of vegetables, have very little food value.

The homemaker must learn to cook the cheaper vegetables in novel and appetizing ways. Cabbage, turnips, squash and carrots hold many surprises for the family of the good cook. Try some of the recipes in this chapter and see!

Most vegetables should be cooked as *quickly* as possible and *in very little water* so that their nutritious substances will not be boiled away. Boiling vegetables in a large quantity of water is no longer considered the best way. The only exceptions to this rule are potatoes, dried beans and peas and the other starchy vegetables which should be cooked slowly in plenty of water. Whenever any water is left from cooking vegetables save it and use it for soup (page 62).

Vegetables contain very little fat. Potatoes, indeed, are mostly starch and dry eating unless fat in some form is added to them. When served with sauces made of Crisco, or mashed and beaten up to a fluff with Crisco and hot milk, or scalloped with Crisco dotted over the top, or prepared in any of the ways suggested in this chapter, the potato takes a new lease on life and grows in popularity.

Not only does the new super-creamed Crisco add food value to vegetables with which it is cooked but, in the recipes where certain vegetables are sautéed, or cooked in a small amount of

Crisco, a most delicious flavor is developed which cannot be obtained by any other method of cookery. Hot Crisco brings out their most delicate characteristics and makes them temptingly crisp and tender.

SUCCESS SECRETS

1. Buy vegetables in their season. Out of season they lack flavor and are expensive.
2. Don't buy vegetables that are old or wilted, moldy or over-ripe.
3. Buy green vegetables in small quantities as you need them. Buy winter vegetables in larger amounts, if you have space to store them.
4. Soak green vegetables in cold water to make them *fresh and crisp*. Soak potatoes in cold water to make them *mealy* when cooked.
5. Wash *all* vegetables carefully in cold water before cooking.
6. Cook vegetables in boiling salted water quickly. Use as *little water as possible*.
7. Don't allow potatoes to stand in water after they are cooked. Drain immediately and keep hot over water.
8. Include vegetables in your diet every day; they are necessary to good health.
9. Save small amounts of left over vegetables for salads, soups, fritters or croquettes.

ASPARAGUS BÉARNAISE

Wash a bunch of asparagus and scrape the lower stalks. Cut the stalks an even length. Divide them in individual portions according to the number to be served and tie in bunches. Cook in boiling salted water 25 to 35 minutes. Drain. Untie and serve each bunch on a slice of toast with Béarnaise Sauce (page 114).

BAKED BEANS

2 cups dried beans	1½ teaspoons salt
¼ cup molasses	⅛ teaspoon pepper
¼ teaspoon mustard	2 cups hot water

2 tablespoons Crisco

Wash and pick over beans and soak over night. Drain. Cook slowly in boiling salted water about 1½ hours. Drain and put in a greased covered baking dish or bean pot. Mix molasses, mustard, salt, pepper and water together and pour over the beans. Dot with small bits of Crisco. Cover and bake in a moderate oven (325 degrees F.) 3 hours or until beans are soft. Uncover the last half hour to allow the beans to brown. Serve with slices of crisp bacon or broiled sausages.

STRING BEANS

Remove strings from green or wax beans. Cut through lengthwise and then in halves crosswise. Cook in a small amount of boiling water until tender, adding a little salt during the last few minutes of cooking. Drain and serve at once.

Left over beans may be reheated in medium White Sauce (page 113).

BEETS PIQUANTE

1 tablespoon Crisco	1 tablespoon sugar
¼ cup water	1 teaspoon salt
¼ cup vinegar	⅛ teaspoon pepper

6 small beets

Cook beets in boiling salted water until tender. Melt Crisco and add water, vinegar, sugar, salt and pepper and bring to the boiling point. Remove skins of beets. Slice and reheat in sauce. Serve very hot.

BRUSSELS SPROUTS

Wash and clean 1 quart of Brussels sprouts and remove any withered leaves. Soak in cold salt water for 1 hour. Drain. Cover with boiling salted water and cook 20 to 25 minutes in uncovered saucepan. Drain and heat in 1½ cups medium White Sauce (page 113).

CABBAGE

Cut a cabbage in quarters and let stand in cold water until crisp. Shred and discard the hard core. Cook in a small amount of boiling salted water 20 minutes. Drain and season with salt and pepper.

DIFFERENT CABBAGE

5 tablespoons Crisco	¼ cup water
6 cups finely shredded cabbage	1 tablespoon sugar
¼ cup milk or cream	¼ teaspoon mustard

½ teaspoon salt

Melt Crisco and fry cabbage in it slowly 10 to 15 minutes. Mix milk, water, sugar, mustard and salt together and add to the cabbage. Mix well and heat thoroughly.

SCALLOPED CABBAGE

3 cups cooked shredded cabbage	1 cup soft bread crumbs
2 cups medium white sauce	½ cup grated cheese

Mix cabbage and White Sauce (page 113) together. Put a layer of cabbage in a greased baking dish, add a layer of crumbs and repeat process until all the ingredients are used. Sprinkle with cheese. Bake in a hot oven (375 degrees F.) about 20 minutes or until brown.

STEAMED CARROTS

Wash and scrape small carrots and cut in thin slices. Allow 1 tablespoon Crisco to 1½ cups carrots. Melt Crisco, add carrots, 1 tablespoon chopped onion and season with salt and pepper. Cover and steam over a low fire until tender. Serve hot.

CAULIFLOWER AU GRATIN

Soak cauliflower in cold water ½ hour. Cook in boiling salted water until tender. Drain. Put in a baking dish and pour 2 cups medium White Sauce (page 113) over it. Sprinkle with ½ cup grated cheese. Bake in a hot oven (375 degrees F.) 25 to 30 minutes.

CREAMED CELERY

1 large bunch celery	¾ teaspoon salt
1½ tablespoons Crisco	⅛ teaspoon pepper
3 tablespoons flour	¾ cup celery stock
¾ cup milk	

Wash celery thoroughly and cut in ½ inch lengths. Boil in salted water 50 to 60 minutes or until tender. Drain and reserve ¾ cup of the stock. Melt Crisco, add flour, salt and pepper. Add the milk and celery stock and bring to the boiling point, stirring constantly. Add the celery and heat thoroughly.

The creamed celery may be put in a baking dish, sprinkled with crumbs and grated cheese and baked 20 minutes in a moderate oven (350 degrees F.).

BAKED CORN

2 tablespoons Crisco	1 tablespoon sugar
1½ tablespoons flour	1 teaspoon salt
1 cup milk	⅛ teaspoon pepper
2 cups cooked or canned corn	2 eggs

Melt Crisco, add flour and mix well. Add milk gradually and bring to the boiling point, stirring constantly. Add corn, sugar, salt and pepper and heat thoroughly. Remove from fire, add well-beaten eggs and pour into a greased baking dish. Bake in a moderate oven (350 degrees F.) 25 minutes, or until corn is firm.

GREEN CORN FRITTERS

2 cups corn	Few grains pepper
1 egg	1 tablespoon Crisco, melted
1 teaspoon sugar	¼ cup flour
½ teaspoon salt	½ teaspoon baking powder

Score the corn with the tines of a fork and scrape kernels from the cob with back of a knife. Add beaten egg, sugar, salt, pepper and melted Crisco. Mix and sift flour and baking powder, add to first mixture and mix well. Melt a little Crisco in frying pan. When hot, but not smoking, drop batter into it by tablespoons and fry on both sides until brown. Drain on unglazed paper. Serve immediately.

CUCUMBERS, SWEET AND SOUR

2 tablespoons Crisco	1 egg yolk
2 tablespoons chopped onion	2 tablespoons sugar
4 large cucumbers, sliced	3 tablespoons vinegar
¼ cup water	1½ teaspoons salt
½ cup sour cream	⅛ teaspoon pepper

⅛ teaspoon paprika

Melt Crisco, add onion and fry until a delicate brown. Add sliced cucumbers and water. Cook until water is absorbed and cucumbers browned. Mix sour cream, beaten egg yolk, sugar, vinegar, salt, pepper and paprika. Add to cucumbers and cook slowly until mixture begins to boil. Serve immediately.

EGGPLANT AU GRATIN

1 large eggplant	⅛ teaspoon pepper
1 cup grated cheese	Few grains cayenne
1 teaspoon salt	2 tablespoons Crisco

Pare eggplant and cut in slices. Cook in boiling salted water until tender. Drain well and mash. Put a layer in a greased baking dish, sprinkle with cheese, salt, pepper and cayenne and dot with small bits of Crisco. Repeat this process until all the ingredients are used, having a layer of cheese on top. Bake in a hot oven (400 degrees F.) 20 minutes or until cheese is brown.

FRIED EGGPLANT

Pare the eggplant and cut in thin slices. Sprinkle with salt and let stand under a weight until some of the juices run out. Drain off liquid and sprinkle with flour. Dip in slightly beaten egg diluted with 2 tablespoons water and seasoned with ½ teaspoon salt and ⅛ teaspoon pepper. Cover with fine dry bread crumbs. Fry in hot Crisco from 8 to 10 minutes. Brown on both sides.

KOHLRABI

Wash and pare and cut in thin slices. Cover with boiling salted water and cook uncovered until tender, about 40 minutes. Drain and heat in medium White Sauce (page 113). Season more if necessary.

BAKED MACÉDOINE

3 tablespoons Crisco	1½ cups boiled rice
1 tablespoon chopped onion	1 hard cooked egg, chopped
2 tablespoons chopped pimento	1 tablespoon chopped parsley
2 tablespoons flour	2 teaspoons salt
2 cups canned or stewed tomatoes	⅛ teaspoon pepper
1 cup cooked corn	1 teaspoon Worcestershire sauce

½ cup grated cheese

Melt Crisco, add onion and pimento and cook 3 minutes. Add flour and mix well. Add tomatoes and stir until mixture thickens slightly. Add corn, rice, egg and seasonings. Put in a baking dish, sprinkle cheese over the top and bake in a hot oven (400 degrees F.) 20 minutes. Any combination of cooked vegetables is good in this dish. Peas, lima beans or carrots may be substituted for the corn.

ONIONS SAUTÉ

2 tablespoons Crisco
6 large white onions

1 teaspoon salt
⅛ teaspoon pepper

⅛ teaspoon paprika

Melt Crisco in a frying pan. Slice onions into it. Add salt, pepper and paprika and mix well. Cover tightly and cook slowly about 35 minutes, stirring occasionally to prevent burning.

STUFFED ONIONS

6 large white onions
¾ cup chopped meat
½ teaspoon salt

⅛ teaspoon pepper
2 tablespoons melted Crisco
2 tablespoons tomato catsup

¼ cup fine bread crumbs

Parboil onions 15 minutes and drain. Mix meat, salt, pepper, Crisco and catsup. Remove centers from onions and fill with the meat mixture. Arrange in a baking dish, cover and bake in a moderate oven (350 degrees F.) about 1 hour. Remove cover, sprinkle tops with crumbs, dot with small bits of Crisco and bake until crumbs are brown.

PARSNIPS SAUTÉ

Wash the parsnips and boil in salted water until tender, about 40 minutes. Scrape off the skins. Cut in slices and sprinkle with salt, pepper and flour. Fry in a small amount of Crisco until a delicate brown.

STUFFED PEPPERS

6 green peppers
1 cup chopped tomatoes
1 cup minced cold meat
1 cup cooked rice (or bread crumbs)

2 tablespoons Crisco, melted
½ teaspoon salt
⅛ teaspoon pepper
1 teaspoon chopped onion

Cut a piece from the stem end of each pepper and remove seeds and partitions. Put peppers in boiling water and parboil 5 minutes. Mix well together the tomatoes, cold meat, rice, Crisco, salt, pepper and onion and fill the peppers with the mixture. Put in a baking dish with a cup of hot water or stock. Bake in a hot oven (400 degrees F.) 30 to 40 minutes.

Almost any combination of vegetables makes a good stuffing for peppers.

POTATOES AU GRATIN

Put a layer of cold potatoes, cut in cubes, in a greased casserole or baking dish, sprinkle with grated cheese, salt and pepper. Dot with small bits of Crisco. Repeat the process until the desired quantity is prepared. Pour over enough milk to almost cover top layer and sprinkle with cheese. Bake in a hot oven (400 degrees F.) 20 to 25 minutes.

BAKED POTATOES

Select medium-sized potatoes. Wash with a vegetable brush to remove all particles of dirt. Soak in cold water 1 hour. Bake in a hot oven (400 degrees F.) 40 to 50 minutes or until soft. Rub skins with Crisco to soften them. Serve at once as they become soggy if allowed to stand.

BOILED PARSLEY POTATOES

Wash potatoes and let stand 1 hour in cold water. Pare and cook in boiling salted water until soft. Drain and keep hot until ready to serve. Do not cover them. Sprinkle with chopped parsley.

DUCHESS POTATOES

Select potatoes of uniform size, wash, pare and let stand in cold water 1 hour. Cook in boiling salted water until tender. Drain off all the water and force through a potato ricer. To 3 cups hot riced potatoes add 2 tablespoons Crisco, 1 teaspoon salt, few grains paprika and the beaten yolks of 3 eggs. Force through a pastry bag into different shapes such as pyramids, roses, circles. Brush over with a beaten egg yolk diluted with 1 tablespoon water. Bake in a moderate oven (350 degrees F.) 15 minutes or until a delicate brown. This is an excellent garnish for planked steak or fish.

FRANCONIA POTATOES

Wash potatoes and let stand in cold water 1 hour. Pare and parboil 10 minutes. Drain and put in pan with roast ¾ of an hour before roast is done. Sprinkle with salt and pepper. Baste them when meat is basted and bake until soft and well browned.

GERMAN FRIED POTATOES

Wash and pare potatoes and slice very thin. Soak them in cold water 1 hour. Drain and dry thoroughly. Put a small amount of Crisco in a frying pan. Add the potatoes, sprinkle with salt and cover with a tight fitting lid. Fry slowly until tender and brown, turning occasionally to prevent burning.

A very easy and quick way to cook raw potatoes.

HASHED BROWNED POTATOES

Melt 2 tablespoons Crisco in a frying pan. Add 2 cups finely chopped cold potatoes, 1 tablespoon chopped parsley, ½ teaspoon salt and few grains pepper. Mix thoroughly, then allow the potatoes to brown on the under side. Fold over like an omelet. Serve immediately.

LYONNAISE POTATOES

Slice 1 small onion thin and fry in 1 tablespoon Crisco until a delicate brown. Add 2 cups cold boiled potatoes, cut in ¼ inch slices. Sprinkle with ½ teaspoon salt and few grains cayenne. Let potatoes brown on the under side, fold over and turn out on hot platter. Sprinkle with 1 teaspoon chopped parsley.

MASHED POTATOES

Select medium-sized potatoes. Wash, pare and let stand in cold water 1 hour. Cook in boiling salted water until tender. Drain off all the water and mash with a potato masher or force through a ricer. To 6 potatoes add 2 tablespoons Crisco, 1 teaspoon salt, few grains pepper and 4 tablespoons hot milk. Beat with a fork until creamy. Pile lightly in a hot serving dish and sprinkle with finely chopped parsley. Serve immediately.

POTATO CAKES

Shape cold mashed potatoes in small flat circular cakes. Sprinkle with flour. Fry on one side until a delicate brown in a small amount of Crisco, turn and fry on the other side.

A good way to use left over potatoes.

SCALLOPED POTATOES

Wash, pare and cut potatoes in thin slices. Soak in cold water ½ hour. Put a layer of potatoes in a greased baking dish, sprinkle with salt, pepper and flour and dot with small bits of Crisco. Repeat the process until all the potatoes are used. Add enough hot milk to almost cover top layer. Bake in a moderate oven (325 degrees F.) 1 to 1½ hours.

POTATO SOUFFLÉ

3 cups hot mashed potatoes	1 teaspoon chopped parsley
2 tablespoons Crisco	1 teaspoon onion juice
1 teaspoon salt	3 egg yolks
Few grains cayenne	3 egg whites

Mix potatoes, Crisco, salt, cayenne, parsley and onion juice together. Add beaten egg yolks and mix well. Fold in the stiffly beaten egg whites. Put in greased baking dish, set in a pan of water and bake in a moderate oven (350 degrees F.) 50 to 60 minutes. Serve immediately.

STUFFED BAKED POTATOES

6 medium-sized potatoes	1 teaspoon salt
2 tablespoons Crisco	⅛ teaspoon pepper
4 tablespoons hot milk	⅛ teaspoon paprika

Wash potatoes with a vegetable brush and soak in cold water 1 hour. Bake in hot oven (400 degrees F.) 40 to 50 minutes. Cut a cross in the side of each potato skin and turn back corners. Scoop out the potatoes with a spoon, being careful not to break the skins. Mash and add Crisco, milk, salt, pepper and paprika. Beat until light and creamy. Fill the potato skins with the mashed potato. Dot each one with a small bit of Crisco and return to the oven to brown. If desired, potatoes may be sprinkled with grated cheese before putting in oven.

GLACÉ SWEET POTATOES

Select medium-sized potatoes. Scrub with a vegetable brush to remove all particles of dirt. Cook in boiling water until tender. Drain off water and remove the skins. Cut in halves, lengthwise, and put them in a greased shallow pan. Make a syrup by boiling ⅔ cup sugar, ⅓ cup water and 1½ tablespoons Crisco 5 minutes. Pour this over the sweet potatoes. Bake in a hot oven (400 degrees F.) 20 minutes or until a delicate brown, basting occasionally with the syrup.

SWEET POTATOES, SOUTHERN STYLE

Select medium-sized potatoes. Scrub with a vegetable brush to remove all particles of dirt. Cook in boiling salted water until tender. Drain off water and cool. Remove skins and cut in ¼ inch slices. Put a layer of potatoes in a greased baking dish. Sprinkle with brown sugar and salt and dot with small bits of Crisco. Add ¼ cup hot water. Cover and bake in a hot oven (400 degrees F.) 20 minutes.

SPINACH AND EGG

2 pounds spinach	⅛ teaspoon pepper
2 tablespoons Crisco	1 teaspoon salt
1 teaspoon chopped onion	2 chopped hard cooked eggs
¼ teaspoon mustard	½ cup spinach water

6 slices bacon

Pick over spinach and wash thoroughly. Cook in saucepan using only the water which clings to the leaves. Add ½ teaspoon salt. When tender, drain and chop. Melt Crisco, add onion, mustard, pepper and salt. Cook until onion is slightly browned. Add spinach, eggs and spinach water. Heat thoroughly. Garnish with crisp bacon.

BAKED SQUASH

Small Hubbard squash	1 teaspoon salt
3 tablespoons Crisco	⅛ teaspoon pepper
2 tablespoons chopped onion	⅛ teaspoon paprika
2 tablespoons chopped green pepper	¼ cup fine bread crumbs

Cut squash in pieces, pare and cook in boiling salted water to cover about 30 minutes or until tender. Drain well and mash. Melt Crisco, add onion and pepper and cook slowly about 5 minutes. Add onion, green pepper, salt, pepper and paprika to the squash. Mix well and turn into a greased baking dish. Sprinkle with crumbs, salt and pepper and bake in a hot oven (400 degrees F.) 20 to 30 minutes.

SQUASH SAUTÉ

Pare summer squash and cut in uniform pieces. Sprinkle with salt, pepper and flour. Dip in slightly beaten egg, diluted with 2 tablespoons water, then in fine dry bread crumbs. Fry in small quantity of Crisco 6 to 8 minutes. Brown on both sides.

BAKED STUFFED TOMATOES

2 cups soft bread crumbs
1 teaspoon salt
⅛ teaspoon pepper

2 tablespoons sugar
3 tablespoons Crisco
6 tomatoes

Mix bread crumbs with salt, pepper, 1 tablespoon sugar and 2 tablespoons melted Crisco. Cut thin slice from stem end of tomatoes and remove a little of the center. Sprinkle with salt, pepper and sugar. Fill with the stuffing. Dot with small bits of Crisco and bake in a moderate oven (350 degrees F.) 1 hour.

BAKED TOMATO EN CASSEROLE

2 Spanish onions
3 tablespoons Crisco
2 cups cooked or canned tomatoes

1 teaspoon salt
⅛ teaspoon paprika
⅛ teaspoon pepper

Cut onions in slices and fry in Crisco until a delicate brown. Add tomatoes, salt, paprika and pepper. Mix well. Put in a baking dish and cook in a quick oven (410 degrees F.) 1 hour, stirring occasionally. Serve on slices of toast.

FRIED TOMATOES, CREAM GRAVY

3 tablespoons Crisco
4 tablespoons flour
2 tablespoons sugar

1½ teaspoons salt
⅛ teaspoon pepper
4 large tomatoes

2 cups milk

Melt Crisco in frying pan. Mix flour, sugar, salt and pepper. Cut tomatoes in ½ inch slices. Dip in flour mixture and fry in Crisco until brown. Remove to a hot platter. Put the milk in the pan and bring to boiling point, stirring constantly until it thickens. Add a little salt, if necessary. Pour over the tomatoes and serve hot.

FLUFFY YELLOW TURNIP

2 tablespoons Crisco
1 tablespoon chopped onion
3 cups yellow turnips, mashed
1 teaspoon salt

1 tablespoon sugar
⅛ teaspoon pepper
Few grains cayenne
2 egg yolks

2 egg whites

Melt Crisco, add onion and fry until a delicate brown. Add turnips, salt, sugar, pepper, cayenne and mix well. Add beaten egg yolks. Fold in the stiffly beaten egg whites. Put in a greased baking dish and bake in a hot oven (400 degrees F.) 20 to 25 minutes.

Left over turnips may be used in this recipe with less seasoning.

CHAPTER XII

Meat, Fish and Vegetable Sauces

TO CHOOSE the right sauce to serve with the right meat, fish or vegetable is no mean accomplishment and the housewife who is noted for her good table will be found to be something of an authority on sauces. She knows that for certain boiled fish and for mutton, caper sauce is a decided success; for fried fish, tartar sauce is the proper thing; for asparagus, Hollandaise; for beefsteak and fillets of beef, mushroom sauce, and so on through the various dishes which can be made culinary masterpieces with skillful handling.

There are two secrets in the making of good sauces! One is the way in which the fat and thickening are blended with the liquid, and the second is the manner in which the flavorings are added to the sauce. If the vegetables, such as onion, parsley and chive, used for flavoring sauces are first browned in Crisco, a decided flavor is brought out. If, on the other hand, a very subtle flavor is wanted the seasoning vegetables should be added to the sauce when it is completely made. Bland foods like asparagus need the more rich, highly seasoned sauces, while foods of pronounced flavor, like mutton, are best with a sauce the flavor of which is sharp and obvious.

The other secret, that of carefully combining the liquid with the fat and thickening, is what gives the sauce its smooth texture and well-cooked flavor. The starchy taste of uncooked flour in a sauce is inexcusable.

Sauces made with the new Crisco have a delicacy of flavor and texture which only Crisco can give them. Hollandaise made with Crisco will be a boon to the housewife who has hitherto felt she could not make it because so much butter was required.

The Crisco chart for White Sauce on next page will be found of great help in varying your menus without too much work and worry.

[112]

SUCCESS SECRETS

1. Serve hot sauces *very hot* and cold sauces *very cold*.

2. Use the Crisco chart for white sauce. It is made to simplify your cooking, as white sauce is the foundation for any number of delicious dishes.

3. Blend Crisco, flour and seasonings thoroughly before adding liquid.

4. Never serve a lumpy sauce. If it isn't perfectly smooth, strain it before serving.

5. Choose the right sauce to serve with the right food— richer sauces for the plainer dishes and simple sauces for the rather rich foods.

6. A perfect sauce is an aid to digestion and a good source of nourishment.

7. To draw out the flavor of vegetables used for flavoring sauces (onions, parsley, carrots, etc.) sauté them first in a small amount of Crisco.

CHART FOR WHITE SAUCE

Ingredients	Thin	Medium	Thick	Very Thick
Crisco	1 tablespoon	1 tablespoon	1 tablespoon	2 tablespoons
Flour	1 tablespoon	2 tablespoons	3 tablespoons	4 tablespoons
Salt	$\frac{3}{4}$ teaspoon	$\frac{3}{4}$ teaspoon	$\frac{3}{4}$ teaspoon	$\frac{3}{4}$ teaspoon
Pepper	$\frac{1}{16}$ teaspoon	$\frac{1}{16}$ teaspoon	$\frac{1}{16}$ teaspoon	$\frac{1}{16}$ teaspoon
Milk	1 cup	1 cup	1 cup	1 cup

Melt Crisco, add flour, salt and pepper and mix well. Add milk slowly and bring to the boiling point, stirring constantly to avoid lumping. Place over hot water until ready to use.

USES FOR WHITE SAUCE

THIN............To cream starchy vegetables such as potatoes. To make cream soups (page 65).

MEDIUM..........To cream non-starchy vegetables such as carrots, onions, peas, cauliflower, etc. To make cream soups (page 65).
To cream chicken, salmon, oysters, etc.

THICK............To prepare scalloped dishes.

VERY THICK......To make croquettes and soufflés.

ALMOND AND RAISIN SAUCE

2 tablespoons Crisco
4 tablespoons flour
3 cups meat stock

1 cup raisins
½ cup almonds, cut in strips
1 tablespoon sugar

¼ cup vinegar

Melt Crisco, add flour and mix well. Add stock and stir until it thickens. Stir in raisins, almonds, sugar and vinegar. Season with salt and pepper if necessary.

Adds a new piquancy to boiled tongue.

BÉARNAISE SAUCE

¼ cup Crisco
4 egg yolks
½ teaspoon salt

Few grains cayenne
1 tablespoon tarragon vinegar
½ teaspoon onion juice

1 tablespoon chopped parsley

Mix Crisco and beaten egg yolks together. Add salt and cayenne and cook over hot (not boiling) water until thick, stirring constantly. Add vinegar and onion juice and cook 20 minutes, still stirring. Remove from fire and add parsley. Serve immediately.

Particularly good with halibut or other fish steak.

CAPER SAUCE

1 tablespoon Crisco
2 tablespoons flour
½ teaspoon salt

⅛ teaspoon pepper
1 cup mutton stock or fish stock
2 tablespoons capers

Melt Crisco, add flour, salt and pepper and mix well. Add stock and bring to the boiling point, stirring constantly. Add capers. Serve hot with boiled lamb, mutton, or any white fish.

CHEESE SAUCE

Follow recipe for medium White Sauce. Add ½ cup grated cheese and stir until melted. Serve hot.

A rich, hearty sauce for bland vegetables or fish.

CUCUMBER SAUCE

Grate a medium-sized cucumber. Drain. Season the cucumber pulp with salt, pepper and 2 teaspoons vinegar.

This sauce is very delicious and will improve any kind of fish.

EGG SAUCE

Follow recipe for medium White Sauce. Add 1 chopped hard cooked egg and 1 teaspoon chopped parsley. Serve hot.

An easily made sauce that is good with any fish.

HOLLANDAISE SAUCE

⅓ cup Crisco
½ teaspoon salt
2 egg yolks

⅓ cup hot water
1 tablespoon lemon juice
Few grains cayenne

Cream Crisco and salt together. Add beaten egg yolks and mix well. Add water gradually and cook over hot water, kept below boiling point, stirring constantly until the sauce thickens. Add lemon juice and cayenne and cook one minute. Remove from the fire and serve at once. If mixture curdles, add a tablespoon of cream and beat thoroughly. This sauce may also be used cold.

This is very delicious and much less expensive than when made with butter. Serve with fish or vegetables.

MOCK HOLLANDAISE SAUCE

2 egg yolks
1 cup thick white sauce

3 tablespoons lemon juice
Few grains cayenne

Add beaten egg yolks to the hot white sauce and mix well. Bring slowly to the boiling point, stirring constantly. Remove from fire, add lemon juice and cayenne.

Serve hot wherever Hollandaise would be good. It is much easier to make.

MUSHROOM SAUCE

Wash, peel and remove stems of ¼ pound of mushrooms. Cut mushroom caps in thin slices and fry in 1½ tablespoons Crisco 5 minutes. Add 2 tablespoons flour and mix well. Put the stems and peelings in a saucepan, cover with water and simmer for 15 minutes. Strain. Add ½ cup mushroom stock and ½ cup milk to the mushrooms and bring to the boiling point, stirring constantly. Season with salt and pepper.

You'll like this especially well served with beef.

PARSLEY SAUCE

Follow recipe for thin White Sauce and add 3 tablespoons chopped parsley.

This gives a touch of color and a delicate flavor to boiled fish.

SPANISH SAUCE

2 tablespoons Crisco
1½ tablespoons chopped onion
2 tablespooons flour
½ teaspoon salt
Few grains cayenne

Few grains pepper
1 cup strained tomato juice
3 tablespoons cooked ham, chopped
3 tablespoons cooked celery, chopped
2 tablespoons cooked carrots, chopped

Melt Crisco, add onion and fry until a delicate brown. Add flour, salt, cayenne and pepper and mix well. Add tomato juice and bring slowly to the boiling point, stirring constantly. Add ham, celery, and carrots. Serve hot.

Use this with a simple meat dish when you want a *different* flavor.

TOMATO SAUCE

2 cups cooked or canned tomatoes
1 teaspoon sugar
2 whole cloves
1 teaspoon salt

Few grains cayenne
3 peppercorns
2 tablespoons Crisco
1½ tablespoons flour

Cook tomatoes, sugar, cloves, salt, cayenne and peppercorns together slowly for 20 minutes. Strain. Melt Crisco, add flour and mix well. Add the tomato juice slowly and bring to the boiling point, stirring constantly.

A tasty way to use tomatoes with meat.

CHAPTER XIII

Quick Breads

Q UICK BREADS, or hot breads as they are sometimes called, are breads which may be prepared in a very short time and are intended to be served at once while they are fresh and hot. Keeping them for any length of time spoils their flavor and lightness.

Because they can be prepared so quickly and because there are endless delicious recipes and variations for them which can be easily followed, quick breads have become a very popular part of the daily menu. In the South many families serve them at every meal and do not consider a menu complete without hot bread in one form or another. Spoon bread and popovers are among their favorites, while in the New England states brown bread and doughnuts hold sway.

Although hot breads are quickly and easily made there are certain principles which must be learned for the very best results. These are: use good materials, measure accurately, mix carefully and bake properly.

To have a good product we must use good material. In using the recipes in this chapter you will discover that the new super-creamed Crisco gives a tender, well-browned crust, imparts a delicious nutty flavor, and makes a particularly rich dough. Use it, too, for greasing the pans so that your muffins will not stick.

There are two general methods of combining the ingredients for quick breads. They differ in the way in which the shortening is added. In one case, unmelted Crisco is worked into the dry ingredients and the liquid then added gradually. This method is used for *soft* doughs of the baking powder biscuit type. The other method is used for thin mixtures, or batters, such as muffins, waffles, griddle cakes and popovers. For these Crisco is melted and added last, after the dry ingredients and liquid have been mixed together until free from lumps.

[117]

Chicken Pie (Page 98)   *Baking Powder Biscuits* (Page 122)

Sweet Milk Griddle Cakes (Recipe on page 127)

The old method of guessing at the heat of your oven is too uncertain. If you have no oven regulator an oven thermometer placed on the baking shelf will tell you just when to put in your biscuits

The handling of hot bread mixtures has a great deal to do with the success or failure of the finished product. Soft doughs should be handled as little as possible—only enough to mix the ingredients thoroughly. Muffin mixtures should be beaten only enough to make them smooth. Too much beating makes the muffins coarse grained and full of holes. Popovers, on the other hand, which depend upon the air beaten into them to make them "pop," should be very thoroughly beaten after all the ingredients are combined.

The next and very important point is the baking—which may "make or break" your reputation as a cook. If possible get an oven regulator; you have only to set it and then forget your oven until the time is up. Or next best, buy an oven thermometer for two dollars and look at it occasionally to see that it stays at the proper temperature. The old method of *guessing* at the heat of your oven is too uncertain and you will find that a heat regulator of some kind will soon pay for itself in saving food material from burning and yourself from worry.

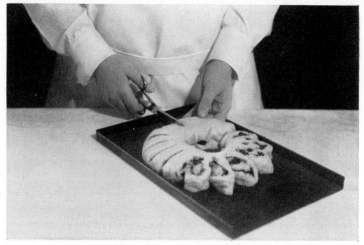

Shaping a Coffee Ring—Place Coffee Ring on a large greased pan and cut gashes two inches apart around outside edge with scissors, spread each section as shown above

SUCCESS SECRETS

1. Use level measurements.
2. Sift flour before measuring.
3. Collect all ingredients before starting to mix.
4. Grease pans with Crisco before beginning to mix.
5. Regulate oven for temperature given in recipe.
6. Bake quick breads as soon as mixed, with the exception of a few loaf breads (see recipes).
7. Keep baking powder tightly covered in a cool, dry place.
8. Break eggs just before using and beat according to directions.
9. Handle baking powder doughs as little as possible.
10. Serve quick breads as soon as possible after they are baked, with the exception of loaf breads which should cool before slicing.

CHART FOR MUFFINS

INGREDIENTS	PLAIN	WHOLE WHEAT	BRAN	CORNMEAL	RICE	BERRIES	NUTS	RAISINS
FLOUR White......	2 cups	1 cup	1 cup	1 cup	1 cup	2 cups	2 cups	2 cups
Whole Wheat..		1 cup						
Bran.......			1 cup					
Cornmeal..				1 cup				
SUGAR........	2 table-spoons	2 table-spoons	2 table-spoons	2 table-spoons	3 table-spoons	4 table-spoons	2 table-spoons	2 table-spoons
BAKING POWDER....	4 tea-spoons	5 tea-spoons	5 tea-spoons	4 tea-spoons	5 tea-spoons	4 tea-spoons	4 tea-spoons	4 tea-spoons
SALT.........	1 tea-spoon	1 tea-spoon	1 tea-spoon	1 tea-spoon	1 tea-spoon	1 tea-spoon	1 tea-spoon	1 tea-spoon
EGGS.........	1	1	1	1	1	1	1	1
MILK.........	1 cup	1 cup	¾ cup	1 cup	1 cup	1 cup	1 cup	1 cup
CRISCO Melted....	3 table-spoons	3 table-spoons	3 table-spoons	3 table-spoons	3 table-spoons	3 table-spoons	3 table-spoons	3 table-spoons
RICE (cooked)					1 cup			
BERRIES......						1 cup		
NUTS.........							½ cup	
RAISINS......								¾ cup

Mix and sift flour, sugar, baking powder and salt. Add the beaten egg and milk and mix well. Add melted Crisco. (Add the rice, berries, raisins or nuts last.) Bake in greased muffin pans in a hot oven (400 degrees F.) 20 to 25 minutes. These recipes make 12 to 14 muffins.

BLUEBERRY TEA MUFFINS

¼ cup Crisco	5 teaspoons baking powder
⅓ cup sugar	1 teaspoon salt
2 eggs	⅔ cup milk
2 cups flour	½ cup blueberries

Cream Crisco and sugar together. Add beaten eggs and mix well. Mix and sift 1½ cups flour, baking powder and salt and add alternately with the milk to the first mixture. Dredge blueberries with ½ cup flour and stir in lightly. Bake in greased muffin pans in hot oven (400 degrees F.) 25 to 30 minutes.

This recipe makes 12 muffins.

SALLY LUNN

Follow recipe for Blueberry Tea Muffins, omitting the berries and using only 4 teaspoons baking powder. Bake in a greased cake pan in a hot oven (400 degrees F.) 20 to 25 minutes.

APPLE GEMS

1¼ cups scalded milk	1 egg
4 tablespoons Crisco	1 cup flour
2 tablespoons sugar	2 teaspoons baking powder
⅔ cup yellow cornmeal	1 teaspoon salt
1½ cups apples, chopped fine	

To the scalded milk add Crisco, sugar and cornmeal. Mix well. Add beaten egg, flour, baking powder and salt. Add apples to the batter and beat thoroughly. Drop into greased gem or muffin pans and bake in a moderate oven (350 degrees F.) 25 to 30 minutes.

This recipe makes 12 to 14 gems.

BAKING POWDER BISCUITS

2 cups flour	½ teaspoon salt
4 teaspoons baking powder	4 tablespoons Crisco
¾ cup milk (variable)	

Mix and sift flour, baking powder and salt. Cut in Crisco with a knife or rub in with the finger tips. Add milk gradually and mix to a soft dough. Roll out on a slightly floured board to ½ inch thickness. Cut with a biscuit cutter. Bake in a quick oven (450 degrees F.) 10 to 15 minutes.

This recipe makes 12 biscuits.

CHEESE BISCUITS

Follow directions for Baking Powder Biscuits and add ½ cup grated cheese before adding the milk.

EMERGENCY BISCUITS

Follow the recipe for Baking Powder Biscuits using one cup milk. Drop by tablespoons into a greased pan.

PARKER HOUSE ROLLS

Follow recipe for Baking Powder Biscuits. Roll out to ¼ inch thickness. Cut with a large cooky cutter. Spread with melted Crisco. Fold over double and press edges together lightly.

OATMEAL BISCUITS

1½ cups flour	1½ teaspoons salt
1 tablespoon sugar	1½ cups uncooked rolled oats
7 teaspoons baking powder	4 tablespoons Crisco
¾ cup milk	

Mix and sift flour, sugar, baking powder and salt. Mix in the rolled oats. Cut in Crisco with a knife or rub in with the finger tips. Add milk gradually and mix to a soft dough. Turn out on floured board and roll, or pat, to ¾ inch thickness. Cut with biscuit cutter. Brush tops with milk and bake in quick oven (450 degrees F.) 15 to 20 minutes.

This recipe makes 14 to 16 biscuits.

SOUR MILK BISCUITS

2 cups flour	2 tablespoons Crisco
3 teaspoons baking powder	½ teaspoon soda
1 teaspoon salt	¾ cup sour milk

Mix and sift flour, baking powder and salt. Cut in Crisco with a knife or rub in with the finger tips. Mix soda with the sour milk. Add slowly to the flour mixture and mix to a soft dough. Roll out on a slightly floured board to ½ inch thickness and cut with a biscuit cutter. Bake in a quick oven (450 degrees F.) 10 to 15 minutes.

This recipe makes 12 biscuits.

SWEET POTATO BISCUITS

2 cups flour	1½ teaspoons salt
6 teaspoons baking powder	3 tablespoons Crisco
2 tablespoons sugar	1½ cups sweet potatoes, mashed
¾ cup milk	

Mix and sift flour, baking powder, sugar and salt. Cut in Crisco with a knife or rub in with the finger tips. Work the sweet potatoes into the flour mixture. Add milk and mix to a soft dough. Roll out on a slightly floured board to ½ inch thickness. Cut with a biscuit cutter. Bake in a quick oven (425 degrees F.) 15 to 20 minutes. This dough will keep for several days if wrapped in wax paper and placed in the ice box.

This recipe makes 14 to 16 biscuits.

SCOTCH SCONES

2 cups flour
1 teaspoon salt
5 teaspoons baking powder

2 tablespoons sugar
4 tablespoons Crisco
2 eggs

⅓ cup milk

Mix and sift flour, salt, baking powder and 1 tablespoon sugar. Cut in Crisco with a knife or rub in with the finger tips. Add the beaten eggs (reserving 1 egg white for the tops). Add milk and mix to a soft dough. Roll out on a slightly floured board to ½ inch thickness and cut in diamond shaped pieces. Brush with white of egg and sprinkle with the remaining tablespoon of sugar. Bake in a quick oven (425 degrees F.) 10 to 15 minutes.

This recipe makes 10 to 12 scones.

SHORTCAKES

2 cups flour
5 teaspoons baking powder
1 teaspoon salt

2 tablespoons sugar
¼ cup Crisco
⅔ cup milk

Mix and sift flour, baking powder, salt and sugar. Cut in Crisco with a knife or rub in with the finger tips. Add milk gradually and mix to a soft dough. Roll out on a slightly floured board to ½ inch thickness. Cut with a large cooky cutter. Bake in a quick oven (425 degrees F.) 15 minutes. Break apart and put sliced and sweetened fruit or crushed berries between and on top of cakes. Serve with whipped cream.

This recipe makes 8 shortcakes.

POPOVERS

1 cup flour
¼ teaspoon salt

1 cup milk
2 eggs

1 tablespoon melted Crisco

Mix and sift flour and salt. Add milk gradually. Add beaten egg and Crisco. Beat batter five minutes with a Dover egg beater. Pour batter into greased hot iron popover pans or hot greased earthen cups. Bake in a hot oven (400 degrees F.) 30 minutes. Reduce heat to a moderate oven (325 degrees F.) and bake 15 minutes. Do not open oven door for the first 15 minutes of baking.

This recipe makes 8 to 10 popovers.

CORNBREAD

1½ cups milk
1 cup cornmeal
1½ tablespoons Crisco

2 eggs
1½ teaspoons baking powder
½ teaspoon salt

2 teaspoons sugar

Scald the milk and pour over the cornmeal and Crisco. Cool. Add beaten eggs, baking powder, salt and sugar and mix well. Pour into a greased shallow pan and bake in a hot oven (400 degrees F.) 25 to 30 minutes.

NUT BREAD

3 cups flour	1 egg
3 teaspoons baking powder	1½ cups milk
1 cup sugar	1 cup nuts, cut in pieces
1 teaspoon cinnamon	1 cup raisins
1 teaspoon salt	2 tablespoons melted Crisco

Mix and sift flour, baking powder, sugar, cinnamon and salt. Beat egg and add milk. Stir liquid into flour mixture and mix well. Add nuts, raisins and Crisco. Pour into bread pan, let stand ½ hour and bake in moderate oven (325 degrees F.) 50 to 60 minutes.

STEAMED BROWN BREAD

1 cup white flour	½ cup sugar
1 cup whole wheat flour	1 teaspoon soda
1 cup cornmeal	½ cup molasses
1½ teaspoons salt	1½ cups buttermilk
2 tablespoons melted Crisco	

Mix flour, whole wheat flour, cornmeal, salt and sugar together. Mix soda with the molasses and add with the buttermilk to the flour mixture. Add Crisco and mix well. Fill a greased pudding mold ¾ full and steam 3 hours.

RAISIN BROWN BREAD

Follow recipe for Steamed Brown Bread. Add ½ cup floured raisins and use ¼ cup sugar instead of ½ cup sugar.

SPOON BREAD

1 cup cornmeal	1 egg
¾ cup boiling water	½ teaspoon soda
1 teaspoon salt	1 cup buttermilk
1 tablespoon sugar	1½ tablespoons melted Crisco

Put the meal into a bowl and pour the boiling water over it. Cover. Let stand until cool. Add salt, sugar, and beaten egg. Dissolve soda in buttermilk and add to the batter. Mix well. Add melted Crisco. Pour into a deep greased baking dish and bake in a hot oven (375 degrees F.) 30 to 35 minutes.

WHOLE WHEAT NUT BREAD

2 cups whole wheat flour	5 tablespoons brown sugar
1 cup flour	½ cup molasses
1 teaspoon soda	¾ cup milk
3 teaspoons baking powder	½ cup water
2 teaspoons salt	1 cup walnuts, cut in small pieces
2 tablespoons melted Crisco	

Mix whole wheat flour, flour, soda, baking powder, salt and sugar together. Add molasses, milk and water and mix well. Add nuts and Crisco and beat thoroughly.   Pour into a greased loaf pan and let stand 20 minutes.   Bake in a slow oven (300 degrees F.) 1 to 1¼ hours.

COFFEE CAKE

3 cups flour	½ cup Crisco
2 cups brown sugar	2 teaspoons baking powder
1 teaspoon salt	2 eggs
1 teaspoon cinnamon	¾ cup milk

Mix and sift flour, salt, sugar and cinnamon.   Cut in Crisco with a knife or rub in with the finger tips.   Reserve 1 cup of this mixture to sprinkle on top of cake.   To the remainder add the baking powder and mix well.   Add the beaten eggs and milk and beat thoroughly.   Pour into two greased layer cake pans and sprinkle top with crumbs reserved for this purpose.   Bake in a hot oven (400 degrees F.) 20 to 25 minutes.

COFFEE RING

3 cups flour	¼ cup Crisco
⅓ cup sugar	1 egg
5 teaspoons baking powder	¾ cup milk
1 teaspoon salt	¾ cup raisins

½ cup nuts, chopped

Mix and sift flour, sugar, baking powder and salt.   Cut in Crisco with a knife or rub in with the finger tips.   Add beaten egg and enough milk to make a soft dough.   Roll out to ¼ inch thickness into a rectangular-shaped piece. Spread lightly with softened Crisco, sprinkle with raisins and nuts and 1 table-spoon sugar.   Roll like a jelly roll lengthwise.   Bring ends together to make a circle and press together.   Put on a large greased pan and cut gashes around outside edge with scissors, 2 inches apart.   Bake in a moderate oven (350 degrees F.) 25 to 30 minutes.   Spread top with Confectioners' Frosting (page 169).

DAINTY ROLLS

2 cups flour	1 egg
4 teaspoons baking powder	½ cup milk
1 teaspoon salt	Crisco
2 tablespoons sugar	Seedless raisins
½ cup Crisco	Chopped nuts

Sugar

Mix and sift flour, baking powder, salt and sugar.   Cut in Crisco with a knife or rub in with the finger tips.   Add beaten egg and enough milk to make a soft dough.   Roll out on slightly floured board to ¼ inch thickness and cut in 3 inch squares.   Spread each lightly with softened Crisco.   Sprinkle with raisins, nuts and a little sugar.   Roll like a jelly roll and press ends together. Brush tops with yolk of egg diluted with 1 teaspoon water.   Bake in a hot oven (400 degrees F.) 20 minutes.

RAISIN ROLLS

2 cups flour
5 teaspoons baking powder
1 teaspoon salt
2 tablespoons sugar
3 tablespoons Crisco
⅔ cup milk
1 teaspoon melted Crisco
½ cup raisins
¼ cup chopped nuts
½ teaspoon cinnamon

Mix and sift flour, baking powder, salt and 1 tablespoon of sugar. Cut in Crisco with a knife or rub in with the finger tips. Add milk gradually and mix to a soft dough. Roll out on a slightly floured board. Brush over with the melted Crisco. Sprinkle with raisins, nuts, 1 tablespoon sugar and the cinnamon. Roll like a jelly roll and cut in ¾ inch slices. Put in a greased baking pan, cut side down, and bake in a quick oven (425 degrees F.) 15 minutes. Serve hot.

This recipe makes 8 rolls.

BUTTERSCOTCH ROLLS

Follow recipe for Raisin Rolls. Line a deep greased pan with 1 cup brown sugar creamed with 2 tablespoons Crisco and 1 tablespoon cold water. Lay the rolls on this mixture. Bake in a hot oven (375 degrees F.) 20 to 25 minutes. Turn biscuits out on a plate and serve hot.

SWEET MILK GRIDDLE CAKES

2 cups flour
1 teaspoon salt
1½ teaspoons baking powder
2 tablespoons sugar
2 cups milk
1 egg
1 tablespoon melted Crisco

Mix and sift flour, salt, baking powder and sugar. Add milk, well-beaten egg and Crisco and mix well. Drop by tablespoons on a hot griddle greased well with Crisco and brown on both sides. Serve hot with marmalade or honey.

SOUR MILK GRIDDLE CAKES

2 cups flour
1 teaspoon salt
1 teaspoon soda
2 cups sour milk
1 egg
1 tablespoon melted Crisco

Mix and sift flour and salt. Dissolve soda in the sour milk and add to the flour mixture. Add beaten egg and Crisco and mix well. Drop by tablespoons on a hot griddle greased well with Crisco and brown on both sides. Serve hot with maple syrup or jam.

WHOLE WHEAT GRIDDLE CAKES

⅔ cup whole wheat flour
1¼ cups flour
3 teaspoons baking powder
1 teaspoon salt
2 tablespoons sugar
1½ cups milk
1 egg
1 tablespoon melted Crisco

Mix whole wheat flour, flour, baking powder, salt and sugar together. Add milk, beaten egg and Crisco and mix well. Drop by tablespoons on a hot griddle, greased well with Crisco and brown on both sides. Serve hot with powdered sugar or maple syrup.

WAFFLES

2 cups flour	1 tablespoon sugar
4 teaspoons baking powder	1¼ cups milk
1 teaspoon salt	2 eggs

2 tablespoons melted Crisco

Mix and sift flour, baking powder, salt and sugar. Add milk and beaten egg yolks and mix well. Fold in the stiffly beaten egg whites. Add Crisco. Heat waffle iron thoroughly on one side, then turn and heat other side. Grease well with Crisco. Put a little of the waffle mixture in the center. The mixture will spread when the iron is closed. Brown on one side, turn and brown on the other. Serve with maple syrup, honey or marmalade.

CHEESE WAFFLES

Follow recipe for Waffles, adding ½ cup grated cheese to the waffle batter.

CHAPTER XIV

Yeast Breads

IN THESE busy days many of us buy our bread at the corner grocery because we think we have no time for bread baking. But if you could be sure that within three hours after you had first set your dough to rise you could take the golden brown, crusty loaves from the oven would you be willing to bake at home?

According to the new "quick method" of bread making you can make your sponge in the morning and have hot bread within three hours—in time for luncheon! For about 30 or 40 minutes of this time you will have been occupied with the bread making; during the remainder of the three-hour period you will have been free to go about your other duties.

Of course more yeast is required by this new method than by the old, over-night process, but the flavor is actually better than that of bread which uses less yeast.

To make bread by the recipes in this chapter will take about three hours, as has been said. In the short process of bread making the all-important thing to watch is your temperature. Keep the dough at 80 degrees or 82 degrees Fahrenheit during the time it is rising, as this is the temperature best suited to yeast growth. Use an ordinary dairy or candy thermometer, put it into the dough and cover with a clean cloth. If the room is cool, place the bowl in a pan of warm water.

The ingredients essential to a good bread are flour, yeast, salt, sugar, liquid and shortening. The flour best suited to bread making is one which contains a large amount of gluten, for gluten produces a dough that is elastic and spongy. The yeast may be either compressed or dry. Among various yeasts, Fleischmann's Compressed Yeast stands out as one of high quality. Furthermore, it can be bought in practically every store. The liquid may be either milk, water, or half milk and

To keep your yeast dough at 80 to 82 degrees F. during the time it is rising, use thermometer, put it into the dough, and cover with a clean cloth. If room is not warm enough place bowl in a pan of warm water and add a little hot water occasionally to regulate temperature

half water. Bread made with whole milk is, of course, more nutritious and should be used whenever possible.

A little salt is usually added to improve the flavor and regulate the fermentation, but too much retards the action of the yeast. Sugar adds flavor and helps to give a delicate brown crust. It also hastens slightly the action of the yeast, so use some and help the yeast along!

Shortening used in bread must be the very best, because on it depends the quality of crumb, the tenderness or toughness of the crust, and the keeping qualities and flavor of the loaf. Crisco makes the crust tender, the crumb flaky and improves the keeping qualities of bread.

A "nutty" flavor is given to the crust if, just before it comes from the oven, it is rubbed over with melted Crisco.

SUCCESS SECRETS

1. Use level measurements.

2. Sift flour before measuring.

3. Be sure to scald milk used in bread making.

4. Dissolve yeast in *lukewarm* water—hot water will kill the yeast and prevent bread from rising.

5. To prevent a hard surface forming on the dough while rising, brush lightly with melted Crisco and cover with a clean cloth.

6. Knead dough thoroughly; the *first* time to blend the ingredients and the *second* time to distribute the gas bubbles produced by the yeast.

7. Use little or *no* flour on the board for second kneading. Extra flour added at this time takes from the lightness of the finished loaf.

8. Keep bread dough at even temperature during mixing and rising—80 degrees to 82 degrees Fahrenheit is the ideal temperature for yeast to grow.

9. After baking remove bread immediately from the pan, place on cake cooler and cover lightly with clean towel.

10. Never wrap bread tightly or put it in bread box while hot—moisture will collect on the surface and it will not keep well.

11. Watch baking carefully—too hot an oven makes a heavy loaf, too slow an oven a loaf of coarse, uneven texture.

BREAD

(OVER-NIGHT PROCESS)

1 cup milk	2½ teaspoons salt
1 cup water	1 yeast cake
3 tablespoons Crisco	¼ cup lukewarm water
2 tablespoons sugar	6 or 7 cups flour

Heat milk and water and add Crisco, sugar and salt. When lukewarm add the yeast cake dissolved in the warm water. Stir in 3 or 4 cups of flour and beat thoroughly. Cover and set in a warm place to rise over night. In the morning add enough flour to make a firm dough. Knead on a slightly floured board until smooth and elastic to touch. Cover and set in a warm place to rise until treble in bulk. Knead again. Shape in loaves and put in greased bread pans. Cover and let rise again in warm place until double in bulk. Bake in a moderate oven (350 degrees F.) 50 to 60 minutes.

BREAD

(QUICK PROCESS)

1 cup milk	1½ teaspoons salt
2 tablespoons Crisco	1 yeast cake
1½ tablespoons sugar	2 tablespoons lukewarm water
2 or 3 cups flour	

Heat milk and add Crisco, sugar and salt. When lukewarm add the yeast cake dissolved in warm water. Add 1 cup of flour and beat thoroughly. Cover and set in a warm place to rise until light, about 1 hour. Add enough flour to make a firm dough. Knead on a slightly floured board until smooth and elastic to touch. Cover and set in a warm place to rise until treble in bulk. Knead again. Shape in a loaf and put in a greased bread pan. Cover, set in a warm place and let rise until double in bulk. Bake in a moderate oven (350 degrees F.) 50 to 60 minutes.

To be sure of perfect results read introduction to this chapter carefully.

RAISIN BREAD

(QUICK PROCESS)

1 cup milk	1 yeast cake
3 tablespoons Crisco	2 tablespoons lukewarm water
4 tablespoons sugar	4 to 5 cups flour
1 teaspoon salt	1 cup raisins

Heat milk and add sugar, Crisco and salt. When lukewarm add the yeast cake dissolved in warm water. Add 2 cups of flour and beat until smooth. Cover and set in a warm place to rise for about 1 hour. Add the raisins and enough flour to make a firm dough. Knead until smooth and elastic to touch. Cover and set in a warm place to rise until double in bulk. Knead until free from air bubbles. Put in a greased loaf pan, cover and set in a warm place to rise until double in bulk. Bake in moderate oven (350 degrees F.) 50 to 60 minutes.

To be sure of perfect results read introduction to this chapter carefully.

WHOLE WHEAT BREAD
(QUICK PROCESS)

1 cup milk	1 yeast cake
2 tablespoons Crisco	2 tablespoons lukewarm water
4 tablespoons sugar	2 cups flour
1 teaspoon salt	1½ to 2 cups whole wheat flour

Heat milk and add Crisco, sugar and salt. When lukewarm add the yeast cake dissolved in the warm water. Add the flour and beat until smooth. Cover and set in a warm place to rise for about 1 hour. Add the whole wheat flour and knead until it is elastic to touch and does not stick to an unfloured board. Cover and set in a warm place to rise until double in bulk. Knead again until free from air bubbles. Put in a greased loaf pan. Cover and set in a warm place to rise until double in bulk. Bake in a moderate oven (350 degrees F.) 50 to 60 minutes.

To be sure of perfect results read the introduction to this chapter carefully.

COFFEE CAKE
(QUICK PROCESS)

½ cup milk	1 yeast cake
3 tablespoons Crisco	2 tablespoons lukewarm water
2 tablespoons sugar	2 to 2½ cups flour
1 teaspoon salt	1 egg
⅓ cup brown sugar	

Heat milk and add Crisco, sugar and salt. When lukewarm add the yeast cake dissolved in warm water. Add ¾ cup flour and beat thoroughly. Cover and set in a warm place to rise until light—about 1 hour. Add beaten egg and brown sugar and enough flour to make a firm dough. Knead on a slightly floured board until smooth and elastic to touch. Cover and set in a warm place to rise until double in bulk. Knead again. Pat dough into a greased pan to ½ inch thickness. Cover and set in a warm place to rise until light. Brush top with melted Crisco, sprinkle with 1 teaspoon cinnamon and 2 table-spoons brown sugar. Bake in a hot oven (400 degrees F.) 15 to 20 minutes.

To be sure of perfect results read the introduction to this chapter carefully.

COFFEE ROLLS
(QUICK PROCESS)

1 cup milk	1 yeast cake
¼ cup Crisco	2 tablespoons lukewarm water
¼ cup sugar	4 to 5 cups flour
1 teaspoon salt	2 eggs

Heat milk and add Crisco, sugar and salt. When lukewarm add the yeast cake, dissolved in warm water. Add 1½ cups flour and beat well. Cover and set in a warm place to rise. When double in bulk add the beaten eggs and mix well. Add enough flour to make a firm dough. Knead on a slightly floured board until smooth and elastic to touch. Cover and set in a warm place to rise until double in bulk. Knead again. Break off small pieces of dough, shape in balls and flatten with hands, like biscuits. Fit into a greased loaf pan, cover and let rise until treble in bulk. Brush tops with melted Crisco and sprinkle with sugar, cinnamon, mace and chopped raisins. Bake in a hot oven (400 degrees F.) 25 to 30 minutes.

To be sure of perfect results read the introduction to this chapter carefully.

PARKER HOUSE ROLLS

(QUICK PROCESS)

2 cups milk	3 teaspoons salt
5 tablespoons Crisco	2 yeast cakes
3 tablespoons sugar	4 tablespoons lukewarm water

6 to 7 cups flour

Heat milk and add Crisco, sugar and salt. When lukewarm add the yeast cakes dissolved in warm water. Add 2 cups flour and beat thoroughly. Cover and set in a warm place to rise until light—about 1½ hours. Add enough flour to make a firm dough. Knead on a slightly floured board until smooth and elastic to touch. Cover and set in a warm place to rise until double in bulk. Knead again. Roll the dough to ¼ inch thickness and cut with a large round cutter. Brush each piece with softened Crisco. Mark through the center with the back of a knife and fold over. Place rolls on a greased shallow pan 1 inch apart. Cover and set in a warm place to rise until double in size. Bake in a hot oven (400 degrees F.) 15 to 20 minutes.

This recipe makes 2½ dozen rolls.

To be sure of perfect results read the introduction to this chapter carefully.

DINNER ROLLS

Follow recipe for Parker House rolls. Roll dough to ½ inch thickness. Cut with a small round cooky cutter. Place rolls in a greased shallow pan 1 inch apart. Continue as for Parker House rolls.

This recipe makes 3 dozen rolls.

CLOVER LEAF ROLLS

Follow recipe for Parker House rolls. Pull off small bits of the dough after the third rising. Shape in small balls. Grease muffin pans and put 3 balls in each pan. Continue as for Parker House rolls.

This recipe makes 3 dozen rolls.

Devil's Food Cake (Recipe on page 157)

Mother's Tea Cakes (Recipe on page 155)

CHAPTER XV

Salads

IF WE are going to serve salads to our family as often as we should—at least once a day according to good health rules—we shall have to give a little time and thought to keeping the salad course out of the rut.

Salad greens must be carefully washed several hours before the meal and put in the ice box or some other cool place to become crisp. A small bag made of cheesecloth is very convenient for holding the washed lettuce and if you keep it filled you will always have a supply of fresh, crisp greens on hand in case of an emergency meal.

When you separate a head of lettuce or Romaine don't discard the outer leaves. Wash and chill them with the rest of the head and use them, shredded, for the foundation of another salad. You will find a pair of scissors very convenient for shredding salad greens.

The other ingredients of the salad, whether they be meat, fruit or vegetables, should be just as carefully prepared and as thoroughly chilled as the greens. Marinate them first. Marinating means to moisten thoroughly with French dressing and let stand for a time—a half hour to an hour—in a cold place in order that the food may absorb some of the flavor of the dressing.

Among the salads which you can serve for special occasions are the molded salads. They are very popular on any occasion, but for the buffet supper, Sunday night tea or bridge party when you want to get everything ready before the guests arrive, you will find them a blessing and your guests will vote them a great treat.

Both the cooked and pineapple dressings are especially good with these more delicate salads as well as with any of the fruit

Rich Cake (Recipe on page 153)

Silver Cake (Recipe on page 155)

salad combinations. New super-creamed Crisco gives just the right touch—a delicate flavor and a smooth, velvety texture.

SUCCESS SECRETS

1. Include at least one salad in your menus every day.
2. Keep a supply of fresh, carefully washed salad greens in a clean cheesecloth bag in your ice box.
3. Do not discard the outer leaves of a head of lettuce or Romaine. Shred them and use for the foundation of another salad.
4. Chill thoroughly all ingredients used for salads, such as meat, fish, vegetables and fruit.
5. Apples, bananas and pears turn dark after slicing, so prepare them at the last minute. Or cover them with French dressing or lemon juice to prevent them from discoloring.
6. Don't think you have to make up a fresh supply of salad dressing for every meal at which a salad is served. Any of the dressings given in this chapter, except those to which whipped cream is added, will keep for several days, if kept in a covered jar in the ice box.
7. Don't put the dressing on salad until immediately before serving. It wilts the greens.
8. Be particular about the appearance of your salad. Remember many of us "eat with our eyes."
9. Vary your salad course frequently by using crisp shredded cabbage instead of lettuce for the foundation.
10. Don't always use the same dressing on the same salad! Dress up an old salad with one of the new dressings in this chapter.
11. Don't think salads have to be elaborate to be good. Any of the following are easy to prepare and delicious served with an appropriate dressing: hearts of lettuce, watercress, chicory, Romaine, shredded lettuce and endive, sliced pine-

apple and cream cheese balls, sliced cucumber and water-cress, stuffed celery and hearts of romaine, shredded cabbage and peanut, grapefruit and orange.

COOKED SALAD DRESSING

½ teaspoon mustard	Few grains cayenne
1½ teaspoons salt	1 egg
1½ teaspoons sugar	1 cup milk
1½ tablespoons flour	4 tablespoons vinegar
⅛ teaspoon paprika	1½ tablespoons Crisco

Mix mustard, salt, sugar, flour, paprika and cayenne together. Add the beaten egg and mix well. Add milk and vinegar and cook over hot water until thick. Add Crisco and stir until melted.

WHIPPED CREAM DRESSING—To the foundation recipe add ½ cup whipped cream. Fold in lightly.

TARRAGON DRESSING—In the foundation recipe use only 2 tablespoons vinegar and add 2 tablespoons tarragon vinegar. Add 2 tablespoons chopped onion and 2 tablespoons chopped parsley.

HORSERADISH DRESSING—To the foundation recipe add 3 tablespoons prepared horseradish.

CELERY DRESSING—To the foundation recipe add ¼ cup chopped celery, 2 tablespoons chopped green pepper and 2 tablespoons chopped red pepper.

FRENCH DRESSING

1 cup salad oil	1 teaspoon sugar
3 tablespoons vinegar	⅛ teaspoon pepper
1 teaspoon salt	⅛ teaspoon paprika

Mix oil, vinegar, salt, sugar, pepper and paprika together and beat thoroughly. Or, put all ingredients in a glass jar and shake well.

LEMON FRENCH DRESSING—In the foundation recipe, substitute 3 tablespoons lemon juice for 2 tablespoons of the vinegar.

CHIFFONADE FRENCH DRESSING—To the foundation recipe add ⅛ cup chopped cooked beets and one chopped hard cooked egg.

THOUSAND ISLAND FRENCH DRESSING—To the foundation recipe add ¼ cup chopped green pepper, 2 tablespoons chopped stuffed olives, 1 tablespoon chopped parsley and 2 tablespoons chopped onion.

CURRY FRENCH DRESSING—To the foundation recipe add ⅛ teaspoon curry powder, mixed with the seasonings.

MAYONNAISE DRESSING

1 egg yolk	¾ teaspoon salt
2 tablespoons vinegar	⅛ teaspoon pepper
¼ teaspoon mustard	1 cup salad oil

Beat egg yolk and add 1 tablespoon vinegar. Add mustard, salt and pepper and mix well. Drop oil a teaspoonful at a time into the egg mixture, beating constantly until ¼ cup oil is added. Then add it in larger quantities, beating thoroughly after each addition. As the mixture thickens, add the remaining vinegar a little at a time. (Half lemon juice and half vinegar may be used.) Keep in a cool place.

FRUIT SALAD MAYONNAISE—To the foundation recipe add ⅓ cup whipped cream. Fold in lightly.

RUSSIAN MAYONNAISE—To the foundation recipe, add ⅓ cup Chili sauce and 2 tablespoons chopped green pepper.

PIQUANTE MAYONNAISE—To the foundation recipe, add ¼ cup chopped sour pickle and 2 tablespoons chopped pickled onions.

TARTAR MAYONNAISE—To the foundation recipe, add 2 tablespoons chopped sour pickle, 2 tablespoons chopped stuffed olives, 1 teaspoon capers and 2 tablespoons chopped parsley.

RED MAYONNAISE—To the foundation recipe, add ¼ teaspoon paprika and ¼ cup catsup.

CUCUMBER MAYONNAISE—To the foundation recipe add ½ cup grated well-drained cucumber.

ASPARAGUS SALAD

Cook 1 bunch of asparagus in boiling salted water 25 to 35 minutes or until tender. Drain and cool. Cut off the stalky ends leaving the tender tips. Marinate tips in French Dressing. Chill. Serve on crisp lettuce leaves with Thousand Island French Dressing.

Canned asparagus may be used instead of fresh.

CHICKEN SALAD

To 3 cups of diced cold chicken add 2¼ cups chopped celery. Season with salt and pepper and marinate in French Dressing. Chill. Moisten well with Mayonnaise Dressing and mound in salad dish. Garnish with lettuce and sprinkle 1 tablespoon capers over the chicken. Decorate with olives or radish roses and slices of hard cooked egg.

RUSSIAN EGG SALAD

6 hard cooked eggs	2 tablespoons chopped cooked ham
1 tablespoon chopped green pepper	½ teaspoon salt
3 tablespoons Chili sauce	⅛ teaspoon pepper
⅛ teaspoon paprika	

Cut eggs in halves lengthwise and remove yolks. Mash them and add green pepper, Chili sauce, ham, salt, pepper and paprika. Mix well. Refill whites of eggs and place on a bed of chopped cabbage. Serve with Cooked Salad Dressing. Any other meat may be used in this recipe.

HAM SALAD

2 cups diced cold ham	1 tablespoon chopped parsley
1 teaspoon chopped onion	1 tablespoon chopped pickle
2 hard cooked eggs, chopped	

Mix ham, onion, parsley, pickle and eggs. Marinate in French Dressing and chill. Garnish with lettuce and strips of pickle. Serve with Mayonnaise Dressing.

POTATO SALAD

5 medium-sized potatoes	1 teaspoon salt
1½ cups celery, cut in pieces	⅛ teaspoon paprika
2 tablespoons chopped parsley	1 hard cooked egg
½ teaspoon chopped onion	Stuffed olives

Wash and boil potatoes in salted water. Drain, and let cool with skins on. Remove skins and cut in small dice. Marinate in French Dressing and chill. Just before serving, add celery, parsley, onion, salt and paprika, and moisten with Mayonnaise Dressing. Garnish with lettuce, slices of hard cooked egg and olives.

MACÉDOINE SALAD

1 cup cooked peas	1 cup celery, cut in small
1 cup cooked carrots, cut	pieces
in cubes	1 cup cooked string beans,
1 small cauliflower, cooked	cut in pieces

Marinate peas, carrots, celery and string beans in French Dressing. Chill thoroughly. Separate cauliflower into small flowerets and marinate separately in French Dressing. Arrange cups of heart leaves of lettuce on a platter and pile vegetables lightly in them. Put a border of cauliflower around the edge of platter and garnish with strips of red and green pepper.

SALMON SALAD

2 cups cooked or canned salmon	½ cup celery, cut in pieces
1 cup chopped cucumber, drained	½ teaspoon salt
1 teaspoon chopped parsley	⅛ teaspoon pepper

Flake the salmon and remove bones. Add cucumber, parsley, celery, salt and pepper and mix well. Moisten with Mayonnaise Dressing. Mound in center of salad dish on crisp lettuce leaves. Garnish with Mayonnaise, slices of cucumber and hard cooked egg. Sprinkle 1 teaspoon capers over the salmon.

STUFFED TOMATO SALAD

6 medium-sized tomatoes
2 cups cooked shrimps
1 cup celery, cut in pieces

1 teaspoon chopped parsley
½ teaspoon salt
⅛ teaspoon pepper

Mayonnaise

Put tomatoes in boiling water for a moment to loosen skins. Peel and chill. Cut slices from the stem end and scoop out some of the pulp. Cut shrimps in pieces and add celery, parsley, salt and pepper. Moisten with Mayonnaise Dressing. Fill the tomatoes with the shrimp mixture. Garnish with a spoonful of Mayonnaise and a whole shrimp. Serve on crisp lettuce leaves.

Crab meat may be used in place of shrimps.

JELLIED TUNA FISH

1 tablespoon lemon juice
1 tablespoon chopped parsley
1 cup chopped celery
½ teaspoon salt

⅛ teaspoon pepper
2 cups flaked tuna fish
1 tablespoon gelatine
¼ cup water

1 cup cooked salad dressing

Add lemon juice, parsley, celery, salt and pepper to the flaked fish. Soak gelatine in cold water 5 minutes and dissolve over hot water. Add to the Cooked Salad Dressing and mix with the other ingredients. Pour into molds which have been dipped in cold water. Chill. Unmold, garnish with lettuce and serve with sliced cucumbers.

JELLIED VEGETABLE SALAD

2¼ tablespoons gelatine
¼ cup cold water
1 cup boiling water
3 tablespoons vinegar
3 tablespoons lemon juice

¼ cup sugar
1 teaspoon salt
1 cup celery, cut in pieces
1 cup shredded cabbage
1 cup cooked peas

Soak gelatine in cold water 10 minutes and dissolve in boiling water. Add vinegar, lemon juice, sugar and salt. Stir in the vegetables and mix thoroughly. Turn into a mold (or individual molds) dipped in cold water. Chill. Remove from mold to a bed of crisp lettuce leaves. Serve with Cooked Salad Dressing and garnish with celery curls and radish roses.

TOMATO JELLY SALAD

3 tablespoons gelatine
⅓ cup cold water
2½ cups canned tomatoes
2 whole cloves

¾ teaspoon salt
2 teaspoons sugar
1 small onion, sliced
Few grains cayenne

Soak gelatine in cold water 10 minutes. Cook tomatoes, cloves, salt, sugar, onion and cayenne together 15 minutes. Add gelatine and stir until dissolved. Strain. Turn into individual molds which have been dipped in cold water. Chill. Remove from molds to cups of crisp lettuce leaves arranged on individual salad plates. Garnish with Cucumber Mayonnaise.

WALDORF SALAD

3 cups diced apples
1 cup celery, cut in pieces

½ cup walnuts, cut in pieces
¾ cup mayonnaise dressing

Mix apple, celery and nuts and moisten with Mayonnaise Dressing. Arrange on crisp leaves of lettuce and garnish with whole nuts and candied cherries.

Salad Accompaniments

CHEESE FINGERS

1 cup flour
½ teaspoon baking powder
⅛ teaspoon cayenne

½ teaspoon salt
2 tablespoons Crisco
4 tablespoons grated cheese

Water

Mix and sift flour, baking powder, cayenne and salt. Cut in Crisco with a knife or rub in with finger tips. Add cheese and enough cold water to hold mixture together. Roll out on floured board to ¼ inch thickness. Cut in very thin strips with a knife or pastry jagger. Bake in a hot oven (400 degrees F.) 20 minutes.

This recipe makes about 50 fingers.

CHEESE STRAWS

Roll out Plain Pastry (page 178) to ⅛ inch thickness. Sprinkle with salt, cayenne and grated American cheese. Fold in 3 layers. Roll out again, spread and roll as before. Cut in strips ½ inch wide and 4 or 5 inches long. Bake in hot oven (400 degrees F.) 5 or 6 minutes.

CHEESE CREAM PUFFS

1 cup boiling water
¼ cup Crisco
½ cup flour

½ teaspoon salt
Few grains cayenne
½ cup grated American cheese

2 eggs

Heat water and Crisco to boiling point. Add flour, salt and cayenne, stirring constantly and cook until mixture leaves sides of pan. Add cheese and mix well. Cool. Add unbeaten eggs one at a time, beating well after each egg is added. Drop by teaspoons on a greased pan, making small balls. Cook in moderate oven (350 degrees F.) 30 to 40 minutes.

This recipe makes 48 puffs.

CHAPTER XVI

Sandwiches

THERE is an interesting bit of culinary history which tells us that the sandwich was named after the English nobleman by whom it was invented. The fourth Earl of Sandwich was so industrious a gambler that he wouldn't leave the card table even to eat. So he devised this new form of eating—the portable meal!

If the story is true we owe him a debt, for sandwiches are a convenient and delicious food for school lunches, afternoon teas, picnics and motor parties. They even are becoming a "square meal" when made of hot meat and thick, rich gravy.

Bread for sandwiches should be a day old so that it will not crumble when cut. For the daintier sandwiches it should be sliced very thin and the crusts cut off. It may then be cut with fancy shaped cutters, or diagonally, or in narrow finger-length oblongs.

A quarter of an inch is not too thick for bread to be sliced for hearty sandwiches, and unless the crust is hard it need not be removed. In cutting bread keep the slices in the order in which they come from the loaf so that they will fit evenly when put together with the filling between.

Instead of spreading your bread with butter try the new Crisco Spread—the first recipe in this chapter. It is a delicious spread for all kinds of sandwiches and much less expensive than butter! It has about the same consistency as mayonnaise dressing and is very much like it in flavor. One great advantage of Crisco Spread is that it may be kept in the ice box in a glass jar *indefinitely*. It is always ready for the hungry school boy's afternoon sandwich or the unexpected caller for whom you want to make a cup of tea. Less filling is needed to make sandwiches savory and appetizing if plenty of Crisco

Spread is used on the slices of bread. It also helps to keep them fresh and moist.

If sandwiches are prepared some time before they are to be served, they should be wrapped in wax paper or, better still, covered with a damp cloth or napkin.

The open sandwich is a rather new idea and offers opportunity for great variety. It consists of a single slice of bread, usually cut in a fancy shape, spread with Crisco Spread and daintily garnished. Canapés are open sandwiches made with highly seasoned fillings such as caviar or anchovy and are served as the first course at dinner or luncheon.

SUCCESS SECRETS

1. Use bread twenty-four hours old for sandwiches.
2. Slice bread very thin for dainty sandwiches.
3. Spread sandwiches with Crisco Spread instead of butter.
4. Always keep a supply of Crisco Spread in the ice box.
5. Get your sandwich filling ready before you cut the bread.
6. Cover sandwiches with a clean damp cloth if they are prepared in advance of serving time.
7. Serve a hearty sandwich occasionally for luncheon or supper. It is a good way to use up left over meat and gravy.
8. Vary your luncheon sandwich by making it of toast.

CRISCO SANDWICH SPREAD

1 cup Crisco	Few grains cayenne
1 egg yolk	1 teaspoon salt
1/4 teaspoon mustard	1/2 teaspoon Worcestershire sauce
1/8 teaspoon paprika	2 tablespoons lemon juice

2 1/2 tablespoons vinegar

Cream Crisco. Add egg yolk slowly and beat well. Mix mustard, paprika, cayenne, salt, Worcestershire sauce and lemon juice together and stir into the first mixture. Add vinegar, beating in a little at a time. Mix thoroughly.

This will keep in a cool place for several weeks. If it becomes hard, warm slightly and beat to proper consistency.

CHEESE AND PICKLE SANDWICH

Cut thin slices of white or graham bread and trim off crusts. Spread lightly with Crisco Spread. Make a filling of 1 cup grated cheese, 4 tablespoons chopped sweet pickle and enough Mayonnaise Dressing to moisten. Spread between two slices of bread. Cut in fancy shapes.

Any home-made pickle or relish may be used.

CHICKEN SALAD SANDWICH

Cut thin slices of white bread and trim off crusts. Spread lightly with Crisco Spread. Make a filling of cold cooked chicken, cut in small cubes, and half the quantity of finely cut celery, seasoned with salt and pepper and moistened with Mayonnaise Dressing. Spread between two slices of bread. Cut in halves diagonally.

CLUB SANDWICH

Cut white bread in ¼ inch slices and toast on one side. Spread untoasted side with Crisco Spread. Lay a crisp lettuce leaf on the bread and spread with Mayonnaise Dressing. On top of lettuce put layers of sliced chicken, sliced tomatoes and crisp bacon or cold ham. Season well with salt and pepper and cover with top piece of toast. Cut in halves diagonally.

EGG AND OLIVE SANDWICH

Cut thin slices of white or whole wheat bread and trim off crusts. Spread lightly with Crisco Spread. Chop 2 hard cooked eggs fine, add ¼ cup chopped olives and enough Mayonnaise Dressing to moisten. Spread between two slices of bread. Cut in fancy shapes.

HOT HAM SANDWICH

Cut slices of white bread and trim off crusts. Spread lightly with Crisco Spread. On one slice arrange a slice of ham and a thin slice of cheese and put another slice of bread on top. Mix ¾ cup milk, 1 beaten egg and ¼ teaspoon salt together, dip sandwich in it and sauté in hot Crisco until brown on both sides. Drain on unglazed paper. Serve hot.

LETTUCE SANDWICH

Cut thin slices of white or whole wheat bread and trim off the crusts. Spread lightly with Crisco Spread. Lay a crisp leaf of lettuce on a slice of bread, spread with Mayonnaise Dressing and sprinkle with salt and pepper. Cover with another slice of bread and cut sandwich in halves diagonally. Serve at once.

BROILED LUNCHEON SANDWICH

Cut white bread in ¼ inch slices and trim off crusts. Spread lightly with Crisco Spread. Cover bread with thin slices of American cheese. Then put slices of tomato on the cheese and sprinkle with salt and pepper. Lay 2 strips of bacon over the top.

Place under the broiler and cook 6 to 8 minutes or until cheese is melted and bacon crisp.

NUT AND RAISIN SANDWICH

Cut thin slices of white or graham bread and trim off crusts. Spread lightly with Crisco Spread. Make a filling of 1 cup chopped raisins and ¼ cup chopped nuts moistened with Mayonnaise Dressing. Spread between two slices of bread. Cut with round cooky cutter.

PEANUT BUTTER SANDWICH

Cut thin slices of white or rye bread and trim off crusts. Spread one slice with peanut butter and the other with Crisco Spread. Put together and cut in halves diagonally.

PICKLED WALNUT AND CHEESE SANDWICH

Cut thin slices of white or whole wheat bread and trim off crusts. Spread lightly with Crisco Spread. Mash 3 pickled walnuts to a paste with ¼ pound of sharp or snappy cheese. Moisten with Mayonnaise Dressing and spread between two slices of bread. Cut with cooky cutter in round or fancy shapes.

SARDINE SANDWICH

Cut thin slices of white or graham bread and trim off crusts. Spread lightly with Crisco Spread. Drain the oil from one can of sardines and remove skin and bones. Mash to a paste and moisten with a little lemon juice. Spread between two slices of bread. Put a crisp leaf of lettuce on top the sardine mixture, just before serving. Cut in halves diagonally.

CANAPÉ DIAGONAL

Cut bread in ¼ inch slices and cut in oblong pieces 1½ inches wide and 4 inches long. Toast on one side. Spread other side lightly with Crisco Spread. Cover with a thin layer of anchovy paste. Sprinkle with yolks of hard cooked eggs pressed through a sieve. Cut anchovies in very thin slices and place them diagonally across the bread. Put a ¼ inch border of chopped hard cooked egg whites around the edge of each piece.

CAVIAR CANAPÉ

Cut bread in ¼ inch slices and cut in oblong pieces 1½ inches wide and 4 inches long. Toast on one side and spread other side lightly with Crisco Spread. Cover with caviar mixed with a little finely chopped onion. Around the edge put a ¼ inch border of yolks of hard cooked eggs pressed through a sieve. Lay a ⅛ inch strip of green pepper in the center.

CANAPÉ SUPREME

Cut bread in ¼ inch slices and cut in circles with a cooky cutter. Spread one side lightly with Crisco Spread, cover with highly seasoned or snappy cheese mashed to a smooth paste.   Place an anchovy in the center of each and put a ¼ inch border of finely chopped hard cooked eggs around the edge.

CHEESE AND OLIVE CANAPÉ

Cut bread in ¼ inch slices and cut in circles with a cooky cutter.   Toast one side.   Spread other side lightly with Crisco Spread.   Cover with cream cheese moistened with Mayonnaise Dressing.   Put a slice of stuffed olive in the center and put a ¼ inch border of finely chopped stuffed olives around the edge.

WIDE OPEN SANDWICHES

1 cup ham, chopped
1 hard cooked egg, chopped
2 tablespoons chopped green pepper

2 tablespoons chopped sour pickle
Few grains pepper
Finger rolls

Mix together ham, egg, green pepper, pickle and pepper.   Moisten with Mayonnaise Dressing.   Split rolls.   Spread both halves lightly with Crisco. Spread and cover with some of the ham mixture.   Decorate tops with thin slices of pickle and strips of green pepper.   Serve open.

CHAPTER XVII

Cakes and Cookies

HAVE you ever wondered where all the cake recipes come from? Every cook book you look over has a chapter on cakes and each recipe looks different!

But if you study these recipes carefully you will find that they are not so different after all and that they are really only variations of *two* kinds of cakes, those made *with* shortening and those made *without* shortening. If we learn the general method of mixing these two kinds of cake it is easy to follow all recipes.

Cakes made with shortening are probably the most popular, so let us discuss first the rules for mixing them. Step number one consists in blending together the shortening and the sugar. If this is done thoroughly the texture of the cake will not be grainy. This process is called "creaming," and is done by pressing Crisco and the sugar against the sides of the bowl with the back of a wooden or metal mixing spoon until the mixture is of a smooth creamy consistency. New super-creamed Crisco is so soft and smooth that it actually cuts creaming time in half.

In many cases, particularly in batters containing whole eggs or yolks, the eggs can be mixed directly with the sugar and Crisco. This is possible only with a shortening that is as soft and creamy as the new super-creamed Crisco. It is desirable not only because it simplifies the mixing process, but also because of the water in the eggs which provides a solvent for the sugar, and thereby helps to produce a more perfectly blended mixture.

The flour is sifted, measured and mixed with any other dry ingredients such as salt, baking powder and spices. This flour mixture is then added to the Crisco mixture. But it is not all put in at once. First, some of the flour goes into the mixing bowl, then some of the milk called for by the recipe and after each addition the ingredients in the bowl are beaten well. When all the flour and milk are in, the batter should have a final beat-

The first step in cake making consists of blending together the shortening and the sugar. This process is called "creaming" and is done by pressing Crisco and sugar against the sides of the bowl with the back of a wooden spoon until the mixture is of a smooth creamy consistency

ing, lasting from one minute for a plain cake to three minutes for a rich one. When not beaten long enough a cake has a porous, open texture with large holes; on the other hand *too much* beating makes a close-grained, tough cake.

The method for mixing the other kind of cakes, those without shortening, starts by separating the yolks from the whites of the eggs. For sponge cakes the yolks are beaten until thick, then the sugar added gradually and last the beaten whites, flour and flavoring are folded in.

Sponge and angel cakes require a slower oven than cakes made with shortening—from 320 to 340 degrees, depending upon the depth of the pan in which they are baked.

For baking any kind of cake an oven thermometer should be used instead of trusting to the "feel" of the oven. We are not all equally sensitive to heat and what may feel "slow" to one person may feel "medium" to another. An accurate temperature for baking cake is next in importance to careful measurements of the ingredients which go into it. A cake baked in too slow an oven rises over the sides of the pan and has a coarse, open texture, while one baked in too hot an oven becomes solid and close-grained with a hard crust.

Loosen cake from pan by slipping a knife around the edge between the cake and the pan, then invert pan and allow cake to cool on a wire rack so that the air can circulate around it

Cakes should be allowed to cool on a wire cooler so the *air* can circulate around them. When turned out on a bread board, or other solid surface, moisture condenses and makes them wet and sticky.

As soon as cake is cool it may be frosted or "iced" and put away in a tin cake box in a cool place. The care of cakes after baking is an important factor in their keeping—the longer they are exposed to the air the more quickly the cake dries out.

Of the cakes made with shortening the plainer ones should be used the same day, or at least by the following day. Layer cakes which are put together with soft "fillings," however, and the richer cakes, made with more Crisco and more eggs, will keep fresh for several days.

Not only do cakes made with new super-creamed Crisco keep well but they have a light, delicate, even texture and a delicious flavor. Crisco blends very easily with sugar in the first step of cake making.

Even in extremely hot weather when it seems desirable to keep Crisco in the refrigerator (at all other times it should be kept at ordinary room temperature) no difficulty in mixing will be en-

As soon as cake is cool it may be frosted or "iced." Use a spatula to spread on the frosting; and a pastry bag—if you have one—to frost small cakes and put fancy touches on large ones

countered. Super-creamed Crisco does not become hard and brittle in cold weather or under refrigerator conditions, but on the contrary keeps its creamy consistency and is always ready to measure and mix without preliminary conditioning.

If you once make your cakes with the new super-creamed Crisco by the following recipes you will never make them with anything else. And think of the money you save by not having to use butter.

SUCCESS SECRETS

1. Use level measurements.
2. Sift flour before measuring.
3. Gather all ingredients together and grease cake pan with Crisco before starting to mix cake.
4. Cream Crisco and sugar together thoroughly—on this depends a good-textured cake.
5. Beat cake batter from one to three minutes, after all the ingredients are in. Rich cakes require longer beating than plain cakes.
6. Don't let cake batter stand around after mixing. Have oven at correct temperature and put cake in at once.

7. When baking without a thermometer, or oven regulator, divide the baking time into quarters, as:

　　1st quarter—Cake batter should rise.

　　2nd quarter—Cake should continue to rise and begin to brown.

　　3rd quarter—Rising should be completed and cake continue to brown.

　　4th quarter—Cake should "settle" and shrink from pan.

8. When cake is done—

　　(a) It will spring back when pressed lightly with the finger.

　　(b) It shrinks from the sides of the pan.

9. Cool cake quickly—on wire rack—but do not let it dry out.

10. Frost cake *as soon as* cool.

11. Keep left over egg whites covered and in a cool place so that they will not dry out.

12. Plan to use up plain cakes quickly as they become stale sooner than rich cakes made with several eggs and plenty of Crisco.

If you have a favorite cake recipe of your own calling for butter, use Crisco instead and double the amount of salt. If no salt is called for use one-quarter teaspoon to each cup of flour.

RICH CAKE

¾ cup Crisco	3 teaspoons baking powder
1½ cups sugar	1 teaspoon salt
4 eggs	¾ cup milk
3 cups flour	2 teaspoons vanilla

Cream Crisco, sugar and egg yolks together. Mix and sift flour, baking powder and salt and add alternately with the milk to the first mixture. Fold in stiffly beaten whites. Add vanilla. Bake in greased cup cake pans in a quick oven (425 degrees F.) 20 minutes, or in 3 layer cake pans in a hot oven (400 degrees F.) 25 minutes. Spread layers and top of cake with Boiled Frosting II to which has been added ½ cup chopped raisins, ⅛ cup chopped candied cherries and ⅓ cup chopped nuts.

ALMOND CAKE

Follow recipe for Rich Cake. Add ½ cup blanched almonds and ¼ cup candied cherries, cut in thin strips. Substitute ½ teaspoon almond flavoring for ½ teaspoon of the vanilla. Bake in a greased loaf pan in a moderate oven (350 degrees F.) 60 to 80 minutes.

RAISIN CAKE

Follow recipe for Rich Cake. Add ¾ cup raisins mixed with a little of the flour. Bake in a greased loaf pan in a moderate oven (350 degrees F.) 60 to 80 minutes.

NUT CAKE

Follow recipe for Rich Cake. Add 1 cup English walnuts, cut in pieces and mixed with a little of the flour. Bake in a greased loaf pan in a moderate oven (350 degrees F.) 60 to 80 minutes. Any kind of nuts may be used in this recipe.

CURRANT SPICE CAKE

Follow recipe for Rich Cake. Add 1 teaspoon cinnamon, ½ teaspoon clove, ¼ teaspoon nutmeg and ¾ cup currants. Mix these with the flour before adding. Bake in a greased loaf or round pan in a moderate oven (350 degrees F.) 60 to 80 minutes.
Cover with Boiled Frosting II.

LAYER CAKE

⅓ cup Crisco	3 teaspoons baking powder
¾ cup sugar	½ teaspoon salt
2 eggs	½ cup milk
1½ cups flour	1 teaspoon vanilla

Cream Crisco, sugar and eggs together. Mix and sift flour, baking powder and salt and add alternately with the milk to the first mixture. Add vanilla and beat thoroughly. Bake in 2 greased layer cake pans in a hot oven (400 degrees F.) 20 to 25 minutes. Cool. Put layers together with any cream filling (chocolate, pineapple, lemon, orange or cocoanut). Ice top with Confectioners' Frosting.

QUICK CAKE

1 cup sugar	¼ cup melted Crisco
1½ cups flour	2 eggs
2 teaspoons baking powder	Milk
½ teaspoon salt	1 teaspoon vanilla

Mix sugar, flour, baking powder and salt and sift three times. Put Crisco in measuring cup, add eggs and fill cup with milk. Add liquid to the sifted flour mixture. Add vanilla and beat thoroughly. Bake in 2 greased layer cake pans in hot oven (400 degrees F.) 15 to 20 minutes. Cool. Put layers together and ice top with Quick Frosting. This cake may also be baked in greased muffin pans.

MOTHER'S TEA CAKES

⅓ cup Crisco	1½ cups flour
1 cup sugar	1 teaspoon baking powder
½ teaspoon salt	½ cup milk
2 eggs	½ teaspoon vanilla

Cream Crisco, sugar, salt and eggs together. Beat until light and soft. Mix and sift flour and baking powder and add to the first mixture alternately with the milk. Add vanilla. Beat thoroughly and pour into well-greased shallow baking pan. Bake in hot oven (375 degrees F.) 30 minutes. When partly cool, dust with powdered sugar, cut in squares and serve while warm.

GOLD CAKE

½ cup Crisco	4 teaspoons baking powder
1 cup sugar	1 teaspoon salt
8 egg yolks	½ cup milk
1½ cups flour	1 teaspoon vanilla

Cream Crisco and sugar together. Add well-beaten egg yolks. Mix and sift flour, baking powder and salt and add alternately with the milk to the first mixture. Add vanilla and beat thoroughly. Bake in 2 greased layer cake pans in a hot oven (400 degrees F.) 20 minutes. When cool, put layers together and ice top and sides with honey frosting.

LADY BALTIMORE CAKE

½ cup Crisco	1 teaspoon salt
1½ cups sugar	1 cup milk
2½ cups cake flour	1 tablespoon lemon juice
2 teaspoons baking powder	4 egg whites

Blend Crisco and sugar until light. (No creaming is needed with super-creamed Crisco.) Sift flour, baking powder, and salt together. Add alternately with the milk. Add lemon juice and then the beaten egg whites. Pour into two round layer pans (9-inch) rubbed with Crisco and dusted with flour, and bake in a moderate oven (350°F.). When cool, spread Lady Baltimore Filling between layers. Ice with Boiled Icing.

LADY BALTIMORE FILLING

¾ cup chopped raisins	½ cup drained and chopped
¾ cup chopped walnuts	maraschino cherries
½ cup chopped steamed figs	¼ cup icing

Mix chopped fruit and nuts together. Add one-quarter cup of icing prepared for top. Blend thoroughly.

BOILED ICING

2 cups sugar	⅛ cup water
⅓ cup light corn syrup	2 egg whites
1 teaspoon vanilla	

Cook sugar, corn syrup, and water, stirring until sugar is dissolved. Boil to 242°F., or until syrup forms a soft ball in cold water. Pour this syrup over egg whites beaten stiff. Beat constantly until mixture holds its shape. Add vanilla.

Currant Spice Cake (Recipe on page 154)

Snicker Doodles (Recipe on page 158)

ORANGE CAKE

⅔ cup Crisco
1½ cups sugar
3 eggs
3 cups flour

3 teaspoons baking powder
1 teaspoon salt
¾ cup orange juice
¼ cup water

Cream Crisco, sugar and egg yolks together. Mix and sift flour, baking powder and salt and add alternately with the combined orange juice and water to the first mixture. Stir in beaten whites. Pour into 3 greased layer cake pans and bake in a hot oven (400 degrees F.) 20 to 25 minutes. Cool. Spread Orange Icing II between layers and on top of cake.

DEVIL'S FOOD CAKE

⅓ cup Crisco *Maltha*
1 cup sugar
2 eggs
⅔ cup milk

3 squares unsweetened chocolate *cocoa*
1½ cups flour
2½ teaspoons baking powder
1 teaspoon salt

1½ teaspoons vanilla

Cream Crisco, sugar and eggs together. Cook the milk and chocolate, cut in pieces, over a slow fire, stirring until thick. Cool. Mix and sift flour, baking powder and salt and add alternately with the chocolate to the first mixture. Add vanilla and beat thoroughly. Bake in 2 layer cake pans in moderate oven (350 degrees F.) 25 to 30 minutes. Cool. Spread Marshmallow Frosting between layers and on top. Sprinkle with chopped nuts.

MARBLE CAKE

¾ cup Crisco
1½ cups sugar
4 eggs
3 cups flour
3 teaspoons baking powder

1 teaspoon salt
1 cup milk
2 teaspoons vanilla
2 squares unsweetened chocolate
¼ cup milk

Cream Crisco, sugar and egg yolks together. Mix and sift flour, baking powder and salt and add alternately with 1 cup milk to the first mixture. Add vanilla and egg whites beaten until light and fluffy but not stiff. Blend thoroughly. Divide the batter in halves. Melt the chocolate over hot water with ¼ cup milk and add to one-half of the batter. Put batter into a greased loaf pan using a spoonful of chocolate mixture and one of the white, alternately, until all is used. Bake in a moderate oven (350 degrees F.) 60 to 80 minutes.

DATE CAKE

⅔ cup Crisco
1½ cups brown sugar
4 eggs
3¼ cups flour
5 teaspoons baking powder

1 teaspoon cinnamon
½ teaspoon nutmeg
1 teaspoon salt
1½ cups dates, stoned and cut in small pieces

¾ cup milk

Cream Crisco, sugar and egg yolks together. Mix and sift flour, baking powder, cinnamon, nutmeg and salt and add alternately with the milk to the first mixture. Stir in well-beaten egg whites. Add dates and mix well. Pour into a greased tube or loaf pan and bake in a moderate oven (350 degrees F.) 50 to 60 minutes. Cool. This cake may be frosted, if desired.

GINGER CAKE

5 tablespoons Crisco	½ cup sour milk
½ cup sugar	1¾ cups flour
1 egg	2 teaspoons ginger
½ cup molasses	1 teaspoon cinnamon
1 teaspoon soda	½ teaspoon salt

Cream Crisco, sugar and egg together. Stir in molasses. Dissolve soda in the sour milk. Mix and sift flour, ginger, cinnamon and salt together and add alternately with the sour milk to the first mixture. Pour into a greased shallow pan and bake in a hot oven (400 degrees F.) 25 to 30 minutes. Serve hot with whipped cream.

SNICKER DOODLES

½ cup Crisco	1 tablespoon hot water
1 cup sugar	2½ cups flour
2 eggs	½ teaspoon salt
⅓ cup seeded raisins	½ teaspoon clove
⅓ cup currants	½ teaspoon mace
⅓ cup nuts	1½ teaspoons cinnamon
1 teaspoon soda	¾ cup sour milk

Cream Crisco, sugar and egg yolks together. Add raisins, currants and nuts, cut fine. Add soda, dissolved in hot water. Mix and sift flour, salt and spices and add alternately with the sour milk to the first mixture. Fold in one stiffly beaten egg white. (Save other white for frosting.) Pour into well-greased muffin pans and bake in a hot oven (375 degrees F.) 15 to 20 minutes.

This recipe makes 18 medium-sized cup cakes.

Frosting

1 egg white	Confectioners' sugar
2 tablespoons sweet cream	¼ teaspoon mace

Add cream to unbeaten egg white and mix well. Add sugar, a little at a time, until frosting is the right consistency to spread. Add mace and mix well.

COFFEE FRUIT CAKE

1 cup Crisco	4 cups flour
2 cups brown sugar	1 teaspoon salt
4 eggs	1 teaspoon clove
1 cup strong coffee	1 teaspoon nutmeg
1 teaspoon soda	2 teaspoons cinnamon
1 cup molasses	1 pound currants

1 pound raisins

Cream Crisco and sugar together. Add eggs one at a time, blending in thoroughly. Stir in coffee. Add soda mixed with molasses. Mix and sift flour, salt and spices. Add enough of the flour mixture to the fruit to keep it from sticking together. Add the remainder to the first mixture. Add fruit and mix thoroughly. Line bottom of a large pan with several layers of greased brown paper and grease sides of pan. Pour in the cake batter and bake in a very slow oven (250 degrees F.) 2 to 3 hours. A small pan of water in the oven helps to keep the cake from burning during the long cooking.

MOLASSES CAKE

½ cup Crisco	1 teaspoon cinnamon
½ cup sugar	¼ teaspoon clove
3 eggs	¼ teaspoon mace
¾ teaspoon soda	1 teaspoon salt
⅔ cup molasses	½ cup milk
2¼ cups flour	½ cup raisins

Cream Crisco, sugar and egg yolks together. Add soda, mixed with the molasses. Mix and sift flour, cinnamon, clove, mace and salt, and add alternately with the milk to the first mixture. Stir in beaten whites. Dredge the raisins lightly with flour and stir in lightly. Pour into a greased loaf pan and bake in a moderate oven (330 degrees F.) 50 to 60 minutes.

POUND CAKE

1 cup Crisco	2 cups flour
1½ cups sugar	1½ teaspoons salt
5 eggs	⅛ teaspoon mace

1 teaspoon vanilla

Cream Crisco and sugar together. Add eggs, one at a time, beating well after the addition of each egg. Add the flour, salt and mace. Add vanilla and beat thoroughly. Bake in a greased tube pan or loaf pan in a moderate oven (350 degrees F.) 60 to 80 minutes.

BREAD CRUMB CAKE

3 egg yolks	1 cup soft bread crumbs
1 cup sugar	2 teaspoons baking powder
3 tablespoons cold water	1 tablespoon melted Crisco
¾ cup walnuts, cut in small pieces	1 teaspoon vanilla

3 egg whites

Beat egg yolks until thick and lemon colored. Add sugar and water. Add the nuts, bread crumbs, baking powder and Crisco and mix well. Add vanilla and fold in stiffly beaten egg whites. Bake in 2 greased layer cake pans in a hot oven (400 degrees F.) 15 to 20 minutes. When cool, spread whipped cream, sweetened and flavored, between layers and on top of cake.

APPLE SAUCE CAKE

½ cup Crisco	1 cup thick apple sauce
1½ cups brown sugar	1 teaspoon salt
1 egg	1 teaspoon cinnamon
1 teaspoon soda	½ teaspoon clove

1½ to 2 cups flour

Cream Crisco, sugar and egg together. Dissolve soda in apple sauce and add. Sift salt, cinnamon and clove with part of the flour and add to the first mixture.

Potato Cakes (Recipe on page 109)

Spanish Omelet (Recipe on page 78)

Dutch Apple Cake (Recipe on page 190)

Apple Fritters (Recipe on page 50)

Add enough more flour to make a fairly stiff batter. (The amount depends upon the thickness of the apple sauce.) Pour into a greased loaf pan and bake in moderate oven (350 degrees F.) 50 to 60 minutes. 1 cup raisins may be added to the batter.

GRAHAM CRACKER CAKE

½ cup Crisco
1 cup granulated sugar
3 eggs
1 cup milk
½ teaspoon salt
2 doz. graham crackers
    (2 cups crumbs)
2 teaspoons baking powder
1 cup chopped nuts

Cream Crisco and sugar together, beat yolks of eggs till light and add to this. Then add milk. Roll the crackers fine. Mix baking powder with cracker crumbs, add this to other mixture together with salt and chopped nuts. Last add beaten whites of eggs. Bake in 2 layers in oven 375 degrees F. When cool spread whipped cream, sweetened and flavored, between layers and on top of cake.

ANGEL CAKE

8 egg whites
1 teaspoon cream of tartar
1 cup sugar
1 cup pastry flour
¼ teaspoon salt
1 teaspoon vanilla

Beat egg whites slightly. Add cream of tartar and beat until stiff. Add the sifted sugar gradually, beating constantly. Fold in the flour and salt which have been sifted together 4 times. Add vanilla. Pour into a tube pan and bake in a moderate oven (325 degrees F.) 50 to 60 minutes. Turn upside down on a cake cooler and let stand until the cake drops out.

SPONGE CAKE

6 egg yolks
1 cup sugar
1½ tablespoons lemon juice
6 egg whites
1 cup flour
½ teaspoon salt

Beat egg yolks until thick and lemon colored. Add sugar gradually and continue beating. Add lemon juice and fold in the stiffly beaten egg whites. Fold in the flour and salt, mixed and sifted together. Pour into a tube pan and bake in a moderate oven (325 degrees F.) 50 to 60 minutes.

CHOCOLATE ROLL

4 egg whites
½ cup sugar
4 egg yolks
4 tablespoons cold water
4 tablespoons cocoa
½ teaspoon vanilla
1 cup flour
1 teaspoon baking powder
½ teaspoon salt
1 cup cream
2 tablespoons confectioners'
    sugar

Beat egg whites until stiff. Add sugar gradually, beating constantly. Add beaten egg yolks and water. Mix and sift cocoa, flour, baking powder and salt and fold into the first mixture. Line a long shallow pan with greased paper. Pour the batter into the pan. Bake in a hot oven (400 degrees F.) 15 to 20 minutes. Turn out on a damp cloth and cool slightly. Spread with the stiffly beaten cream sweetened with confectioners' sugar and flavored with vanilla. Roll like jelly roll. Sprinkle with powdered sugar.

SOUR CREAM CAKES

1 tablespoon Crisco	½ cup sour cream
1 cup sugar	1½ cups flour
2 eggs	1½ teaspoons salt
½ teaspoon soda	½ teaspoon cream of tartar
	⅛ teaspoon mace

Cream Crisco, sugar and eggs together. Beat until very light. Dissolve soda in sour cream. Mix and sift flour, salt, cream of tartar and mace, and add alternately with the cream to the first mixture. Beat thoroughly. Bake in small greased cup cake pans in a hot oven (400 degrees F.) 15 to 20 minutes.

This recipe makes about 18 small cakes.

CUP CAKES

½ cup Crisco	2 teaspoons baking powder
1 cup sugar	½ teaspoon salt
3 eggs	½ cup milk
1¾ cups flour	1 teaspoon vanilla

Cream Crisco, sugar and eggs together. Mix and sift flour, baking powder and salt and add alternately with the milk to the first mixture. Add vanilla and beat thoroughly. Pour into greased muffin or cup cake pans and bake in quick oven (375 degrees F.) 15 to 20 minutes.

This recipe makes 15 to 20 cakes.

FILLED CUP CAKES

Follow recipe for Cup Cakes. When cool split in halves crosswise and remove portion of the cake. Fill center with stiffly whipped cream, flavored and sweetened. Put halves together and ice all over with Boiled Frosting I or Creamy Chocolate Frosting.

FILLED CHOCOLATE CAKES

Follow recipe for Devil's Food Cake. Bake in small, greased cup cake pans in a quick oven (425 degrees F.) 15 to 20 minutes. While hot remove a square from the top of each cake and substitute a marshmallow in place of the cake removed. Ice with Boiled Frosting I.

SUGAR COOKIES

⅔ cup Crisco	1½ teaspoons salt
1¼ cups sugar	2 teaspoons baking powder
2 eggs	Grated rind 1 orange
3 cups flour	1 tablespoon orange juice

Cream Crisco, sugar and eggs together. Mix and sift flour, salt and baking powder and add to the first mixture. Add orange rind and juice and mix to a smooth dough. Chill. Roll out thin on slightly floured board and cut with cooky cutter. Sprinkle with sugar and bake in a moderate oven (325 degrees F.) 12 to 15 minutes. This recipe makes about 60 cookies.

SAND TARTS

Follow recipe for Sugar Cookies. Use 1 teaspoon vanilla for flavoring instead of orange juice and rind. Cut into diamonds or squares and brush with white of egg. Sprinkle with sugar, dust with cinnamon and decorate with a blanched almond in center.

SPICE COOKIES

Follow recipe for Sugar Cookies. Sift ⅛ teaspoon clove, ¼ teaspoon nutmeg and ½ teaspoon cinnamon with the flour. Use 1 teaspoon vanilla flavoring instead of orange juice and rind.

FILLED COOKIES

Follow recipe for Sugar Cookies. Roll out cooky dough very thin and cut into circles. Put a small teaspoon of jam in the center of one circle. Cover with another circle of dough, pressing the edges firmly together.

CHOCOLATE COOKIES

Follow recipe for Sugar Cookies. Add ½ cup cocoa, moistened with 3 tablespoons hot water or coffee, when the eggs are added. Use 1 teaspoon vanilla flavoring instead of orange juice and rind.

PEANUT COOKIES

Follow recipe for Sugar Cookies. Add 1 cup finely chopped peanuts to the cooky dough.

COCOANUT COOKIES

Follow recipe for Sugar Cookies. Add 1 cup shredded cocoanut to the cooky dough.

RAISIN COOKIES

Follow recipe for Sugar Cookies. Press 4 Sultana raisins in each cooky before baking. Sprinkle with sugar.

NUT COOKIES

Follow recipe for Sugar Cookies. Brush with egg white, before baking, and sprinkle with sugar and chopped nuts.

MOLASSES CRISPS

¼ cup Crisco	¾ cup molasses
½ cup sugar	1 cup flour

¾ teaspoon salt

Melt Crisco, add sugar and molasses and bring to boiling point. Cool slightly and add flour and salt. Drop by teaspoons 2 inches apart on a greased sheet.

Cook in moderate oven (325 degrees F.) 15 minutes. Remove from the pan when beginning to cool and turn quickly around the finger to form rolls.

This recipe makes about 36 cookies.

HERMITS

1 cup Crisco	1½ teaspoons salt
1½ cups sugar	1 teaspoon cinnamon
3 eggs	1 teaspoon allspice
½ teaspoon soda	1 teaspoon clove
2 teaspoons water	1 teaspoon nutmeg
3 cups flour	1½ cups raisins

½ cup nuts, cut in pieces

Cream Crisco, sugar and eggs together. Dissolve soda in water and add. Mix and sift flour, salt and spices and add to the first mixture. Add raisins and nuts and mix thoroughly. Drop by teaspoons on greased pans. Bake in moderate oven (350 degrees F.) 15 to 20 minutes. These cookies improve on keeping in stone crock or cooky jar.

This recipe makes about 70 hermits.

OATMEAL COOKIES

1½ cups rolled oats	½ teaspoon cinnamon
½ cup brown sugar	½ teaspoon soda
¾ cup white flour	¼ cup boiling water
1 teaspoon salt	½ cup melted Crisco

Mix oats, sugar, flour, salt and cinnamon together. Add soda, dissolved in boiling water, and Crisco. Mix well. Chill. Roll out thin on slightly floured board. Cut with cooky cutter and bake in moderate oven (350 degrees F.) 12 to 15 minutes.

This recipe makes about 30 cookies.

LACE WAFERS

2 tablespoons Crisco	½ teaspoon nutmeg
1 cup sugar	2½ cups rolled oats
2 eggs	2½ teaspoons baking powder
½ teaspoon salt	1 teaspoon vanilla

¼ teaspoon maple or almond flavoring

Cream Crisco, sugar and eggs together. Mix salt, nutmeg, rolled oats and baking powder. Add to the first mixture and mix thoroughly. Add flavoring. Drop by teaspoons on greased pans, two inches apart. Bake in a moderate oven (350 degrees F.) 12 to 15 minutes.

This recipe makes about 60 cookies.

DATE BARS

1 cup stoned dates	1 tablespoon melted Crisco
1 cup nuts	1 tablespoon lemon juice
1 cup powdered sugar	4 tablespoons flour
2 eggs	½ teaspoon salt

Put dates and nuts through food chopper. Add sugar and beaten eggs and mix well. Add melted Crisco, lemon juice, flour and salt and mix thoroughly.

Spread evenly in a greased shallow pan, having mixture ¼ inch deep.   Bake in a moderate oven (325 degrees F.) about 30 minutes.   While hot cut in strips and roll in powdered sugar before serving.

CHOCOLATE INDIANS

½ cup Crisco	½ cup flour
1 cup sugar	1 cup walnuts, cut in pieces
2 eggs	2 squares unsweetened chocolate
1 teaspoon salt	1 teaspoon vanilla

Cream Crisco and sugar together.   Add beaten eggs, salt and flour.   Add nuts, melted chocolate and vanilla and mix well.   Spread evenly in a greased shallow pan, having mixture ¼ inch deep.   Bake in a moderate oven (350 degrees F.) 20 to 25 minutes.   While hot cut in squares.

MARGUERITES

Follow recipe for Boiled Frosting I.   Add 1 cup of chopped nuts and 1 table-spoon melted Crisco.   Beat the mixture until it will hold its shape.   Drop by teaspoons on soda or salted crackers.   Bake in a moderate oven (350 degrees F.) 15 minutes or until a delicate brown.

ALMOND MACAROONS

3 egg whites	½ lb. finely chopped almonds
1 cup sugar	10 drops almond extract
1 tablespoon melted Crisco	

Beat egg whites.   Add sugar gradually, beating constantly.   Add almonds, flavoring and Crisco.   Mix well.   Drop by teaspoons on wet paper which has been placed on inverted pan or bread board.   Bake in slow oven (275 degrees F.) 30 to 40 minutes.

This recipe makes about 45 macaroons.

Frostings and Fillings

BOILED FROSTING I

1¾ cups sugar	2 egg whites
½ cup water	1 teaspoon vanilla

Cook sugar and water together, stirring until the sugar is dissolved.   Boil without stirring to 238 degrees F. (or until the syrup forms a soft ball when tested in cold water).   Pour over the stiffly beaten egg whites and beat constantly until the mixture holds its shape.   When cool add vanilla.

BROWN SUGAR FROSTING

Follow the recipe for Boiled Frosting I, substituting brown sugar for the white sugar and cook until 240 degrees F. is reached.

MAPLE SUGAR FROSTING

Follow the recipe for Boiled Frosting I, substituting maple sugar, broken into small pieces, for the white sugar. 1¾ cups maple sugar weighs about 12 ounces.

HONEY FROSTING

Follow the recipe for Boiled Frosting I. After the syrup has been beaten into the egg whites add ½ cup honey.

COCOANUT MARSHMALLOW FROSTING

Follow the recipe for Boiled Frosting I. Add 1 cup marshmallows cut in small pieces and ½ cup shredded cocoanut.

BOILED FROSTING II

2 cups sugar	⅓ cup water
⅓ cup light corn syrup	2 egg whites
1 teaspoon vanilla	

Cook sugar, syrup and water together, stirring until sugar is dissolved. Boil without stirring to 244 degrees F. (or until syrup forms a rather firm ball when tested in cold water). Pour this syrup slowly over the stiffly beaten egg whites, beating constantly. Continue beating until mixture holds its shape. Add vanilla. This frosting will keep in a covered jar in a cool place. If it becomes hard on standing, add a very small amount of hot water and beat well.

CHOCOLATE FROSTING

Follow the recipe for Boiled Frosting II, adding 3 squares of melted unsweetened chocolate after all the syrup is added.

LADY BALTIMORE FROSTING AND FILLING

Follow the recipe for Boiled Frosting I. Divide the frosting in halves and reserve a half for top and sides of cake. To the remainder (to be used between the layers), add

1 cup chopped raisins	½ cup chopped citron
1 cup chopped walnuts	1 cup chopped figs
½ cup blanched and chopped almonds	¼ cup chopped candied cherries

ORNAMENTAL FROSTING

1½ cups sugar	2 egg whites
⅔ cup water	¼ teaspoon cream of tartar
1 teaspoon vanilla	

Cook sugar and water together, stirring until the sugar is dissolved. Boil without stirring to 240 degrees F. (or until the syrup forms a rather firm ball when tested in cold water). Pour the syrup slowly over the stiffly beaten egg whites, beating constantly. Place the bowl of frosting in a pan of hot water and beat until there is a slight scraping noise along the sides of the bowl and the frosting holds its shape. Spread between layers and on top of cake. Reserve some to force through a pastry bag to decorate top of cake.

QUICK FROSTING

1 cup sugar	1 egg white
¼ cup water	½ teaspoon vanilla

Put sugar, water and unbeaten egg white in saucepan and cook over boiling water. Beat constantly until frosting is the proper consistency to spread. Add vanilla.

APPLE SNOW FROSTING

1 cup sugar	1 egg white
¼ cup water	1 apple, grated
½ teaspoon vanilla	

Cook sugar and water together, stirring until sugar is dissolved. Cook to 240 degrees F. (or until it forms a rather firm ball when tested in cold water). Pour syrup gradually over the stiffly beaten egg whites. Add apple and continue beating until the mixture will hold its shape. Add vanilla.

CARAMEL FROSTING

3 cups brown sugar	1 cup milk
½ teaspoon salt	½ cup chopped pecan or
2 tablespoons Crisco	walnut meats
1 teaspoon vanilla	

Put sugar, salt, Crisco and milk over the fire and stir until sugar is dissolved, and then only occasionally to prevent burning. Cook to 236 degrees F. (or until it forms a soft ball when tested in cold water). Cool slightly. Add nuts and vanilla. Beat until the frosting is the proper consistency to spread.

CREAM MAPLE FROSTING

1 pound maple sugar	¾ cup cream

Break sugar into small pieces. Add cream and cook, stirring until the sugar is dissolved and then only occasionally to prevent burning. Cook over a slow fire to 238 degrees F. (or until it forms a soft ball when tested in cold water). Remove from fire and beat until it will hold its shape.

CREAMY CHOCOLATE FROSTING

1½ cups milk	1½ cups powdered sugar
4 squares unsweetened chocolate	1 teaspoon vanilla
Few grains salt	

Cook milk with chocolate, cut in pieces, over a slow fire, stirring until thick and smooth. Add sugar and cook again until very thick, stirring constantly. Cool and add vanilla and salt.

FUDGE FROSTING

1½ cups brown sugar	¾ cup evaporated milk, or milk
1½ cups sugar	1 teaspoon vanilla
3 squares unsweetened chocolate	⅛ teaspoon salt
1 tablespoon Crisco	

Cook sugar, chocolate cut in pieces, and milk together, stirring constantly until sugar is dissolved and then only occasionally to prevent burning. Cook to

238 degrees F. (or until it forms a soft ball when tested in cold water). Add Crisco, vanilla and salt, and beat until it is the proper consistency to spread.

MARSHMALLOW FROSTING

½ pound marshmallows
1 cup sugar
¼ cup water

1 egg white
½ teaspoon vanilla
Few grains salt

Cut marshmallows in pieces and melt over hot water. Cook sugar and water together to 240 degrees F. (or until the syrup forms a rather firm ball when tested in cold water). Pour the syrup slowly over the stiffly beaten egg whites and beat until stiff. Add melted marshmallows and beat until smooth and thick enough to spread. Add vanilla and salt.

CONFECTIONERS' FROSTING

1½ tablespoons Crisco
1½ cups confectioners' sugar
1 teaspoon vanilla

3 tablespoons milk or cream
⅛ teaspoon salt

Cream Crisco, add sugar gradually and cream together thoroughly. Add enough milk or cream to make the frosting the proper consistency to spread. Add salt and vanilla and mix well.

MOCHA FROSTING

Follow the recipe for Confectioners' Frosting, adding 2 tablespoons cocoa and using strong coffee in place of milk.

CHOCOLATE FROSTING

Follow the recipe for Confectioners' Frosting, adding 2 tablespoons melted chocolate, or 3 tablespoons cocoa, to the sugar.

ALMOND FROSTING

Follow the recipe for Confectioners' Frosting, adding ¼ teaspoon almond flavoring and using ½ teaspoon vanilla instead of 1 teaspoon.

ORANGE FROSTING I

2 cups confectioners' sugar
Grated rind of 1 orange

3 tablespoons orange juice

Mix sugar, orange juice and rind together. Beat until smooth.

LEMON FROSTING

Follow the recipe for Orange Frosting I, using lemon juice and rind instead of the orange juice and rind.

ORANGE FROSTING II

1 egg
Juice of ½ orange

Grated rind of ½ orange
4 cups confectioners' sugar

Beat egg and add orange juice and rind. Add enough confectioners' sugar to make it the right consistency to spread. Beat until smooth.

BANANA FILLING AND FROSTING

1 cup cream   1 cup banana pulp
½ cup confectioners' sugar   ½ teaspoon vanilla
                Few grains salt

Beat cream until stiff and add sugar. Fold in banana pulp, vanilla and salt.

CREAM FILLING

⅓ cup sugar   1 egg
3 tablespoons flour 1 cup milk
⅛ teaspoon salt   1 teaspoon vanilla

Mix sugar, flour and salt. Add beaten egg. Add milk and cook over boiling water until thick. Cool and add vanilla. Spread between layers of cake.

COFFEE FILLING

Add 2 tablespoons ground coffee to the milk, and bring to the boiling point. Strain. Follow the recipe for Cream Filling.

CHOCOLATE FILLING

Follow the recipe for Cream Filling. Melt 1 square unsweetened chocolate in the milk and add ¼ cup extra sugar.

FRUIT FILLING

¾ cup finely chopped figs   ½ cup sugar
½ cup finely chopped dates   ½ cup boiling water
¼ cup finely chopped raisins   3 tablespoons lemon juice

Mix figs, dates and raisins. Add sugar, water and lemon juice and cook over hot water until thick. Spread while hot between layers of cake.

ORANGE FILLING

1 cup sugar   ⅓ cup orange juice
5 tablespoons flour   Grated rind of 1 orange
⅛ teaspoon salt   ½ cup water
1 egg   ½ tablespoon Crisco
                1 tablespoon lemon juice

Mix sugar, flour and salt together. Add the beaten egg, orange juice, rind and water. Cook in a double boiler or over hot water until thick. Add Crisco and lemon juice and mix well. Cool and spread between layers of cake.

LEMON FILLING

Follow the recipe for Orange Filling, using ¼ cup lemon juice and grated rind of 1 lemon instead of the orange juice and rind.

PINEAPPLE FILLING

½ cup sugar	1 egg
4 tablespoons flour	1 cup pineapple, cut in pieces
⅛ teaspoon salt	¾ cup pineapple juice

1 tablespoon Crisco

Mix sugar, flour and salt. Add beaten egg, pineapple and juice. Cook in a double boiler or over boiling water until thick, stirring constantly. Add Crisco and mix well. Cool and spread between layers of cake.

FEATHERWEIGHT CAKE

This recipe is published here in answer to a special demand for it by many of our old Crisco customers with whom it has been popular for many years, as an inexpensive but delicious plain white cake.

1 cup sugar	2 teaspoons baking powder
½ cup Crisco	⅔ cup milk
2 cups flour	3 egg whites
½ teaspoon salt	1 teaspoon vanilla

Cream Crisco with sugar until the mixture is very light. Mix and sift flour, salt and baking powder, and add alternately with the milk to the first mixture. Fold in egg whites which have been beaten until stiff but not dry. Add vanilla. Turn batter into two greased layer pans. Bake in a moderate oven (350° F.). Ice with any desired icing.

CHAPTER XVIII

Pastry

THE proof of the pudding is in the eating and the proof of the pastry, too. There are pastries and pastries, all built on the same simple foundation of flour, shortening and water with a dash of salt, yet varying in results all the way from the young bride's first soggy pie to the experienced house-wife's light-as-thistledown puff paste.

Two important principles underlie pastry making. They are short and easily remembered. In colloquial language they are, "Keep the water out" and "Get the air in." In other words, pastry that is made with too much water is tough and hard, while pastry that is kneaded and prodded and crushed beneath a rolling pin makes a fine substitute for shoe leather.

So when you make pastry use the smallest amount of liquid that will hold the ingredients together.

Then handle it quickly and gently. There is an old ballad which goes:

> "Would you gain the tender creature
> Gently, softly, kindly treat her,"

and pastry is just like that. A heavy touch spoils everything. Air must be worked *into* pastry, not forced *out* of it, for when the heat of the oven is applied the air will expand and make a light, air-filled crust.

Closely related to the question of liquid in pastry is the amount and kind of shortening used. Generally speaking, the less water and the more shortening, the more tender the pastry will be.

Flakiness is somewhat dependent on the temperature of the shortening. If a very flaky crust is desired, the Crisco should be thoroughly chilled before using. Instead of melting and con-tributing its share of moisture to the dough, it remains in tiny pieces which melt only in the heat of the oven and produce the

[172]

Be sure the ingredients for pastry are very cold.   Cut the Crisco into the flour with a knife until the flour appears MEALY, *that is, until the Crisco is cut into* VERY *fine pieces and is thoroughly mixed through the flour*

In making Puff Pastry, most of the Crisco, instead of being cut into the dough is shaped into a flat circular piece and rolled and folded in, in order to enclose as much air as possible.   (See Puff Paste recipe, page 179)

much-desired "shortness." Some people find it worth while to keep a small can of Crisco in the refrigerator just for this purpose.

If a short, mealy crust is preferred it is better not to chill the Crisco, but rather to work it into the flour in its natural soft, creamy state. Whether you chill it or not, you will find that the new super-creamed Crisco makes all pie crust more delicious and digestible, more tender and easier to cut.

There are two classes of pastry—plain pastry and puff pastry. In the latter most of the shortening instead of being cut into the dough is rolled and folded in. Puff pastry is more complicated than plain pastry. It is a *de luxe* product which the novice may hesitate to undertake, but once the art of making it is acquired, it offers all sorts of delightful possibilities and adds very much to a housewife's prestige as a cook.

The baking of pastry plays a very important part in its success. The colder the pastry when it goes in the oven, the flakier it will be. The oven should be hot enough to start it rising quickly, then the heat reduced for the remainder of the time in order that the filling may be thoroughly cooked. The upper crust of covered pies should be pricked to allow the steam to escape. The edges may be trimmed with a sharp knife and a fancy edge made by pinching with the fingers, or you may buy a little cutter that trims and makes a fancy edge at the same time.

When you are baking the empty shell for an open pie be very careful not to stretch the pastry as you lay it over the pan. Ease it in gently and trim it off a little beyond the edge of the pan to allow for shrinkage. Prick the bottom and side with a fork so that it will not blister while baking.

SUCCESS SECRETS

1. Use level measurements.
2. Sift flour before measuring. Use a reliable pastry flour if you cannot make good pastry with ordinary bread flour.
3. *All* pastry ingredients must be very cold.
4. Use only enough water to hold ingredients together. On this depends the tenderness of the pastry.

*When baking the empty shell for an open pie be careful not to stretch
the pastry as you lay it over the pan.   Ease it in gently and trim it off
with a sharp knife a little beyond the edge of the pan*

*Patty shells or tarts may be made of plain or puff pastry. Cut
rounds of pastry and bake over the bottom of inverted pans; or line
tart pans with the pastry and prick bottom and sides with a fork*

Cranberry Roll (Recipe on page 191)

Grandmother's Apple Crow's Nest (Recipe on page 190)

Brown Betty (Recipe on page 193)

Apple Delights (Recipe on page 190)

5. Handle pastry as little and as quickly as possible.   Do not knead it with the hands.
6. Roll pastry out with a light, quick motion of the rolling pin.
7. Dust the board with flour when necessary, but use no more flour than is absolutely necessary to keep pastry from sticking.
8. Brush the lower crust of juicy fruit pies with white of egg before putting in the filling.   It prevents a soggy under crust.
9. Bake pastry shells (without filling) in a quick oven.   Prick them well with a fork so crust will not blister while baking.
10. Cool pastry shells before putting the filling in.
11. Crisco is the best shortening for pastry because it will remain solid at ordinary room temperature.   The fat for good, flaky pastry should be cut through the flour into very tiny particles and never allowed to melt before it reaches the oven.
12. Pastry will keep in the ice box covered with wax paper for two or three days—or even longer in cold weather.

PLAIN PASTRY

2 cups flour
¾ teaspoon salt

⅔ cup Crisco
Cold water

Mix and sift flour and salt.   Cut in the Crisco with a knife.   Add only water enough to hold the ingredients together.   Do not knead.   Divide dough in 2 parts and roll out thin on a slightly floured board.   Line a pie pan with one-half the pastry.   Pinch pastry with the fingers to make a fancy edge and prick bottom and sides with a fork.   Bake in a very hot oven (460 degrees F.) 10 to 15 minutes.   For a 2 crust pie, line pie pan with pastry, put in a filling, cover with top crust and bake as directed for pies.

If a less rich pastry is desired, use only ½ cup Crisco.

DANISH PASTRY

2½ cups flour
1½ teaspoons salt

¾ cup Crisco
1 egg

Ice water

Mix and sift flour and salt.   Cut in Crisco with a knife.   Add beaten egg and only enough water, a few drops at a time, to make the paste hold together.

Chill. Break off small pieces of paste, roll out on floured board to ⅛ inch thickness and fit over inverted muffin pans. Trim to fit. Prick with a fork and bake in a quick oven (425 degrees F.) 10 to 15 minutes.

FLAKY PASTRY

2 cups flour   ⅔ cup Crisco
1 teaspoon salt   Cold water

Mix and sift flour and salt. Cut in 2 tablespoons of the Crisco with a knife. Add enough water to make a stiff dough. Roll out in an oblong piece on a slightly floured board and dot with bits of Crisco, using ⅓ the remaining quantity. Fold over ends to the center and fold again to make 4 layers. Press ends together and roll out. Dot again with Crisco, fold and roll. Repeat this process a third time. Chill thoroughly.

This pastry may be used wherever plain pastry is called for.

PUFF PASTE

2 cups flour   1½ teaspoons salt
1 cup Crisco   Water

Mix and sift flour and salt. Cut in 2 tablespoons of the Crisco with a knife. Add only enough water, a few drops at a time, to make the paste hold together. Knead the dough 5 minutes, cover and chill. Roll out to ¼ inch thickness, keeping the paste a little wider than long and corners square. Place remaining Crisco, softened and shaped into a circular piece in center of one-half of paste. Fold other half over it, pressing edges firmly to enclose as much air as possible. Fold right side over and left side under the enclosed Crisco. Chill. Roll out, keeping the paste always rectangular in shape and rolling away from you. Fold ends towards center, making 3 layers. Chill. Roll out, fold again, chill and repeat process 4 times. (Paste is better made the day before it is baked and should be icy cold when put in the oven.)

PATTY SHELLS

Roll out Puff Paste to ¼ inch thickness. Cut with a round cutter, floured. Remove centers from ½ of these circles with a smaller cutter. Wet the edges of the whole circles and place the rings on them. Brush the tops carefully with slightly beaten egg mixed with 1 tablespoon water, taking care not to moisten the sides. Chill in ice box until paste is stiff. Bake in a hot oven (400 degrees F.) about 20 minutes. Bake the small centers in a quick oven (450 degrees F.) 10 minutes and use them as tops after the shells are filled.

TART SHELLS

Roll out Puff Paste to ⅛ inch thickness. Fit over inverted pie, muffin or patty pans. Prick bottom and sides all over with fork. Place on a baking sheet and bake in a quick oven (425 degrees F.) 15 to 20 minutes.

APPLE DUMPLINGS

Roll out Plain Pastry to ⅛ inch thickness. Cut in large circles. Cut tart apples in thin slices, and put a small amount in the center of each circle of pastry.

Sprinkle with sugar and a little nutmeg and dot with a small bit of Crisco. Moisten edge of pastry with water. Bring opposite edges to the center and press tightly together. Prick top to allow the steam to escape. Bake in a quick oven (425 degrees F.) 10 minutes. Reduce the heat to a moderate oven (350 degrees F.) and bake 15 to 20 minutes.

PEACH DUMPLINGS

Follow recipe for Apple Dumplings, using peaches instead of apples, and a few drops of lemon juice instead of nutmeg.

BERRY DUMPLINGS

Follow recipe for Apple Dumplings, using berries instead of the apples. Mix the berries with a little flour to thicken the syrup. Omit the nutmeg.

APPLE PIE

5 or 6 large tart apples	1 tablespoon Crisco
Plain pastry	$\frac{1}{4}$ teaspoon nutmeg
1 cup sugar	$\frac{1}{8}$ teaspoon cinnamon

Wash, pare and cut apples in quarters. Remove cores and slice thin. Line a pan with Plain Pastry and put apples into it. Pour sugar over them and dot with bits of Crisco. Sprinkle with nutmeg and cinnamon. Moisten edge of pastry, cover with a top crust, trim and press edges together. Prick top to allow steam to escape. Bake in a quick oven (425 degrees F.) 10 minutes. Reduce heat to moderate oven (325 degrees F.) and bake 25 minutes.

ONE CRUST APPLE PIE

4 large tart apples	1 tablespoon Crisco
$\frac{1}{2}$ cup sugar	Plain pastry
Few grains nutmeg	Whipped cream

Wash, pare and core apples and cut in thin slices. Put them in the bottom of pie pan and sprinkle with sugar and nutmeg. Dot with small bits of Crisco. Roll Plain Pastry thin and fit over the apples. Trim off edge of the pastry and press with fingers or fork to make a fancy edge. Prick top to allow steam to escape. Bake in a quick oven (425 degrees F.) 10 minutes. Reduce heat to a moderate oven (325 degrees F.) and bake 20 minutes. Cool. Turn out upside down on a serving dish. Cover with whipped cream, sweetened and flavored.

COBBLESTONE PIE

4 large tart apples	1 tablespoon Crisco
Plain pastry	$\frac{1}{4}$ teaspoon nutmeg
1 cup sugar	$\frac{1}{8}$ teaspoon cinnamon

Wash, pare and cut apples in quarters. Remove the cores. Line a pie pan with Plain Pastry, pinch with fingers to make a fancy edge, and fit apples into it to represent cobblestones. Pour the sugar over them and dot with small bits of Crisco. Sprinkle with nutmeg and cinnamon. Bake in a quick oven (425 degrees F.) 10 minutes. Reduce the heat to moderate oven (325 degrees F.) and bake 20 minutes, or until apples are tender.

BLUEBERRY PIE

2½ cups blueberries   1 cup sugar
Plain pastry   2 tablespoons flour
          1 teaspoon lemon juice

Wash and pick over blueberries. Drain. Line a pie pan with Plain Pastry. Mix sugar, flour and lemon juice with blueberries. Turn into the pie pan and moisten edge of pastry with water. Cover with a top crust, trim and press edges together. Prick top with a fork to allow the steam to escape. Bake in a quick oven (425 degrees F.) 10 minutes. Reduce the heat to moderate oven (350 degrees F.) and bake 20 minutes.

CHOCOLATE PIE

Plain pastry   1 cup sugar
2 squares unsweetened chocolate   2 tablespoons soft bread crumbs
3 eggs   ½ cup chopped nuts
          1 cup cream

Line a pie pan with Plain Pastry and pinch with fingers to make a fancy edge. Cut chocolate in pieces and melt over hot water. Beat eggs well and add sugar, bread crumbs and melted chocolate. Mix well. Pour into the pie pan. Bake in a hot oven (375 degrees F.) 20 minutes, or until filling is firm. When cold, sprinkle with chopped nuts. Spread with whipped cream and decorate with cherries and whole nuts.

CHOCOLATE CREAM PIE

2 tablespoons Crisco   ¼ teaspoon salt
6 tablespoons flour   2 egg yolks
1½ cups milk   1 teaspoon vanilla
2 squares unsweetened chocolate 2 tablespoons confectioners' sugar
¾ cup sugar   2 egg whites
          Baked pie shell

Melt Crisco. Add flour, milk, chocolate (cut in pieces), sugar and salt, and bring slowly to the boiling point, stirring constantly until thick and smooth. Remove from the fire and add beaten egg yolks and vanilla. Pour into a baked pie shell (see Plain Pastry). Cover with a meringue made by beating the confectioners' sugar into the stiffly beaten egg whites. Bake in a moderate oven (325 degrees F.) 15 minutes or until a delicate brown.

Whipped cream may be used instead of the meringue.

CREAM PIE

1 tablespoon Crisco	1 teaspoon vanilla
8 tablespoons flour	2 tablespoons confectioners' sugar
⅔ cup sugar	2 cups milk
¼ teaspoon salt	2 egg whites
2 egg yolks	Baked pie shell

Melt Crisco. Add flour, sugar, salt, milk and beaten egg yolks and cook over hot water until thick, stirring constantly. Add vanilla. Pour into a baked pie shell (see Plain Pastry). Cover top with a meringue made by beating the confectioners' sugar into the stiffly beaten egg whites. Bake in a moderate oven (325 degrees F.) 15 minutes, or until a delicate brown.

CUSTARD PIE

1½ tablespoons flour	2 cups scalded milk
4 tablespoons sugar	½ teaspoon vanilla
⅛ teaspoon salt	Few grains nutmeg
2 eggs	Plain pastry

Mix flour, sugar, salt and well-beaten eggs together. Add the scalded milk, vanilla and nutmeg. Line a pie pan with Plain Pastry and pinch with fingers to make a fancy edge. Pour in the custard mixture and bake in a quick oven (425 degrees F.) 10 minutes. Reduce heat to a slow oven (300 degrees F.) and bake 20 minutes, or until custard is firm. When done, a silver knife, inserted, will come out clean.

COCOANUT CUSTARD PIE

Follow recipe for Custard Pie. Add ¼ cup dried cocoanut to the custard mixture.

DEEP DISH HUCKLEBERRY PIE

Wash and pick over 3 cups huckleberries. Drain. Mix with 1 cup sugar, 2 tablespoons flour, 1 teaspoon lemon juice and a few grains salt. Put berries in a deep pie plate. Cover with Plain Pastry, trim and press with fingers or fork to make a fancy edge. Prick top with fork to allow the steam to escape. Bake in a quick oven (425 degrees F.) 10 minutes. Reduce heat to moderate oven (325 degrees F.) and bake 25 minutes.

LEMON MERINGUE PIE

1½ tablespoons Crisco	2 egg yolks
8 tablespoons flour	Juice of 1 lemon
1 cup sugar	Grated rind of ½ lemon
¼ teaspoon salt	2 tablespoons confectioners' sugar
2 cups water	2 egg whites
	Baked pie shell

Melt Crisco, add flour, sugar, salt, water and beaten egg yolks. Mix well. Cook over hot water until thick, stirring constantly. Remove from fire, add lemon juice and rind and mix well. Pour into the baked pie shell. (See Plain

Pastry.) Cover top with a meringue made by beating the confectioners' sugar into the stiffly beaten egg whites. Bake in a moderate oven (325 degrees F.) 15 minutes or until a delicate brown.

The same filling may be used for lemon tarts.

MINCEMEAT

2 pounds lean meat, cut from round	1 tablespoon cinnamon
1 pound suet, chopped fine	1/2 tablespoon mace
5 tart apples, cut in small pieces	1/2 tablespoon cloves
3 pounds raisins	1/2 tablespoon allspice
2 pounds currants	2 teaspoons nutmeg
3 ounces citron, cut in pieces	1 tablespoon salt
1/4 ounce candied orange peel	2 pounds brown sugar
1/4 ounce candied lemon peel	1 quart hard cider

1 pint grape juice

Cover meat with boiling water and simmer until tender. Let cool in the liquor. When cold remove meat from pot and chop fine. (Save broth for soup.) Add suet and apples to the meat with the raisins, currants, citron and chopped orange and lemon peel. Mix spices, sugar and salt, and add to the meat mixture. Add cider and grape juice, mix thoroughly, and cook slowly for 2 hours. Stir frequently to prevent burning. Seal in sterilized, air-tight jars. When ready to make pies, add more cider or grape juice, if additional liquid is needed.

This recipe makes 8 quarts mincemeat.

MINCE PIE

Line a pie pan with Plain Pastry. Fill pie pan 2/3 full of mincemeat and moisten edge of pastry. Cover with a top crust, trim and press edges together. Prick top crust with a fork to allow the steam to escape. Bake in a quick oven (425 degrees F.) 10 minutes. Reduce heat to hot oven (400 degrees F.) and bake 20 minutes.

MOCK CHERRY PIE

2 cups cranberries, coarsely chopped	1 cup sugar
1 cup seeded raisins	1/8 teaspoon salt
3 tablespoons flour	1 tablespoon Crisco

Plain pastry

Mix cranberries and raisins. Add flour, sugar and salt. Line a pie pan with plain pastry, and fill with the cranberry mixture. Dot with small bits of Crisco. Moisten edge of pastry, cover with a top crust, trim and press edges together. Prick the top with a fork to allow the steam to escape. Bake in a quick oven (425 degrees F.) 10 minutes. Reduce heat to hot oven (375 degrees F.) and bake 25 minutes.

PEACH PIE

Remove skins from 8 peaches and cut in thin slices. Cook with 1/3 cup water for 10 minutes. Add sugar to taste (according to the tartness of the peaches).

Line a pie pan with plain pastry and pour the filling into it. Dot with small bits of Crisco. Moisten edge of pastry, cover with a top crust and press edges together. Prick top with a fork to allow steam to escape. Bake in a quick oven (425 degrees F.) 10 minutes. Reduce heat to moderate oven (350 degrees F.) and bake 15 to 20 minutes.

PINEAPPLE PIE

½ cup flour
1 cup sugar
¼ teaspoon salt
⅔ cup pineapple juice
1 cup hot water
1 tablespoon Crisco

2 cups cooked or canned pineapple, cut in small pieces
3 egg yolks
3 tablespoons confectioners' sugar
3 egg whites
Baked pie shell

Mix flour, sugar and salt together. Add the pineapple juice and water and bring slowly to the boiling point, stirring constantly. Cook 15 minutes over hot water. Remove from fire, add Crisco and well-drained pineapple. Pour this mixture on the beaten egg yolks and mix well. Pour the filling into a baked pie shell (see Plain Pastry). Cover with a meringue made by beating the confectioners' sugar into the stiffly beaten egg whites. Bake in a moderate oven (325 degrees F.) 15 minutes or until a delicate brown.

This filling may be used for pineapple tarts.

ORANGE PIE

Follow recipe for Pineapple Filling using orange juice and pulp instead of pineapple juice and pineapple, adding 1 tablespoon lemon juice just before pouring over the beaten egg yolks.

PUMPKIN PIE

Plain pastry
2 cups cooked and strained pumpkin
1 cup milk
3 egg yolks
½ cup sugar

1¼ teaspoons cinnamon
¼ teaspoon cloves
¼ teaspoon ginger
¼ teaspoon nutmeg
1 teaspoon salt

3 egg whites

Line a pie pan with Plain Pastry and pinch with fingers to make a fancy edge. Mix the pumpkin and milk together. Add the beaten egg yolks. Add the sugar mixed with the cinnamon, clove, ginger, nutmeg, and salt. Mix well. Fold in the stiffly beaten egg whites. Turn into the pie pan. Bake in a quick oven (450 degrees F.) 10 minutes, reduce heat to hot oven (375 degrees F.) and bake 20 minutes longer or until the filling is firm.

RHUBARB PIE

3 cups rhubarb
Plain pastry
1 cup sugar

2 tablespoons flour
⅛ teaspoon salt
2 eggs

Peel rhubarb and cut in one-half inch pieces before measuring. Line a pie pan with Plain Pastry. Mix sugar, flour, salt and beaten eggs. Add to the rhubarb and pour into the pie pan. Moisten edge of pastry with water. Cover with a top crust, trim and press edges together. Prick top with a fork to allow steam to escape. Bake in a quick oven (425 degrees F.) 10 minutes. Reduce heat to a moderate oven (325 degrees F.) and bake 25 to 30 minutes.

APRICOT TARTS

Turn the contents of 1 can of apricots into a saucepan with $\frac{1}{2}$ cup sugar and cook slowly until apricots are slightly transparent, about 20 minutes. Remove apricots and cook syrup until thick. Bake tart shells of Danish Pastry. Just before serving place an apricot in each baked tart shell. Pour a little of the syrup over it. Garnish with whipped cream.

BANBURY TARTS

$\frac{1}{4}$ cup chopped raisins	1 tablespoon flour
$\frac{1}{4}$ cup chopped dates	1 egg
$\frac{1}{4}$ cup chopped figs	Juice of 1 lemon
$\frac{1}{4}$ cup chopped nuts	Grated rind of 1 lemon
1 cup light brown sugar	Plain pastry

Mix raisins, dates, figs and nuts, sugar and flour together. Add beaten egg, lemon juice and rind. Mix well. Roll out Plain Pastry to $\frac{1}{8}$ inch thickness and cut in pieces 3 inches square. Put a little of the mixture on each piece. Moisten edges with cold water, fold over diagonally and press edges together with tines of a fork. Bake in a hot oven (400 degrees F.) 15 to 20 minutes or until pastry is brown.

FRIED BANBURY TARTS

Follow recipe for Banbury Tarts, using Plain Pastry, made with $\frac{1}{2}$ cup Crisco. Fry in deep hot Crisco 10 minutes or until brown. Drain on unglazed paper. Sprinkle with confectioners' sugar. Serve hot.

BUTTERSCOTCH TARTS

1 cup brown sugar	2 tablespoons cornstarch
1 tablespoon Crisco	1 egg yolk
2 tablespoons water	$\frac{1}{2}$ teaspoon vanilla
1 cup milk	1 tablespoon confectioners' sugar

1 egg white

Boil brown sugar, Crisco and water together until sugar is dissolved. Mix milk, cornstarch and beaten egg yolk together and add to the sugar syrup. Cook over hot water until thick, stirring constantly. Cool. Add vanilla. Pour into baked Tart Shells. Decorate tops with meringue made by beating the confectioners' sugar into the stiffly beaten egg white. Bake in a moderate oven (325 degrees F.) 15 minutes or until a delicate brown.
   This recipe fills 6 tarts.

GOOSEBERRY TARTS

Wash 4 cups of gooseberries and drain. Cook slowly with 1½ cups sugar and ¼ cup water until berries are tender, stirring constantly until sugar is melted. Add 1 tablespoon Crisco and 1 teaspoon grated lemon rind. Cool. Pour into baked Tart Shells. Garnish with whipped cream, flavored and sweetened.

PEACH TARTS

Remove skins and slice peaches thin. Cook in a small amount of water until tender. Drain liquid from peaches. To 1 cup liquid add ½ cup sugar and cook until thick. Cool. Just before serving put peaches in a baked pie shell (see Plain Pastry) and pour the syrup over the peaches. Cover with whipped cream, flavored and sweetened.

COCOANUT DATE STRIPS

Plain pastry	3 tablespoons brown sugar
2 tablespoons Crisco	3 tablespoons cocoanut, shredded
⅛ teaspoon salt	¼ cup chopped dates

Make up half the recipe for Plain Pastry. Roll out on slightly floured board in rectangular sheet about ¼ inch thick. Spread with softened Crisco and sprinkle with salt. Mix sugar, cocoanut and dates and sprinkle over one-half the pastry. Fold over the other half and cut into strips 1 inch wide, making them uniform in length. Bake in a hot oven (400 degrees F.) 10 to 15 minutes.

Left over pie trimmings may be used in making these dainty pastries.

FRUIT PASTRIES

Roll out Plain Pastry to ¼ inch thickness. Cut in circles. Put a tablespoon of fruit filling in center of 1 piece of pastry, moisten the edge and cover with another circle. Press edges firmly together with tines of fork. Bake in a quick oven (425 degrees F.) 15 to 20 minutes.

FRUIT FILLING

½ cup chopped raisins	1 tablespoon lemon juice
¼ cup chopped figs	2 tablespoons brown sugar
¼ cup chopped nuts	2 tablespoons corn or maple syrup

Mix the raisins, figs and nuts. Add the lemon juice, sugar and syrup and mix well.

PEANUT CREAM PASTRIES

2 tablespoons flour	1 cup milk
¼ cup sugar	½ teaspoon vanilla
⅛ teaspoon salt	Plain pastry
1 egg	Chopped peanuts

Mix flour, sugar and salt. Add beaten egg and milk. Cook over hot water until thick, stirring constantly. Cool. Add vanilla.

Roll out Plain Pastry to ¼ inch thickness. Cut in square, round or rectangular shaped pieces. Prick with a fork and bake in a quick oven (450 degrees F.) 12 to 15 minutes. Cool. Serve 2 as a portion, with the custard filling between and on top of pastries. Sprinkle thickly with chopped peanuts.

PUMPKIN FANCHONETTES

Cut large circles from Plain Pastry rolled to ⅛ inch thickness. Fit into small fluted pans. Pinch with fingers to make a fancy edge. Fill with pumpkin pie filling. Bake in quick oven (425 degrees F.) 15 to 20 minutes. Garnish before serving with a spoonful of whipped cream.

CHAPTER XIX

Desserts and Sauces

DESSERT is the topping off of the meal, and the family's hunger having been satisfied, the homemaker is justified in giving rein to her imagination for this course. The recipes in this chapter are, some of them, practical; others are a bit of fluff. But they are *all* good.

If the first part of your meal consists of rather heavy food you will choose one of the lighter desserts, Bavarian cream, pineapple sherbet or boiled custard pudding. Pie or pudding would be a bad aftermath for a hearty feast, although on high days and holidays some latitude would be permissible. For the ending of a light meal your children (including your husband!) would rejoice at brown Betty or steamed chocolate pudding.

Fruits have become more and more popular as desserts since we realized their very real value as a food. Yet, having learned this lesson, we are apt to depend upon the fresh fruits and to neglect the dried fruits which are available in all places and at all seasons. Made into steamed puddings, whips, sherbets, jellies, tapioca and cornstarch combinations they lend endless variety to your dessert repertory.

A sauce gives even the simplest pudding a festive air and the housewife who wants to be ready for the unexpected guest or to keep her family's appetite whetted will learn how to make some of the good pudding sauces. Sauces are either hard or liquid, the latter offering many varieties with a basis of fruit juices, egg, cornstarch, chocolate, or caramel.

Crisco may be used successfully in any of these and makes a rich, delicious sauce; and the nicest part about it is that you can make a large enough quantity to satisfy the sweetest tooth in your household without going bankrupt for butter.

SUCCESS SECRETS

1. Choose a light dessert to serve after a hearty meal.

2. Serve cold desserts *thoroughly chilled;* hot desserts *very hot.*

3. Unmold a gelatine dessert before serving. To do so loosen the edge slightly with a pointed knife, then turn upside down on the plate or platter on which it is to be served.

4. Don't have gelatine mixtures too stiff. When too much gelatine is used the dessert will be tough and rubbery.

5. Cook custards over hot water, stirring constantly. If custard separates, remove it from the fire and beat with an egg beater to "bring it back" again.

6. Do not fill the molds for steamed puddings more than three-quarters full as the mixture will rise in the can.

7. Keep the water boiling in the vessels in which you steam puddings. If more water is needed during the cooking add *boiling* water.

8. Vary the same desserts by garnishing with whipped cream, marshmallows or chopped nuts, or serving with a different sauce.

COTTAGE PUDDING

¼ cup Crisco	3 teaspoons baking powder
¾ cup sugar	½ teaspoon salt
2 eggs	¾ cup milk
2¼ cups flour	1 teaspoon vanilla

Cream Crisco, sugar and eggs together. Mix and sift flour, baking powder and salt and add alternately with the milk to the first mixture. Add vanilla and beat thoroughly. Pour into a greased pan, having batter 1 inch deep in pan. Bake in a hot oven (400 degrees F.) 20 to 25 minutes. Cut in squares and serve with Lemon or Custard Sauce. This batter may also be baked in muffin pans and served as individual portions.

CHOCOLATE COTTAGE PUDDING

Follow recipe for Cottage Pudding. Add 1½ squares melted, unsweetened chocolate, or ⅓ cup cocoa mixed to a smooth paste with hot water.

FRUIT COTTAGE PUDDING

Follow recipe for Cottage Pudding. Add ¾ cup berries or chopped fruit, well drained and mixed with a little of the flour.

DUTCH APPLE CAKE

Follow recipe for Cottage Pudding. Arrange thinly sliced apples in rows on top of batter. Sprinkle with sugar and cinnamon and dot with small bits of Crisco. Bake in a moderate oven (350 degrees F.) 45 minutes or until apples are tender.

APPLE DELIGHTS

2 cups flour	¼ cup Crisco
1½ teaspoons baking powder	1 cup milk
½ teaspoon salt	1 egg

6 soft ripe apples

Mix and sift flour, baking powder and salt. Cut in Crisco with a knife. Add milk and beaten egg and mix well. Drop tablespoons of batter into well greased muffin pans. Peel apples, cut in halves and take out cores. Put on top of batter, cut side up, and fill the holes with sugar. Bake in a hot oven (400 degrees F.) 25 minutes or until apples are tender. Serve hot with sweetened whipped cream, dusted with cinnamon.

This recipe makes 12 delights.

GRANDMOTHER'S APPLE CROW'S NEST

4 medium sized tart apples	¼ teaspoon salt
1 cup flour	¼ cup sugar
2 teaspoons baking powder	3 tablespoons Crisco
1¼ teaspoons cinnamon	¼ cup milk (about)

Slice apples into a greased pie pan and dot with bits of Crisco. Sprinkle with sugar and cinnamon. Mix flour, baking powder, salt and sugar and sift twice. Cut in Crisco with a knife. Add enough milk to make a soft dough. Spread over apples. Bake in hot oven (400 degrees F.) 25 minutes or until apples are tender. Turn out on a plate, upside down. Mix ½ cup sugar and 1 teaspoon cinnamon and stir into apples with a fork. Serve hot with whipped cream. Dust over cream with a little cinnamon and a few finely chopped nuts.

ROLY-POLY PUDDING

2 cups flour	5 tart apples, sliced
4 teaspoons baking powder	½ teaspoon cinnamon
1 teaspoon salt	½ teaspoon nutmeg
5 tablespoons Crisco	½ cup sugar

½ cup milk

Mix and sift flour, baking powder and salt. Rub in 3 tablespoons Crisco with finger tips. Add milk and mix to a soft dough. Turn out on floured board and pat into oblong shape. Spread with remaining 2 tablespoons softened Crisco. Cover with a layer of thinly sliced apples and sprinkle with cinnamon, nutmeg and sugar. Roll lengthwise like jelly roll, and bake in a moderate oven (350 degrees F.) 30 to 40 minutes. Cut in slices and serve hot with Lemon Sauce.

CRANBERRY ROLL

2½ cups flour
4 teaspoons baking powder
1 teaspoon salt
¼ cup sugar

2 tablespoons Crisco
1 egg
½ to ¾ cup milk
2 cups whole cranberries

Mix and sift flour, baking powder, salt and sugar. Cut in Crisco with a knife. Add beaten egg and milk enough to make a rather soft dough. Roll out on slightly floured board to ½ inch thickness. Spread surface with Crisco and cover with cranberries. Roll up, handling it lightly. Place in center of a well greased pan. Brush top and sides of the roll with melted Crisco. Put in a quick oven (450 degrees F.); when it begins to brown reduce heat to moderate oven (350 degrees F.) and bake about 45 minutes longer. Cut in slices and serve with Lemon Sauce or Hard Sauce.

PEACH BASKET TURNOVER

2 egg yolks
1 cup sugar
⅓ cup hot water
2 egg whites
1 cup flour

1 teaspoon baking powder
½ teaspoon salt
1 teaspoon vanilla
1 cup brown sugar
2 tablespoons Crisco

1 can sliced peaches, drained

Beat egg yolks and ½ cup sugar together until light. Add hot water and remaining sugar and beat 5 minutes. Fold in stiffly beaten egg whites. Mix and sift flour, baking powder and ¼ teaspoon salt. Add to first mixture and mix well. Add vanilla. Cream brown sugar and Crisco, add peaches and ¼ teaspoon salt, and put in a shallow greased baking pan. Pour cake batter over the mixture and bake in hot oven (400 degrees F.) 45 minutes. Turn out on a platter and serve with the fruit juice and whipped cream.

BREAD PUDDING

2 eggs
1½ cups soft bread crumbs
3 cups scalded milk
1 tablespoon Crisco

⅔ cup sugar
¼ teaspoon salt
½ teaspoon vanilla
½ cup nuts, cut in pieces

Beat eggs, add bread crumbs, milk, Crisco, sugar and salt and mix well. Add vanilla and nuts. Pour into a greased baking pan and bake in a moderate oven (325 degrees F.) 45 minutes or until firm. Serve hot or cold with whipped cream.

CHOCOLATE BREAD PUDDING

Follow recipe for Bread Pudding and add 3 squares melted unsweetened chocolate. Serve with whipped cream.

BLUEBERRY PUDDING

¼ cup Crisco	2 teaspoons baking powder
¾ cup sugar	½ teaspoon salt
1 egg	½ cup milk
2¼ cups flour	1 cup blueberries or huckleberries

Cream Crisco, sugar and egg together. Mix and sift flour, baking powder and salt. Reserve ¼ cup to flour blueberries. Add the remainder alternately with milk to the first mixture. Beat thoroughly. Stir in the blueberries. Pour into a greased shallow pan and bake in moderate oven (350 degrees F.) 40 to 45 minutes. Cut in squares and serve hot with Lemon Sauce.

RICE PUDDING

3 tablespoons rice	¼ teaspoon salt
3 tablespoons sugar	Few grains nutmeg
2 tablespoons Crisco	4 cups milk

Wash and drain rice. Add sugar, Crisco, salt and nutmeg and stir into the milk. Put into a pudding dish and bake in a slow oven (275 degrees F.) 2 hours. Stir occasionally during the first hour of cooking. Serve hot or cold. ½ cup raisins may be added to this recipe.

BAKED INDIAN PUDDING

¼ cup cornmeal	½ teaspoon salt
5 cups milk	⅛ teaspoon ginger
¼ cup molasses	¼ teaspoon cinnamon
1 tablespoon Crisco	

Mix cornmeal with 1 cup milk. Scald the remaining milk in a double boiler, or over hot water. Add cornmeal, molasses, salt, ginger, cinnamon and Crisco and mix well. Pour into a greased baking dish and cook in a slow oven (275 degrees F.) 2 hours. Serve with cream or Custard Sauce.

STEAMED CHOCOLATE PUDDING

1 tablespoon Crisco	1½ teaspoons baking powder
¾ cup sugar	½ teaspoon salt
1 egg	½ cup milk
1½ cups flour	2 squares unsweetened chocolate

Cream Crisco, sugar and egg together. Mix and sift flour, baking powder and salt and add alternately with the milk to the first mixture. Beat thoroughly. Add melted chocolate and mix well. Fill greased pudding mold ¾ full, cover tightly and steam 1 hour. Serve with whipped cream.

STEAMED MOLASSES PUDDING

1 egg	1½ cups flour
¾ cup molasses	½ teaspoon salt
1 teaspoon soda	1 cup raisins
½ cup water	2 tablespoons melted Crisco

Beat egg and add molasses. Dissolve soda in water and stir into the egg mixture. Sift flour and salt, add and beat thoroughly. Dredge raisins with flour and stir in lightly. Add Crisco. Fill greased pudding mold ¾ full, cover tightly and steam 1¼ hours. Serve with hot Foamy Sauce.

STEAMED FIG PUDDING

⅓ cup Crisco	1 teaspoon baking powder
½ cup sugar	½ teaspoon salt
2 cups bread crumbs	¼ teaspoon cinnamon
1¼ cups scalded milk	¼ teaspoon clove
3 eggs	¼ teaspoon nutmeg
¼ cup flour	½ cup chopped figs

½ cup Sultana raisins

Cream Crisco and sugar, add bread crumbs and scalded milk. Mix well. Cool. Add beaten eggs. Sift flour, baking powder, salt and spices together, and mix with figs and raisins. Add to the first mixture and stir well. Fill greased pudding mold ¾ full. Cover tightly and steam 3 hours. Serve with Custard Sauce.

BROWN BETTY

3 cups dried bread crumbs	⅛ teaspoon nutmeg
3 cups sliced tart apples	¾ teaspoon cinnamon
⅓ cup brown sugar	½ teaspoon salt
⅓ cup white sugar	3 tablespoons Crisco

½ cup water

Put a layer of bread crumbs in the bottom of a greased baking dish and cover with a layer of apples. Mix sugar with nutmeg, cinnamon and salt. Sprinkle apples with part of the sugar mixture and dot with small bits of Crisco. Repeat the process until all the ingredients are used, having a layer of crumbs on top. Dot with Crisco. Pour the water over it and bake in moderate oven (350 degrees F.) 45 to 50 minutes. Serve with Foamy Sauce.

MOCK PLUM PUDDING

¾ teaspoon soda	2 tablespoons chopped citron
1 cup grated raw potato	2 tablespoons chopped orange peel
1 cup grated raw carrot	2 tablespoons melted Crisco
1 cup sugar	1 teaspoon salt
1 cup flour	1 teaspoon cinnamon
½ cup chopped nuts	½ teaspoon nutmeg
1 cup raisins	Few grains clove

Stir soda into the raw potato and mix well. Add carrot, sugar, flour, nuts, raisins, citron, orange peel, Crisco, salt and spices. Mix thoroughly. Fill greased mold ¾ full. Cover tightly and steam 2 hours. Serve with Marshmallow Sauce.

BOILED CUSTARD

2 cups rich milk	3 tablespoons sugar
1 tablespoon Crisco	½ teaspoon vanilla
3 egg yolks	Few grains salt

Scald the milk and Crisco in double boiler or over hot water. Beat egg yolks and sugar together until light. Pour scalded milk on the eggs and sugar and stir until well mixed. Return to boiler; cook until custard coats the spoon, stirring constantly. Remove at once from fire. Cool; add vanilla and salt.

Custard must be very carefully cooked. If not cooked enough it will be too thin, and if cooked too much it will separate.

MACAROON CUSTARD

Follow the recipe for Boiled Custard. Add ¼ pound crumbled macaroons just before removing from the fire. Serve cold with whipped cream.

BAKED CUSTARD

2 eggs	2 cups scalded milk
2 tablespoons sugar	½ teaspoon vanilla
Few grains salt	Few grains nutmeg

Beat eggs, add sugar and salt. Add scalded milk, vanilla, and nutmeg. Mix well. Pour into custard cups. Set cups in pan of hot water and bake in a slow oven (300 degrees F.) 25 minutes. Test with silver knife. When it is done, the custard will not stick to the knife.

COCOANUT CUSTARD

Follow the recipe for Baked Custard, allowing 1 teaspoon of cocoanut to each cup custard.

PLUM PUDDING

¼ cup Crisco	3 eggs
1 cup sugar	¾ cup scalded milk
3 cups soft bread crumbs	2 tablespoons chopped orange peel
1 teaspoon baking powder	2 tablespoons chopped lemon peel
1 teaspoon salt	1½ cups raisins
¼ teaspoon nutmeg	¼ cup currants
½ teaspoon cinnamon	¼ cup chopped figs
¼ teaspoon mace	½ cup nuts, cut in pieces
¼ teaspoon clove	½ cup grape juice

Cream Crisco and sugar together, add bread crumbs, baking powder, salt and spices. Add beaten eggs and mix thoroughly. Add scalded milk. Add orange and lemon peel, raisins, currants, figs, nuts and grape juice to the first mixture, and beat thoroughly. Fill greased pudding mold ¾ full, cover tightly and steam for 4 hours. Serve with Orange or Hard Sauce.

VANILLA BLANC MANGE

½ cup sugar	3 cups scalded milk
3 tablespoons cornstarch	2 egg yolks
3 tablespoons flour	1 teaspoon vanilla
¼ teaspoon salt	2 egg whites

Mix sugar, cornstarch, flour and salt together. Add milk and mix well. Cook over boiling water until thick, stirring constantly. Cover and cook 15 minutes longer. Remove from fire, pour on the beaten egg yolks and cook 2 minutes longer over boiling water, stirring constantly. Add vanilla and fold in stiffly beaten egg whites. Pour into a large mold or individual molds which have been dipped in cold water. Chill. Serve with fresh fruit or Chocolate Sauce.

CHOCOLATE BLANC MANGE

Follow recipe for Vanilla Blanc Mange. Add 1½ squares melted unsweetened chocolate with the milk. Serve with whipped cream.

LEMON JELLY

2½ tablespoons gelatine
½ cup cold water
1 cup sugar

2 cups boiling water
½ cup lemon juice
Grated rind of ½ lemon

Soak gelatine in cold water 5 minutes. Add sugar to gelatine and pour the boiling water on it, stirring until dissolved. Add lemon juice and rind and mix well. Strain through cheesecloth into a mold. Chill thoroughly. Serve plain or with Custard Sauce.

PLAIN BAVARIAN CREAM

2½ tablespoons gelatine
½ cup cold milk
3 egg yolks
½ cup sugar

Few grains salt
1½ cups scalded milk
1 teaspoon vanilla
½ pint cream, whipped

Soak gelatine in the cold milk 5 minutes. Beat egg yolks, sugar and salt together until light. Add scalded milk and stir until well mixed. Cook in double boiler or over hot water, stirring constantly, until mixture coats the spoon. Add gelatine and stir until dissolved. Set in pan of cold water and stir until mixture begins to thicken. Add vanilla and fold in whipped cream. Turn into a mold which has been dipped in cold water. Chill until firm.

SPANISH CREAM

Follow the recipe for Bavarian Cream, folding in the stiffly beaten whites of three eggs instead of whipped cream.

LEMON ICE

4 cups water
2¼ cups sugar

Juice of 4 lemons
Juice of 1 orange
Grated rind of 1 lemon

Boil water and sugar together 10 minutes. Strain the lemon and orange juice into the sugar syrup. Add grated rind and mix well. Cool. Turn into freezer and freeze, using 1 part rock salt to 5 parts finely cracked ice. Turn freezer constantly until mixture stiffens. Remove dasher from freezer and repack, using 1 part salt and 3 parts ice.

ORANGE ICE

4 cups water
2 cups sugar

Juice 6 oranges
Juice 1 lemon
Grated rind of 1 orange

Boil water and sugar together 10 minutes. Strain the orange and lemon juice into the syrup. Add grated rind and mix well. Cool. Turn into freezer and freeze, using 1 part rock salt to 5 parts finely cracked ice. Turn freezer constantly until mixture stiffens. Remove dasher from freezer and repack, using 1 part salt and 3 parts ice.

PINEAPPLE SHERBET

4 cups water	2 cups shredded pineapple
1½ cups sugar	Juice of 1 lemon

1 egg white

Boil water and sugar together 10 minutes. Drain pineapple and add with the lemon juice. Cool. Turn into a freezer and freeze, using 1 part rock salt to 5 parts finely cracked ice. When partly frozen fold in stiffly beaten egg whites. Turn freezer constantly until mixture stiffens. Remove dasher and repack, using 1 part salt and 3 parts ice. If canned pineapple is used, only half the amount of sugar will be needed.

VANILLA ICE CREAM

4 cups rich milk	Few grains salt
3 eggs	1 cup sugar

1 tablespoon vanilla

Scald milk in a double boiler or over hot water. Beat eggs, salt and sugar together until light. Pour the scalded milk over them and stir until well mixed. Return to boiler and cook until the mixture coats the spoon, stirring constantly. Remove from fire and cool. Add vanilla. Turn into a freezer and freeze, using 1 part rock salt to 8 parts finely cracked ice. Turn freezer constantly until mixture stiffens. Remove dasher and repack, using 1 part salt and 3 parts ice.

CHOCOLATE ICE CREAM

Follow recipe for Vanilla Ice Cream, adding 3 squares melted unsweetened chocolate and ½ cup extra sugar with the scalded milk.

FRENCH ICE CREAM

2 cups milk	1 cup sugar
5 egg yolks	2 cups cream
Few grains salt	1 tablespoon vanilla

Scald the milk in a double boiler or over hot water. Beat egg yolks, salt and sugar together until light. Pour the scalded milk on them and stir until well mixed. Return to boiler and cook until the mixture coats the spoon, stirring constantly. Remove from fire, add cream and stir well. Cool. Add vanilla. Turn into a freezer and freeze, using 1 part rock salt to 8 parts finely cracked ice. Turn freezer constantly until mixture stiffens. Remove dasher and repack, using 1 part salt and 3 parts ice. Serve with chocolate sauce.

COFFEE ICE CREAM

Follow recipe for French Ice Cream, adding ¾ cup strong black coffee.

CUSTARD SAUCE

1 cup milk   2 tablespoons sugar
2 egg yolks   1/8 teaspoon salt
1/4 teaspoon vanilla

Scald milk in double boiler or over hot water. Beat yolks, sugar and salt together until light, and pour scalded milk on them. Return to boiler and cook until mixture coats the spoon, stirring constantly. Chill and add vanilla.

To make a fluffy sauce, reserve 1 egg white, beat stiff and add to the custard just before taking from fire.

COCOANUT SAUCE

Follow recipe for Custard Sauce, adding 1/2 cup shredded cocoanut.

FOAMY SAUCE

1/4 cup sugar   1 egg yolk
2 tablespoons flour   2 tablespoons sherry flavoring
1/2 teaspoon salt   Few grains nutmeg
1 cup milk   2 egg whites

Mix sugar, flour and salt together. Add milk and beaten egg yolk and cook over hot water until thick. Add flavoring and nutmeg. Fold in the stiffly beaten egg whites.

LEMON SAUCE

1/2 cup sugar   1 cup boiling water
1 tablespoon cornstarch   2 tablespoons Crisco
1/8 teaspoon salt   2 tablespoons lemon juice
1 egg yolk

Mix sugar, cornstarch and salt. Add boiling water slowly, stirring constantly. Boil 5 minutes. Take from the fire and add Crisco, lemon juice and beaten egg yolk.

ORANGE SAUCE

Follow recipe for Lemon Sauce, substituting 1 cup orange juice for the water.

COFFEE SAUCE

Follow recipe for Lemon Sauce, substituting 1 cup hot coffee for water and omitting lemon juice. Add 1/4 teaspoon vanilla.

HOT CHOCOLATE SAUCE

1 1/4 cups milk   1 cup powdered sugar
2 squares unsweetened chocolate   1 teaspoon vanilla
1/2 tablespoon Crisco   1/8 teaspoon salt

Cook milk, chocolate and Crisco over a slow fire and stir until chocolate melts and the mixture is thick. Add sugar and cook until it thickens again, stirring constantly. Add vanilla and salt.

HOT MARSHMALLOW SAUCE

1 cup sugar   ¼ pound marshmallows
½ cup water   1 tablespoon sherry flavoring
                    ½ teaspoon vanilla

Put sugar and water in a saucepan. Place over the fire and stir until sugar is
dissolved. Cook without stirring until the sugar will spin a thread when
dropped from the tip of a spoon (238 degrees F.). Add marshmallows which
have been softened in the oven, but not browned. Beat until sauce is smooth.
Add flavoring. Keep hot over water. If too thick, thin with a few drops of
boiling water.

CHAPTER XX

Candy

AMERICANS spend something over seven dollars per capita each year for candies and confections, and the candy shops increase and flourish. The skilled candy-maker consequently has a real asset at her command, whether she uses it commercially or merely to give pleasure to her family and friends.

Home-made candy does not mean amateur candy. If one takes the trouble to master a few of the bed-rock rules of candy-making, luck gives way to assured success.

A thermometer is essential if you go in for candymaking on any scale, because cooking to just the right temperature is the first principle of success.

Fudge with its variations is by all odds the most popular of home-made candies and anyone can acquire the simple art of making it. Just be careful not to overcook it and you will have a smooth, creamy candy, instead of the grainy kind from which we have all suffered. If a little corn syrup is added—about two tablespoons to two cups of sugar—an unusually nice texture will result and the fudge will keep fresh longer.

Let the candy cool before beating it, because beating it when it is very hot also tends to make it grainy.

Crisco used in candy gives delightful results and you can use large quantities without extravagance. A little salt should be added to the candy.

Home-made confections always make a much-appreciated gift. There are any number of varieties such as caramels, nut brittles and even fudge and penuchi which can be made in advance of the last of the Christmas rush.

A thermometer is essential if you go in for candymaking, because cooking to just the right temperature is the first principle of success

SUCCESS SECRETS

1. Cook candy in a perfectly smooth saucepan large enough to allow it to "boil up."
2. Cook creamy candies *without stirring* after the sugar has dissolved.
3. Wash down sugar crystals from side of pan with cheesecloth wrapped on a fork and dipped in cold water.
4. Cool creamy candies before beginning to beat. This will prevent sugaring.
5. For taffies and brittles stir only enough to keep candy from burning.
6. Use a candy thermometer, if possible; if not, drop a little of the mixture into cold water and test as follows:

Soft Ball..................236 to 240 degrees F.
Firm Ball..................242 to 248 degrees F.

Hard Ball................250 to 265 degrees F.
Brittle......................270 to 290 degrees F.
Very Brittle..............295 to 310 degrees F.

7. Fudge and Penuchi kept in tightly covered cans will remain fresh for two weeks.

8. Wrap caramels as soon as they are cold.

9. Heat nuts before using to give them a sweet flavor.

10. Break nuts for candy instead of chopping them. When chopped the fine particles cloud the candy.

CHOCOLATE FUDGE

2 cups sugar	3 squares unsweetened chocolate
⅔ cup milk	2 tablespoons Crisco
2 tablespoons corn syrup	1 teaspoon vanilla

Put sugar, milk, syrup and chocolate, cut in small pieces, into a saucepan and stir until sugar is dissolved. Cook slowly until the temperature is 236 degrees F., or until mixture forms a soft ball when tested in cold water. Remove from fire and add Crisco. When lukewarm, add vanilla and beat until thick. Pour into greased shallow pan. When cold cut in squares.

CHOCOLATE MARSHMALLOW FUDGE

Double the recipe for Chocolate Fudge. Pour one-half the fudge into a greased square pan and lay marshmallows on it. Pour the other half over them. When cool cut in squares.

CHOCOLATE NUT FUDGE

Follow recipe for Chocolate Fudge. Just before pouring into pan add ¾ cup nuts, broken in pieces, and mix well.

CHOCOLATE COCOANUT FUDGE

Follow recipe for Chocolate Fudge. Just before pouring into pan add ⅔ cup dried cocoanut.

PENUCHI

2 cups brown sugar	1 teaspoon vanilla
½ cup evaporated milk	⅛ teaspoon salt
2 tablespoons Crisco	1 cup nuts, broken in pieces

Cook sugar and milk together in a saucepan, stirring until the sugar is dissolved. Continue to cook slowly, stirring constantly until 236 degrees F. is reached, or until mixture forms a soft ball when tested in cold water.   Add Crisco.   Cool slightly, add vanilla, salt and nuts and beat until creamy.   Pour into a greased pan and when cold cut in squares.

MEXICAN KISSES

Follow recipe for Penuchi, substituting ½ cup candied cherries, cut in pieces, for ½ cup of the nuts.   Continue beating until it will hold its shape.   Drop by teaspoons on waxed paper.

SANDWICH PENUCHI

Follow recipes for Fudge and Penuchi.   Pour fudge into a greased shallow pan. Spread with a layer of Penuchi.   Cool and cut in squares.

VANILLA CARAMELS

2 cups sugar	1½ cups milk
1 cup brown sugar	⅓ cup Crisco
1 cup light corn syrup	¼ teaspoon salt
1 cup condensed milk	1½ teaspoons vanilla

Cook sugar, corn syrup, condensed milk and milk together in a saucepan, stirring constantly until the sugar is dissolved.   Cook slowly, stirring occasionally to prevent burning, until the temperature is 248 degrees F., or until mixture forms a firm ball when tested in cold water.   Remove from fire, add Crisco, salt and vanilla and mix well.   Pour into a greased pan.   When cold remove from pan, cut in cubes and wrap each caramel in waxed paper.

CHOCOLATE CARAMELS

Follow recipe for Vanilla Caramels, cooking 5 squares unsweetened chocolate, cut in pieces, with the other ingredients.

MAPLE NUT BRITTLE

2 cups nuts, broken in pieces	¾ cup water
1½ cups maple sugar, cut in pieces	2 tablespoons Crisco
1½ cups light corn syrup	¼ teaspoon salt

Brown nuts slightly in the oven.   Cook sugar, syrup, and water together in a saucepan, stirring until the sugar is dissolved.   Add Crisco.   Continue cooking without stirring until the temperature is 290 degrees F., or until syrup becomes brittle when tested in cold water.   Add nuts and pour on an inverted greased pan in a very thin sheet.   Do not scrape the bottom and sides of the saucepan. Break into pieces.

COCOANUT BRITTLE

Follow recipe for Maple Nut Brittle.   Add 2 cups dried cocoanut instead of the nuts.

MOLASSES MINT TAFFY

2 cups molasses	1/8 teaspoon salt
2 teaspoons vinegar	1/2 teaspoon soda
1 1/2 tablespoons Crisco	7 drops oil of peppermint

Cook molasses and vinegar in a saucepan slowly, stirring constantly, until the temperature is 270 degrees F., or until syrup becomes brittle when tested in cold water. Remove from fire and add Crisco, salt and soda. Stir until mixture ceases to foam. Pour into a greased pan. When cool enough to pull pour the peppermint in the center of the candy and draw the corners toward the center. Remove from pan and pull until light in color and firm. Roll into a thin rope. Cut in pieces and wrap in waxed paper.

POPCORN BALLS

1 1/4 cups sugar	2/3 cup water
1 1/4 cups brown sugar	1 tablespoon Crisco
1/2 cup light corn syrup	3 1/2 quarts popped corn
1 1/4 teaspoons salt	

Put sugar, brown sugar, syrup and water in a saucepan, stirring until sugar is dissolved. Add Crisco and continue cooking without stirring until the temperature 240 degrees F. is reached, or until mixture forms a soft ball when tested in cold water. Put popped corn in a large bowl and sprinkle with salt. Pour the hot syrup over it and mix thoroughly. Shape in small balls, wrap in wax paper.

SALTED ALMONDS

Blanch 1/2 pound shelled almonds in boiling water and remove skins. Put 1 teaspoon Crisco in a pie pan and place in a hot oven (375 degrees F.). When it is melted put the almonds into it and stir until well coated with Crisco. Cook until a delicate brown, stirring often so that they may brown evenly without burning. Drain on unglazed paper and sprinkle with salt. Do not enclose in box or tin until perfectly cold.

Almonds may also be browned in deep Crisco, drained and salted.

CHAPTER XXI

Large Quantity Cooking

IT OFTEN happens that it is the busiest housewife who is called on most frequently for "outside" duties such as taking charge of church suppers, class luncheons or the men's club dinner.

A difficulty likely to confront her at the outset is the lack of adequate oven and stove-top space for cooking for fifty or more persons. So she must plan the menu with this in mind. Questions like marketing, serving, and collecting china, silver and linen for such a hungry mob fade into insignificance before the actual cooking!

If, then, lack of equipment or cooking space is a factor she must plan a meal for which part of the food may be prepared beforehand. Such things as pies, cakes and doughnuts may be made outside and brought in at serving-time. The menu should consist of at least one hot dish and a hot beverage, and if it is possible to bake hot biscuit or rolls, they will cause blessings to be showered on your head. The rest of the food may be cold—salads, cold meats, relishes and desserts, of which last ice cream and pie know no rivals.

The planning and ordering for a large number of people should be done as far ahead as practicable so that materials will be on hand and any gaps filled before the last minute. If roasts or hams are to be served they may be partly cooked the day before, the hams boiled and prepared with spices and sugar for a final baking. Beans may always be baked the previous day and reheated with no loss of flavor or delicacy. Macaroni dishes may be made ready for the oven, and vegetables may be prepared for boiling early in the day and allowed to soak in cold water. The ingredients for salad may be prepared and left in the ice box to chill.

Although most recipes may be doubled with very satisfactory results it is not always possible to increase them successfully in any larger proportion than that. There are many scientific reasons for this and it is well to realize that a fresh start must be made with a reliable recipe which has been worked out on a larger scale.

In large quantity cooking the ingredients should be of the best grade or the finished product will tell the tale. Crisco is an invaluable ally in the church or club kitchen. It may be bought in large cans and kept over from one affair to the next without danger of becoming rancid.

SUCCESS SECRETS

1. Plan menus with reference to the equipment available and the amount of stove space on which to cook.
2. Do as much preparation as possible the day before.
3. Use large shallow pans rather than deep ones for baking and so hasten the process.
4. Bake cakes in large sheets—allow them to cool in the pan, frost, and cut in squares for serving.
5. Keep a new clothes boiler for making coffee. To serve, dip out with large pitcher and fill cups before putting them on the saucers.

VEGETABLE SOUP

5 gallons water	2 cups rice
3 quarts cooked or canned tomatoes	6 onions
¼ cup salt	1½ quarts celery
3 teaspoons pepper	3 quarts potatoes
2 bay leaves	1 quart carrots
2 cups Crisco	1 pint turnips

Put water and tomatoes in a large soup kettle. Add seasonings, Crisco and rice. Chop vegetables fine, add and cook slowly 2 hours. Add more seasoning if necessary. Do not strain.

Any meat or vegetable stock may be used instead of part of the water.

This recipe makes about 50 to 60 servings.

MASHED POTATOES

15 pounds potatoes	¼ cup salt
1½ quarts milk (scalded)	⅓ cup melted Crisco

Wash and pare potatoes and boil or steam until tender.   Mash until free from lumps and add milk, salt and Crisco.   Beat until light.   Serve immediately.

This recipe makes about 50 servings.

BAKED BEANS

4 quarts pea beans	2 teaspoons mustard
¼ cup soda	2 teaspoons paprika
1 cup molasses	6 tablespoons salt
½ cup sugar	2 cups Crisco

3 quarts hot water

Soak beans over night.   Drain.   Cover with water, add soda and cook slowly until almost tender.   Drain.   Add molasses, sugar, mustard, paprika, salt, Crisco and hot water.   Bake in shallow pans in a moderate oven (325 degrees F.) 1 to 1½ hours.

This recipe makes about 75 servings.

WHITE SAUCE

2 cups Crisco	1 teaspoon pepper
3 cups flour	1 teaspoon paprika
¼ cup salt	5 quarts milk

1 quart water

Melt Crisco and add flour, salt, pepper and paprika.   Mix well.   Scald milk and water.   Add a little at a time to the flour mixture, stirring constantly to prevent lumping.   Cook, stirring until thick and smooth.

This recipe makes 6 quarts of sauce.

MACARONI AND CHEESE

5 pounds macaroni	6 quarts thin white sauce
2 gallons water	2 pounds cheese, cut in small pieces
¼ cup salt	1 quart soft bread crumbs

½ cup Crisco

Break macaroni in pieces.   Cook in boiling salted water until tender.   Drain. Add white sauce and cheese to the macaroni.   Put in greased shallow baking pans.   Cover with crumbs and dot with small bits of Crisco.   Bake in moderate oven (350 degrees F.) 50 to 60 minutes.

This recipe makes about 50 servings.

CHICKEN À LA KING

6 quarts cooked chicken*
1 small can pimento, chopped
2 tablespoons salt
2 teaspoons pepper

4 tablespoons parsley, chopped
1 pound mushrooms
2 tablespoons Crisco
3 quarts white sauce

Cut chicken in cubes before measuring. Add pimento, salt, pepper and parsley. Peel mushrooms, slice thin and cook in Crisco 10 minutes. Add them with the white sauce to the chicken mixture. Heat over boiling water. Serve on toast or in patty shells.
This recipe makes about 50 servings.
*(4 or 5 six pound fowls will give 6 quarts cooked meat.)

CHICKEN SALAD

4 quarts cooked chicken, cut in small pieces
4 quarts celery, cut in small pieces
1 tablespoon salt

1 teaspoon pepper
2 quarts salad dressing
8 hard cooked eggs

Mix chicken, celery, salt and pepper. Moisten with French Dressing and let stand several hours. Mix with Boiled Salad Dressing or Mayonnaise Dressing. Serve on lettuce leaves and garnish with slices of hard cooked eggs.
This recipe makes about 50 servings.

POTATO SALAD

8 quarts potatoes
1½ quarts celery, cut in small pieces

2 tablespoons salt
½ cup chopped parsley

Wash and pare potatoes and cut in cubes. Cook in boiling salted water until tender. Drain and cool. Add celery, salt and parsley. Moisten with French Dressing and let stand several hours. Place on lettuce leaves and garnish with Mayonnaise Dressing and stuffed olives.
This recipe makes about 50 to 60 servings.

BOILED SALAD DRESSING

1½ cups flour
½ cup cornstarch
1½ cups sugar
2 tablespoons mustard
1 teaspoon paprika

⅛ teaspoon cayenne
¼ cup salt
3 quarts milk
¾ cup Crisco
1¼ quarts vinegar

8 eggs

Mix flour, cornstarch, sugar, mustard, paprika, cayenne and salt together. Mix to a paste with a little of the milk. Scald remaining milk with the Crisco in a double boiler or over hot water. Add the first mixture to the milk gradually and cook until smooth and thick, stirring constantly. Pour on to the beaten eggs. Return to the fire and cook 3 minutes. Add vinegar a little at a time beating after each addition. Stir until dressing is well mixed and blended. Cool.
This recipe makes 4½ quarts of salad dressing.

BAKING POWDER BISCUITS

6½ quarts flour   ¾ cup baking powder
½ cup salt   3 cups Crisco
                    2 quarts milk

Mix and sift flour, salt and baking powder together. Cut in Crisco with a knife or rub in with the finger tips. Add milk slowly to make a soft dough. Roll out on slightly floured board to ¾ inch thickness and cut with a biscuit cutter. Put on a greased baking sheet and bake in a quick oven (425 degrees F.) 10 to 15 minutes.

This recipe makes about 100 biscuits.

SOUTHERN CORNBREAD

2 quarts flour   3½ cups cornmeal
½ cup sugar   6 eggs
¾ cup baking powder   1½ tablespoons soda
4 tablespoons salt   1½ quarts buttermilk
                1 cup melted Crisco

Mix and sift flour, sugar, baking powder and salt. Stir in cornmeal and mix well. Add beaten eggs. Add soda, dissolved in buttermilk and Crisco. Beat thoroughly. Bake in greased shallow pans in quick oven (425 degrees F.) 35 minutes.

This recipe makes about 50 servings.

CHOCOLATE CAKE

1 cup Crisco   4 tablespoons baking powder
6 cups sugar   2 cups milk
9 egg yolks   9 squares unsweetened chocolate
8 cups flour   1 tablespoon vanilla
2½ teaspoons salt   9 egg whites

Cream Crisco, sugar and egg yolks together. Mix and sift flour, salt and baking powder and add alternately with the milk to the first mixture. Add melted chocolate and vanilla and beat thoroughly. Fold in stiffly beaten egg whites. Pour into greased shallow pans and bake in a moderate oven (350 degrees F.) 20 to 30 minutes. When cool cover with any desired frosting.

This recipe makes about 50 servings.

APPLE PIES

PIE CRUST

6 pounds flour   3 pounds Crisco
4 tablespoons salt   Water

Mix and sift flour and salt. Cut in Crisco with a knife or rub in with finger tips. Moisten with just enough cold water to hold the mixture together. Chill thoroughly. Roll out thin on a slightly floured board.

PIE FILLING

16 pounds tart apples
2 tablespoons cinnamon

7 pounds sugar
1 cup flour

½ cup Crisco

Pare and core apples and cut in thin slices. Add cinnamon, sugar and flour and mix well. Line pie pans with pastry and fill with apple mixture. Dot with Crisco. Cover with top crust, trim and press edges together to make a fancy edge. Prick top to allow steam to escape. Bake in a quick oven (425 degrees F.) 10 minutes, reduce heat to moderate oven (350 degrees F.) and bake 20 to 30 minutes.

This recipe makes 14 pies.

GINGER SNAPS

1 cup molasses
1 cup Crisco
1 cup sugar
1 teaspoon soda

2 tablespoons water
1 teaspoon cinnamon
2 teaspoons ginger
1 teaspoon salt

4 cups flour (about)

Heat molasses, Crisco and sugar together until Crisco is melted. Cool. Add soda dissolved in water. Sift cinnamon, ginger and salt with part of the flour. Stir into the first mixture and then add the rest of the flour gradually until dough is stiff enough to roll. Chill. Roll on slightly floured board until very thin. Cut with a cooky cutter and bake in a moderate oven (325 degrees F.) 10 to 12 minutes.

This makes about 100 cookies.

COFFEE FOR 100 PERSONS

8 cups ground coffee

18 quarts water

Tie the coffee in thick cheesecloth bags, leaving plenty of room for coffee to swell. Let stand in the water several hours. Bring slowly to boiling point and boil 5 minutes. Remove the bags and keep coffee hot for serving.

COCOA FOR 100 PERSONS

3 cups cocoa
4 cups sugar
½ teaspoon salt

1 quart warm water
2 quarts boiling water
16 quarts hot milk

Mix cocoa, sugar, salt and warm water together until smooth. Add boiling water and boil 10 minutes. Pour into the hot milk, bring to boiling point, stirring constantly, and beat with an egg beater for a few minutes. Keep hot over boiling water. Serve with whipped cream.

CHOCOLATE FOR 100 PERSONS

2 pounds chocolate
3 pounds sugar

4 quarts boiling water
16 quarts hot milk

½ teaspoon salt

Melt chocolate, add sugar and boiling water and stir until smooth. Boil 10 minutes. Add salt. Pour into the hot milk. Beat well with an egg beater and keep hot over boiling water. Serve with whipped cream.

HOW TO PREPARE FOR FIFTY PERSONS

DESSERTS		AMOUNT NEEDED
	Ice Cream	6 quarts (brick) or 8 quarts (loose)
	Steamed Puddings	8 quart mold 2 quarts sauce
	Strawberry Shortcake	*Biscuit dough 6 quarts berries 2½ cups sugar 1 quart whipped cream
MEAT	Meat Pie	10 pounds stew meat 1 quart potatoes, cut in pieces *Biscuit dough
	Hamburg Steak	10 pounds meat 2 cups bread crumbs 1 quart stock or milk
	Hash	6 quarts chopped meat 4 quarts chopped potatoes 3 quarts stock or water
	Roast Lamb	16 pounds
	Roast Beef	16 pounds
	Roast Chicken	25 pounds
	Creamed Chicken	6 quarts chicken, cut in cubes 3½ quarts white sauce

*Recipe given in this chapter.

HOW TO PREPARE FOR FIFTY PERSONS

SALADS	Chicken	AMOUNT NEEDED 4 quarts chicken, cut in cubes 4 quarts celery, diced *2 quarts salad dressing
	Fish	4 quarts flaked fish 4 quarts celery *2 quarts salad dressing
	Fruit	7 quarts prepared fruit (drained) *1 quart salad dressing
SOUPS		4 gallons
VEGETABLES	Creamed Peas (or any creamed vegetable)	5 quarts peas *2½ quarts white sauce
	Scalloped Potatoes	8 quarts sliced potatoes 3 quarts milk
	*Mashed Potatoes	15 pounds potatoes 1½ quarts milk
	*Macaroni and Cheese	5 pounds uncooked macaroni, broken in pieces *6 quarts white sauce 3 cups grated cheese

*Recipe given in this chapter.

CHAPTER XXII

Specialty Dishes

IN THE heart of every true homemaker lies the desire to be a good hostess. It is as natural as the desire to be beautiful!

There are still occasions and meals that call for formality and ceremony, but they are becoming more and more rare. Whether you aspire to entertain formally or merely to gather a few congenial friends around your table or hearth, or perhaps just to give your family a special treat once in a while when you have a little extra time, you will want to be able to prepare some *one* food superlatively well.

Perhaps you have a "knack" for cooking desserts, or meats or salads, or hearty, heartening vegetables. Or perhaps you are a terribly busy person who has budgeted your time so carefully that you can give only a few minutes to "very special" cooking.

Whichever you are, you will find in this little chapter some one specialty dish that appeals to you. We have selected one or two that are appropriate for Sunday night suppers, for afternoon teas, for party luncheons, a man's dinner, chafing dish parties, weddings and birthdays. Each of them is delicious and not at all hard to prepare.

PLANKED STEAK

The steak should be 1½ inches thick. Put on a broiler well greased with Crisco. Spread steak with Crisco and season with salt and pepper. Broil over a quick fire about 12 to 15 minutes, turning every few minutes. Heat the plank, grease with Crisco and put the steak on it. Put Duchess Potatoes (page 108) around the edge with a pastry tube. Arrange Stuffed Onions (page 107) and Baked Stuffed Tomatoes (page 111) around steak. Brush tops of potatoes and onions with beaten egg yolk, diluted with 1 tablespoon milk. Place in a hot oven (400 degrees F.) and cook about 6 to 8 minutes to brown the potatoes and finish cooking the steak. Take from the oven and arrange hot cooked carrots, string beans and peas inside the potato border.
Serve at once with Mushroom Sauce (page 115).

PLANKED BLUEFISH

Fish plank   2 tablespoons Crisco
Blue fish (3½ to 4 lbs.)   ½ teaspoon salt
⅛ teaspoon pepper

A fish plank should be made of hard wood, about 16 inches long and 12 inches wide. Heat plank very hot and grease with Crisco. Remove head and tail of fish. Split and clean. Place on the plank, skin side down. Spread with melted Crisco and sprinkle with salt and pepper. Place under the broiler and cook 15 to 20 minutes, depending upon the size of the fish. Decorate with Duchess Potatoes (page 108) put through a pastry bag. Return to oven and cook until potatoes are brown. Garnish top of fish with chopped parsley and slices of lemon. Arrange hot cooked carrots, creamed Brussels sprouts and pickled beets cut in fancy shapes, inside the potato border. Serve from the plank.

LOBSTER PATTIES

Follow recipe for Boiled Lobster (page 84). Crack claws and remove meat. Discard the stomach which lies under the head, also the woolly gills. Save the fatty green substance and coral (if any) to mix with the meat. Pick out all the meat and cut in uniform pieces. To 2 cups of lobster add 2 cups Medium White Sauce (page 113) using 1 cup thin cream in place of 1 cup of the milk and heat thoroughly. Add 1 tablespoon chopped parsley and 1 well-beaten egg yolk before taking from the fire. Serve in Patty Shells (page 179). Garnish with watercress.

SHRIMP NEWBURG

2 tablespoons Crisco   ½ cup cream
1½ tablespoons flour   ¼ cup milk
¾ teaspoon salt   2 cups cooked shrimps
Few grains cayenne   2 egg yolks
1 tablespoon sherry flavoring

Melt Crisco, add flour, salt and cayenne and mix well. Add cream and milk gradually and bring to the boiling point, stirring constantly. Add shrimps.

Just before serving add the beaten egg yolks and flavoring. Serve on rounds of Puff Paste (page 179). Garnish with parsley and thin strips of pimento.

SWEETBREADS BÉCHAMEL

2 pairs sweetbreads	4 tablespoons flour
1 sprig parsley	1 cup stock
1 stalk celery	1 cup rich milk
½ teaspoon salt	1 tablespoon chopped parsley
2 tablespoons Crisco	1 egg yolk

Soak sweetbreads in salt water for 1 hour. Drain. Put in saucepan with parsley, celery and salt and enough water to cover. Bring to boiling point. Reduce heat and cook slowly 30 minutes. Strain off and measure the stock. Discard the fat and connective tissues from the sweetbreads and cut them in small pieces. Melt Crisco, add flour and stir until blended. Add milk and stock and stir until thick. Add sweetbreads and keep hot over hot water. Add parsley and beaten egg yolk just before serving. Serve in Croustades (page 51) or on points of toast.

ARTICHOKES HOLLANDAISE

Cut stem and tough outside leaves from French artichokes. Remove the thistle-like center or "choke." Soak in salted water ½ hour. Boil about 25 minutes in salted water to which 1 tablespoon vinegar has been added. Drain. Serve with Hollandaise Sauce (page 115).

These may be served cold with cold Hollandaise.

BRIOCHE

1 cup milk	1 yeast cake
⅓ cup Crisco	2 tablespoons lukewarm water
½ cup sugar	3 eggs
1½ teaspoons salt	1 teaspoon lemon extract
4½ to 5 cups flour	

Heat milk and add Crisco, sugar and salt. When lukewarm add the yeast cake dissolved in warm water. Add 1 cup flour and beat thoroughly. Cover and set in a warm place to rise until light—1 hour. Add beaten eggs and lemon extract and enough flour to make a firm dough. Knead on a slightly floured board until smooth and elastic to touch. Roll out to ¼ inch thickness into a rectangular shape. Spread lightly with melted Crisco. Fold edges to the center and fold again. Cover and set in a warm place to rise until light. Cut in pieces ½ inch wide. Twist each piece from the ends in opposite directions. Bring ends together and press into center of strip. Put on a greased pan 1 inch apart. Cover and set in a warm place to rise. Bake in a hot oven (400 degrees F.) 15 to 20 minutes. While hot spread with 2 cups confectioners' sugar moistened with a little milk and flavored with vanilla.

This recipe makes about 24 brioche.

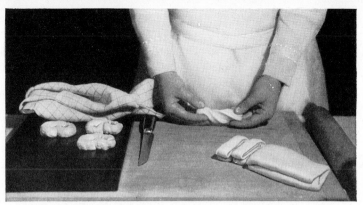

The characteristic shape of French Brioche is obtained by twisting small pieces of dough in opposite directions, bringing ends together and pressing them into center of strip

ORANGE BISCUITS

2 cups flour
4 teaspoons baking powder
½ teaspoon salt

4 tablespoons Crisco
½ tablespoon grated orange rind
⅔ cup milk

Juice of 1 orange

Mix and sift flour, baking powder and salt. Cut in Crisco with a knife or rub in with the finger tips. Add orange rind and enough milk to make a soft dough. Roll out on a slightly floured board to ½ inch thickness. Cut with a biscuit cutter. Dip loaf sugar in orange juice. Put a piece of sugar on each biscuit. Bake in a quick oven (425 degrees F.) 10 to 15 minutes.

(Cut with a small cutter, these biscuits are most attractive for afternoon tea.)

This recipe makes 12 biscuits.

FRUIT SALAD

1 grapefruit
3 oranges

1 banana
3 slices pineapple

½ pound Malaga grapes

Peel grapefruit and oranges. Remove sections, discarding the white membrane. Cut banana and pineapple in small pieces. Skin grapes and remove seeds. Mix all the fruit together. Drain. Pile lightly on heart leaves of lettuce. Serve with Pineapple Dressing.

PINEAPPLE DRESSING

4 tablespoons flour
3 tablespoons sugar
Juice from 1 can sliced pineapple

1 tablespoon Crisco
2 eggs
1 cup cream, whipped

Mix flour and sugar, adding pineapple juice a little at a time, until the mixture will pour. Heat remaining juice and add flour mixture. Cook directly over fire, stirring until slightly thickened. Place over hot water, add Crisco and well-beaten eggs. Cook again until quite thick, stirring constantly. Chill. Fold in whipped cream just before serving.

COFFEE MOUSSE

2 cups cream
Few grains salt

½ cup powdered sugar
½ cup strong coffee
1 tablespoon mocha essence

Whip the cream, sugar and salt together until stiff. Add coffee and mocha essence and mix well. Turn mixture into a mold. Cover tightly. Pack in 1 part rock salt to 3 parts finely cracked ice and let stand 4 or 5 hours. Serve with whipped cream.

CHOCOLATE MOUSSE

Follow recipe for Coffee Mousse, using 2 ounces melted unsweetened chocolate instead of coffee. Add 1 teaspoon vanilla instead of mocha essence.

FRUIT MOUSSE

Follow recipe for Coffee Mousse and add two cups slightly sweetened, chopped and drained fruit and 1 teaspoon vanilla, omitting the coffee and mocha essence.

MOCK NESSELRODE PUDDING

2½ tablespoons gelatine
1 cup cold milk
4 egg yolks
¾ cup sugar
3 cups scalded milk

¾ cup chopped raisins
10 macaroons, rolled
1 teaspoon vanilla
½ teaspoon almond extract
2 tablespoons sherry flavoring

4 egg whites

Soak gelatine in cold milk 5 minutes. Beat egg yolks and sugar together and pour the scalded milk on them. Put in a double boiler, or over hot water and cook, stirring constantly until custard coats the spoon. Add gelatine and milk and stir until dissolved. Take from the fire and add raisins, macaroon crumbs, vanilla, almond extract and sherry flavoring. Mix well. Fold in stiffly beaten egg whites. Set in a pan of ice water and beat until thick. Pour into a mold which has been dipped in cold water and chill thoroughly. Turn out of mold onto a plate and decorate with whipped cream and Maraschino cherries.

CHOCOLATE SOUFFLÉ

2 tablespoons Crisco	3 squares unsweetened chocolate
3 tablespoons flour	3 tablespoons hot water
1 cup milk	3 egg yolks
½ cup sugar	1 teaspoon vanilla
½ teaspoon salt	3 egg whites

Melt Crisco, add flour and mix well. Add milk gradually and bring to the boiling point, stirring constantly. Add sugar, salt and melted chocolate which has been mixed with the hot water. Cool. Add egg yolks and beat well. Add vanilla and fold in the stiffly beaten egg whites. Pour into a greased baking dish. Set in a pan of hot water and bake in a moderate oven (325 degrees F.) 50 to 60 minutes. Serve immediately with Custard Sauce (page 197), or whipped cream.

CREAM PUFFS

½ cup Crisco	1½ cups flour
1 cup water	5 eggs

Put Crisco and water in a saucepan and bring to the boiling point. Add flour and mix well. Cook 2 minutes, stirring constantly. Cool. Add eggs one at a time beating after each egg is added. Beat for 5 minutes. Drop by tablespoons on a greased shallow pan 2 inches apart. Flatten with back of spoon into circles, leaving center a little thicker. Bake in a moderate oven (350 degrees F.) 30 to 35 minutes. Cool. Make a slit with a sharp pointed knife near the bottom of the puff and fill with Cream Filling (page 170), or whipped cream.

ECLAIRS

Follow the recipe for Cream Puffs. Press the dough through a pastry bag onto a greased shallow pan, making strips 4 inches long and 1 inch wide and keeping them 2 inches apart. Or bake in greased lady finger pans.

MERINGUE CAKE

6 egg whites	1 teaspoon vinegar
2 cups sifted granulated sugar	Few grains salt
1 teaspoon vanilla	

Beat egg whites until stiff, add sugar, 1 tablespoon at a time, then vinegar, salt and vanilla, beating constantly (about 30 minutes altogether). Cover bottom of 2 round pans with 2 layers of wet wrapping paper. Pour in the egg mixture and bake in very slow oven (250 degrees F.) 45 minutes to 1 hour. Serve with preserved fruit, whipped cream or ice cream between the layers, and whipped cream on top.

This meringue may be made in individual portions.

BIRTHDAY CAKE

½ cup Crisco	1 teaspoon salt
1½ cups sugar	3 teaspoons baking powder
3 eggs	⅔ cup milk
2¼ cups flour	1 teaspoon almond extract

Cream Crisco, sugar and eggs together. Mix and sift flour, salt and baking powder and add alternately with the milk to the first mixture. Add almond extract and beat thoroughly. Pour into a greased tube pan. Wrap a button, thimble, ring and dime in separate pieces of wax paper and put into the cake batter. Bake in a moderate oven (350 degrees F.) 50 to 60 minutes. Cover and decorate with Ornamental Frosting (page 167).

WEDDING CAKE

½ pound Crisco	1 tablespoon mace
¾ pound brown sugar	½ tablespoon ginger
6 eggs	½ tablespoon clove
½ cup molasses	3 pounds raisins
1 cup grape juice	1 pound currants
½ pound flour	½ pound lemon and orange peel,
1½ tablespoons cinnamon	chopped

½ pound citron, chopped

Cream Crisco and sugar together. Add the beaten eggs, molasses and grape juice and mix well. Mix and sift flour, cinnamon, mace, ginger and clove. Add enough of the sifted flour mixture to the fruit to keep it from sticking together. Add remaining flour and fruit to the first mixture and beat thoroughly. Line bottom of a large round pan with greased paper and grease sides of pan. Pour mixture into it and bake in a very slow oven (225 degrees F.) 3 to 4 hours. A small pan of water in the oven helps to keep the cake from burning during the long cooking. Ice and decorate with Ornamental Frosting (page 167).

ROLLED PECAN WAFERS

½ cup Crisco	4 tablespoons flour
1 cup brown sugar	½ cup pecans, chopped
2 eggs	½ teaspoon salt

½ teaspoon maple flavoring

Cream Crisco and sugar together. Beat in eggs, one at a time. Stir in flour and mix well. Add nuts, salt and flavoring. Drop by teaspoons on greased cooky sheet about 5 inches apart. Spread out very thin with back of spoon. Bake in slow oven (300 degrees F.) 10 to 12 minutes. Remove with a spatula or broad-bladed knife and roll while hot over round handle of wooden spoon. If the cookies get too cool to roll, reheat in oven. (If difficulty is found in rolling, they may be served as wafers.)

This recipe makes about 36 rolls.

SCOTCH FANS

1 cup Crisco   2¼ cups flour
¾ cup brown sugar   1 teaspoon salt
                          1 egg yolk

Cream Crisco and sugar together. Add flour and salt and knead until ingredients hold together. Roll out on slightly floured board to ¼ inch thickness. Cut in circles with large fluted cooky cutter, then cut each circle in 3 fan shaped pieces. Brush with egg yolk diluted with 1 tablespoon water. Bake in a slow oven (300 degrees F.) 15 to 20 minutes.

This recipe makes about 30 fans.

HAZELNUT COOKIES

¼ pound sweet chocolate   2 egg whites
¼ pound finely chopped hazelnuts   ¼ teaspoon cinnamon
¼ pound finely chopped almonds   Few grains ground clove
⅔ cup powdered sugar   2 tablespoons melted Crisco

Melt chocolate over hot water. Add chopped nuts and sugar and mix well. Add stiffly beaten egg whites, spices and Crisco. Mix well. Chill. Roll out thin, a small quantity at a time, on slightly floured board. Cut with cooky cutter. Place on greased pans and bake in moderate oven (325 degrees F.) 12 to 15 minutes.

This recipe makes about 50 cookies.

CHAPTER XXIII

Spring-Summer Menus

SUNDAY

BREAKFAST

Stewed Rhubarb
Puffed Rice

Popovers   Marmalade
        Coffee   Cocoa

DINNER

Roast Spring Lamb, Mint Sauce
New Potatoes   Green Peas
        Watercress Salad
    Lemon Ice   Sand Tarts
            Coffee

SUPPER

Stuffed Tomato Salad
Baking Powder Biscuit   Cottage Cheese
    Berries   Silver Cake
        Tea   Milk

MONDAY

BREAKFAST

Blueberries
Shredded Wheat

Crisp Bacon   Toast
        Coffee

LUNCHEON

Jellied Tuna Fish
Cheese Biscuit   Potato Chips
    Fruit Salad, Pineapple Dressing
    Tea   Milk

DINNER

Minced Lamb en Casserole
Radishes   Steamed Brown Rice
        String Beans
    Romaine Salad, Tarragon Dressing
    Baked Custard, Caramel Sauce

TUESDAY

BREAKFAST

Cantaloupe
Bran Flakes
Sautéed Lamb Kidneys   Toast
Coffee   Cocoa

LUNCHEON

Cream of Tomato Soup
String Bean Salad   Sardine Sandwiches
Sliced Peaches   Cup Cakes
Tea   Milk

DINNER

Broiled Beefsteak
French Fried Potatoes   Baked Stuffed Tomatoes
Endive Salad, Celery Dressing
Blueberry Pudding, Foamy Sauce

WEDNESDAY

BREAKFAST

Fresh Apricots
Wheatena
Poached Eggs on Toast
Coffee   Cocoa

LUNCHEON

Cheese Fondue
Cabbage Salad   Sour Milk Biscuit
Peach Jam
Milk   Iced Tea

DINNER

Cream of Watercress Soup
Beefsteak Hash, Mushroom Sauce
Parsley Potatoes   Baked Corn
Pineapple Sherbet
Nut Cookies   Coffee

THURSDAY

BREAKFAST

Sliced Watermelon
Puffy Omelet
Toast   Marmalade
Coffee   Cocoa

LUNCHEON

Creamed Beef on Toast
Tomato Salad
Brown Sugar Cookies   Iced Cocoa or Milk

DINNER

Chicken Chop Suey
Corn Fritters   Crisp Rolls
Asparagus Salad
Peach Shortcake   Coffee

FRIDAY

BREAKFAST

Blueberries
Hominy
Shirred Eggs   Bran Muffins
Coffee   Cocoa

LUNCHEON

Rice Cakes, Cheese Sauce
Fresh Peas   Popovers
Waldorf Salad, Whipped Cream Dressing
Iced Cocoa   Milk

DINNER

Cream of Asparagus Soup
Broiled Mackerel
Scalloped Potatoes   Swiss Chard or Beet Tops
Sliced Cucumbers
Cottage Pudding, Lemon Sauce
Coffee

SATURDAY

BREAKFAST

Oranges
Corn Flakes
Crisp Bacon   Coffee Ring
Coffee   Cocoa

LUNCHEON

Italian Spaghetti
Heart of Lettuce Salad   Emergency Biscuit
Raspberries
Milk   Iced Tea

DINNER
Cream of Pea Soup

Veal Cutlets   Mashed Potatoes

Steamed Carrots

Chocolate Layer Cake

Coffee

SUNDAY

BREAKFAST
Pears

Wheatena

Waffles and Honey

Coffee   Cocoa

DINNER
Roast Duck

Currant Jelly   Celery

Parsley Potatoes   Brussels Sprouts

Lettuce Salad

Vanilla Ice Cream, Fresh Strawberries

Coffee

SUPPER
Jellied Vegetable Salad

Scotch Scones   Olives

Sliced Peaches and Cream

Marble Cake   Milk   Cocoa

MONDAY

BREAKFAST
Blackberries

Puffed Wheat

Poached Eggs on Toast

Coffee   Cocoa

LUNCHEON
Cheese Soufflé

Fried Tomatoes   Graham Gems

Strawberry Jam

Milk   Iced Cocoa

DINNER
Rolled Flank Steak

Potato Puffs   Different Cabbage

Cucumber Salad

Deep Huckleberry Pie   Cheese

Coffee

TUESDAY

BREAKFAST
Cantaloupe
Fried Eggs and Bacon   Toast
Coffee   Cocoa

LUNCHEON
Corn Chowder
Egg Plant au Gratin
Bran Muffins   Honey
Cocoa   Milk

DINNER
Duck with Rice en Casserole (left-over)
String Beans   Baked Stuffed Tomatoes
Watercress and Radish Salad
Peach Basket Turnover
Coffee

WEDNESDAY

BREAKFAST
Orange Juice
Shredded Wheat
Spanish Omelet   Corn Muffins
Coffee   Cocoa

LUNCHEON
Broiled Luncheon Sandwich
Asparagus Salad
Strawberries and Cream   Nut Cookies
Milk or Iced Cocoa

DINNER
Boiled Salmon with Horseradish Sauce
Lyonnaise Potatoes   Beets Piquante
Green Pepper Salad
Macaroon Custard Pudding
Coffee

THURSDAY

BREAKFAST
Plums
Hominy
Egg Fluff   Toast
Marmalade
Coffee

LUNCHEON
Creamed Chicken on Toast
Emergency Biscuit   Currant Jam
Iced Cocoa
Pecan Cakes

DINNER
Cream of Tomato Soup
Veal Loaf with Mushroom Sauce
Scalloped Potatoes   Green Peas
Grapefruit and Orange Salad
Coffee

FRIDAY

BREAKFAST
Strawberries and Cream
Codfish Balls
Toast

Coffee   Cocoa

LUNCHEON
Russian Egg Salad

Nut Muffins   Cocoa

Caramel Custard

DINNER
Broiled Bluefish
Baked Stuffed Tomatoes   French Fried Potatoes
Cucumber Salad
Cherry Pie

SATURDAY

BREAKFAST
Pears
Shredded Wheat
Boiled Eggs   Muffins
Coffee   Cocoa

LUNCHEON
Scalloped Fish in Ramekins (Left Over)
Baking Powder Biscuit   Tomato Salad
Iced Tea   Cookies

DINNER
Braised Sweetbreads on Toast
Creamed Potatoes   Baked Summer Squash
Heart of Lettuce Salad
Molasses Cake, Whipped Cream
Coffee

CHAPTER XXIV

Autumn-Winter Menus

SUNDAY

BREAKFAST
Orange Juice

Sausages   Baked Potatoes

Griddle Cakes and Maple Syrup

Coffee   Cocoa

DINNER
Roast Beef, Yorkshire Pudding

Franconia Potatoes   Baked Squash

Olives   Currant Jelly

Asparagus Salad, Thousand Island Dressing

Butterscotch Pie

Coffee

SUPPER
Shrimp Newburg

Sweet Pickles   Scotch Scones

Canned Peaches

Caramel Layer Cake

Tea

MONDAY

BREAKFAST
Baked Apples

Cream of Wheat

Shirred Eggs   Plain Muffins

Coffee   Cocoa

LUNCHEON
Cream of Tomato Soup

Macaroni and Cheese   Fruit Salad, Pineapple Dressing

Tea   Milk

DINNER
Shepherd's Pie

Steamed Carrots   Spinach Salad, French Dressing

Clover Leaf Rolls

Spanish Cream   Coffee

*T*UESDAY

BREAKFAST
Oranges

Oatmeal   Crisp Bacon
  Bran Muffins   Grape Jam
    Coffee   Cocoa

LUNCHEON
Corn Chowder

Cabbage and Celery Salad   Parker House Rolls
  Stewed Peas   Peanut Cookies

DINNER

Virginia Baked Ham   Potato Soufflé
        Creamed Parsnips
        Pickle Relish
    Rice Pudding with Raisins
          Coffee

*W*EDNESDAY

BREAKFAST
Stewed Prunes

Wheatena   Scrambled Eggs
  Toast   Marmalade
    Coffee   Cocoa

LUNCHEON
Ham Soufflé (Left Over)

Baking Powder Biscuit   Waldorf Salad
    Tea   Milk

DINNER
Lamb Chops

Sweet Potatoes, Southern Style   Scalloped Cabbage
          Mint Jelly

  Pumpkin Pie   Cheese
            Coffee

*T*HURSDAY

BREAKFAST
Bananas

Shredded Wheat   Griddle Cakes and Honey
    Coffee   Cocoa

LUNCHEON
Egg and Spinach en Casserole

Grapefruit Salad   Rice Muffins
    Tea   Milk

DINNER

Braised Liver with Bacon
Mashed Potatoes   Baked Stuffed Onions
Heart of Lettuce Salad, Russian Dressing
Dutch Apple Cake, Lemon Sauce
Coffee

FRIDAY

BREAKFAST

Grapes
Cornmeal Mush   Puffy Omelet
Toast   Coffee   Cocoa

LUNCHEON

Cream of Potato Soup
Baked Macédoine   Stewed Apricots
Oatmeal Cookies
Tea   Milk

DINNER

Baked Stuffed Haddock
Potato Puffs   Spinach and Egg
Celery and Nut Salad
Steamed Chocolate Pudding, Custard Sauce
Coffee

SATURDAY

BREAKFAST

Grapefruit
Farina
Toast   Marmalade
Coffee   Cocoa

LUNCHEON

Creamed Haddock (Left Over)
Baked Potatoes
Cornmeal Muffins   Grape Jam
Tea   Milk

DINNER

Baked Beans   Steamed Brown Bread
Pineapple and Cheese Salad
Lady Baltimore Cake
Coffee

*S*UNDAY

*B*REAKFAST
Grapefruit
Fried Scallops
Waffles and Syrup

Coffee   Cocoa

*D*INNER
Roast Chicken, Chestnut Stuffing
Celery   Cranberry Jelly
Potato Puffs   Cauliflower au Gratin
Heart of Lettuce Salad
Vanilla Ice Cream, Chocolate Sauce
Coffee

*S*UPPER
Cheese Rarebit on Toast
Baking Powder Biscuit   Stewed Apricots
Hermits
Cocoa   Milk

*M*ONDAY

*B*REAKFAST
Apples   Wheatena
Crisp Bacon
Toast
Coffee   Cocoa

*L*UNCHEON
Egg Croquettes, Cheese Sauce
Plain Muffins   Jam
Tea   Milk

*D*INNER
Chicken Pot-Pie (Left Over)
Cranberry Jelly
Sweet Potato Croquettes   Scalloped Cabbage
Grapefruit Salad
Cottage Pudding, Chocolate Sauce
Coffee

*T*UESDAY

*B*REAKFAST
Bananas   Bran Flakes
Fried Smelts
Cornmeal Muffins
Coffee   Cocoa

LUNCHEON

Chicken Soup
Salmon Salad, Cooked Dressing
Waffles, Maple Syrup
Tea   Milk

DINNER

Veal Cutlets
Parsley Potatoes   Eggplant au Gratin
Celery   Cranberry Sauce
Lemon Meringue Pie
Coffee

WEDNESDAY

BREAKFAST

Sliced Oranges   Oatmeal
French Omelet
Toast   Jam
Coffee   Cocoa

LUNCHEON

Baked Green Peppers,
Stuffed with Veal and Tomato (Left Over)
Sweet Potato Biscuit
Apple Sauce   Molasses Cake

DINNER

Curried Lamb with Rice
Vegetable Fritters   Pickle Relish
Lettuce Salad
Roly-Poly Pudding, Foamy Sauce
Coffee

THURSDAY

BREAKFAST

Stewed Figs   Puffed Rice
Crisp Bacon
Toast
Coffee   Cocoa

LUNCHEON

Oyster Chowder
Whole Wheat Muffins
Cabbage and Green Pepper Salad
Doughnuts
Milk   Tea

DINNER

Beef Kidney Stew, Dumplings
Glacé Sweet Potatoes   Asparagus Béarnaise
Cranberry Jelly   Celery
Chocolate Soufflé
Custard Sauce
Coffee

*F*RIDAY

BREAKFAST

Stewed Prunes
Codfish Balls   Muffins
Coffee   Cocoa

LUNCHEON

Cheese Soufflé
Emergency Biscuit
Jam
Tea   Milk

DINNER

Fillet of Sole, Tartar Sauce
Potato Soufflé   Baked Stuffed Tomatoes
Romaine Salad, Horseradish Dressing
Cocoanut Layer Cake
Coffee

*S*ATURDAY

BREAKFAST

Bananas   Cream of Wheat
Scrambled Eggs and Bacon
Toast
Coffee   Cocoa

LUNCHEON

Ham Salad, Cooked Dressing
Baking Powder Biscuit
Cake
Tea   Milk

DINNER

Pork Chops and Sweet Potatoes en Casserole
Baked Squash
Tomato Jelly Salad
Apple Fritters with Lemon Sauce
Coffee

CHAPTER XXV

Menus for Special Occasions

THANKSGIVING

Fruit Cocktail

Celery   Olives

Cream of Corn Soup with Crisp Crackers

Roast Turkey, Chestnut Stuffing

Mashed Potatoes   Baked Stuffed Onions

Cranberry Sauce

Pumpkin Pie   Cheese

Coffee

CHRISTMAS

Oysters on Half-Shell

Stuffed Celery   Ripe Olives

Cream of Mushroom Soup

Bread Sticks

Roast Goose or Duck, Fried Apples

Glacé Sweet Potatoes   Creamed Cauliflower

Dinner Rolls   Currant Jelly

Heart of Lettuce Salad

Mince Pie   French Ice Cream

Nuts   Mints

Coffee

COMPANY LUNCHEON WITHOUT A MAID

Fruit Cocktail

Chicken Pie   Potatoes Julienne

Scotch Scones   Currant Jelly

Romaine Salad

Meringue Cake

Coffee   Salted Nuts

COMPANY LUNCHEON WITH A MAID

Cream of Mushroom Soup

Sweetbreads Béchamel   Potatoes Surprise

Asparagus Hollandaise

Lettuce and Cucumber Salad   Parker House Rolls

Mock Nesselrode Pudding

Salted Almonds   Coffee

[232]

COMPANY DINNER WITHOUT A MAID

Oysters on Half-Shell
Consommé
Planked Steak
Hearts of Lettuce Salad   Dinner Rolls
Celery
Fruit Mousse   Coffee
Mints   Salted Nuts

COMPANY DINNER WITH A MAID

Canapés
Bouillon
Filet of Sole, Tartar Sauce
Parsley Potato Balls
Roast Capon   Creamed Peas in Timbale Cases
Dinner Rolls   Cranberry Jelly
Watercress and Endive Salad
Orange Ice
Coffee   Mints

PICNICS—MOTOR LUNCHES

Cold Fried Chicken
Chopped Watercress Sandwiches
Vegetable Salad   Egg and Olive Sandwiches
Coffee or Tea in Thermos Bottle
Orange Layer Cake

Cold Ham and Tongue
Potato Salad   Pickles
Buttered Rolls   Hot Coffee
Fruit   Cake

CAMPFIRE PARTIES

Broiled Steak
Baked Potatoes
Rolls   Doughnuts   Coffee

Broiled Bacon Sandwiches
Scrambled Eggs   Roasted Corn
Coffee   Fruit
Cake

CHURCH SUPPERS

Oyster Stew
Baked Beans   Asparagus Salad
Ice Cream and Cake
Coffee

CHURCH SUPPERS—(*Continued*)

Macaroni and Cheese
Parker House Rolls   Tomato Salad
Apple Pie
Coffee

Chicken à la King
Baking Powder Biscuit
Hearts of Lettuce with Russian Dressing
Strawberry Shortcake
Coffee

Potato Salad
Cold Baked Ham   Southern Cornbread
Chocolate Cake with Whipped Cream
Coffee

CROSS INDEX

What to Serve and How to Serve It

BREAKFAST

Main Dishes

LUNCHEON

Egg and Casserole Dishes

Fish

LUNCHEON (Continued)

Meat

Salads

Hearty Sandwiches

DINNER

Fish

Meat

DINNER (Continued)

Meat (Continued)

DESSERTS

Pastry

Puddings

DESSERTS (*Continued*)

AFTERNOON TEA

"COMPANY" SUPPER

Hot Dishes

Oyster Chowder	68	Fried Oysters	56
Lobster Bisque	66	Lobster Patties	213
Cheese Dreams	74	Shrimp Newburg	213
Cheese Soufflé	74	Sweetbreads Béchamel	214
Welsh Rarebit	75	Chicken Croquettes	53
Eggs and Mushrooms en Casserole	80	Artichokes Hollandaise	214
Egg Soufflé	79	Potato Surprise	59
Broiled Oysters	84	Asparagus Béarnaise	103
Hollandaise Sauce	115	Green Corn Fritters	105
Scalloped Oysters	85	Stuffed Peppers, Baked	107
Soft Shell Crabs	54	Stuffed Tomatoes, Baked	111
Fried Clams in Batter	55		

Salads and Salad Accompaniments

Fruit Salad, Pineapple Dressing	215	Jellied Vegetable Salad	142
Chicken Salad	140	Cheese Fingers	143
Stuffed Tomato Salad	142	Cheese Straws	143
Jellied Tuna Fish	142	Cheese Cream Puffs	143

Breads

Blueberry Tea Muffins	122	Coffee Cake	126
Scotch Scones	124	Coffee Rolls	133
Shortcakes	124	Brioche	214
Popovers	124	Orange Biscuits	215
Butterscotch Rolls	127	Swedish Timbales	61
Waffles	128		

Sandwiches

Chicken Salad Sandwich	146	Broiled Luncheon Sandwich	146
Club Sandwich	146		

Cakes and Pastry

Meringue Cake	217	Lady Baltimore Cake	155
Cream Puffs	217	Devils' Food Cake	157
Eclairs	217	Chocolate Roll	162
Rolled Pecan Wafers	218	Filled Cup Cakes	163
Scotch Fans	219	Filled Chocolate Cakes	163
Hazelnut Cookies	219	Filled Cookies	164
		French Crullers	51

SCHOOL AND PICNIC LUNCH BOX

Breads

Bran Muffins	121	Raisin Rolls	127
Blueberry Tea Muffins	122	Butterscotch Rolls	127
Nut Bread for Sandwiches	125	Parker House Rolls (yeast)	134
Steamed Brown Bread	125	Coffee Cake (yeast)	133
Raisin Brown Bread	125		

Roasting

KIND OF FOOD	TEMPERATURE	TIME
Beef—uncovered roaster.		
Rare	500° F. first 20 minutes reducing to 400° F. for remaining time.	8–12 minutes per lb.
Medium	500° F. first 20 minutes reducing to 400° F. for remaining time.	12–15 minutes per lb.
Well done	500° F. first 20 minutes reducing to 400° F. for remaining time.	15–20 minutes per lb.
Chicken	450° F. for 15 minutes reducing to 350° F. for remaining time.	15 minutes per lb.
Lamb (leg) (shoulder)	460° F. for 15 minutes reducing to 350° F. for remaining time.	15–20 minutes per lb.
Pork	460° F. for 15 minutes reducing to 350° F. for remaining time.	20–25 minutes per lb.
Poultry	450° F. for 15 minutes reducing to 350° F. for remaining time.	20–25 minutes per lb.
Veal	500° F. for 15 minutes reducing to 400° F. for remaining time.	20–25 minutes per lb.

Broiling

Chicken. Split in half		15–20 minutes
Lamb Chops		10–12 minutes
Shad, Bluefish, etc. (split for broiling)		18–20 minutes
Steak 1 inch thick { Rare		8–10 minutes
Well-done		10–15 minutes

Boiling

Asparagus..20–25 minutes
Beans (Lima)...30–40 minutes
Beans (string)...45–50 minutes
Beets (young)......................................45 minutes (or more)
Brussels Sprouts.......................................20–25 minutes
Cabbage (shredded or quartered)........................15–20 minutes
Carrots (young)..15–20 minutes
Carrots (old)..30–40 minutes
Cauliflower.. 20 minutes
Corn (green)...15–20 minutes
Kohlrabi...30–40 minutes
Parsnips...30–40 minutes
Peas (fresh)...20–30 minutes
Potatoes...20–30 minutes
Onions...30–40 minutes
Spinach..15–20 minutes
Squash (summer)..15–20 minutes

MEAT (Cook just below boiling point)

Chicken....................per pound...................15–20 minutes
Corned Beef................per pound...................30–40 minutes
Fowl.......................per pound...................20–30 minutes
Ham........................per pound...................18–20 minutes
Mutton.....................per pound................... 15 minutes
Pot Roast..................per pound...................35–40 minutes

FISH

Cod........................per pound................... 8–10 minutes
Haddock....................per pound................... 10 minutes
Halibut....................per pound...................10–15 minutes
Salmon.....................per pound...................10–15 minutes

Table of Equivalent Measures

3 teaspoons	=1 tablespoon
16 tablespoons	=1 cup
½ cup	=1 gill
2 cups	=1 pint
2 pints	=1 quart
4 quarts	=1 gallon

Table of Weights and Measures

2⅓ cups Crisco...............................1 pound
2 cups granulated sugar.........................1 pound
    (2 tablespoons—1 ounce)
2 cups butter...............................1 pound
    (2 tablespoons—1 ounce)
4 cups flour...............................1 pound
    (4 tablespoons—1 ounce)
3 cups cornmeal...............................1 pound
2 cups rice...............................1 pound
2 cups dry beans...............................1 pound
5 cups coffee (ground)...............................1 pound
8 cups tea (dry leaves)...............................1 pound
    (2 ounces—1 cup)
1 cake (8 squares) chocolate.....................½ pound
4 cups cocoa (dry)...............................1 pound
4 cups shelled walnuts...............................1 pound
    (1 pound walnuts in shell equals about ½ pound shelled)
1 cup raisins or currants........................1 pound

Temperature Chart

Very slow	.225° to 250°
Slow	.250° to 300°
Moderate	.300° to 350°
Hot	.350° to 400°
Quick	.400° to 450°
Very hot	.450° to 550°
Broil	.600°

INDEX